MODERN YIDDISH CULTURE

YIDDISH

CULTURE

The Story of the
Yiddish Language Movement

פרייז אין אדעסא:

אין גאנץ אימפעריע:

קול מבשר

КОЛЪ-М'ВАССЕРЪ

Приложеніе къ „Гамелицу"

на нѣмецко-еврейскомъ языкѣ

№ 11.   1869   הוספה להמליץ שנה השיעית

אירבאלם: אדעססא. — מאר סענקעל. —
ואהן, (פאריסטונעמוננ). — וויא נעשיכטען פון יום־
טוב. א. קימפאנינין. — ערב"רכ. — מדעווה. —
פעלליעטאן: דיא מטירה.

ערב א נ סא 13 מארץ 1869
(יג ניסן תרכ"ט).

Front page of *Kol Mevaser*, March 13, 1869.

MODERN YIDDISH CULTURE

The Story of the Yiddish Language Movement

Emanuel S. Goldsmith

FORDHAM UNIVERSITY PRESS
New York

LC-97-45515
ISBN 0-8232-1695-0
Published by arrangements with Associated University Presses
First edition 1976
Revised reprint 1987
Expanded edition 1997
Reprinted 2000

Library of Congress Cataloging in Publication Data

Goldsmith, Emanuel S., 1935–
    Modern Yiddish culture : the story of the Yiddish language
movement / Emanuel S. Goldsmith. — Expanded ed.
        p.   cm.
    Includes bibliographical references and index.
    ISBN 0-8232-1695-0
    1. Yiddish language—History.   2. Jews—Languages—History.
I. Title.
PJ5113.G67   1997
439.1'09—dc21   96-45515
                                                              CIP

To my wife
Shirley Zebberman Goldsmith

מיט ליבשאַפֿט

CONTENTS

LIST OF ILLUSTRATIONS

1

FOREWORD

by Robert M. Seltzer
Professor of History,
Hunter College of The City University of New York

Emanuel S. Goldsmith's account of the series of writers and
ideologists he has called "architects of Yiddishism" is a sympathetic and comprehensive depiction of a striking phase in the
modernization of Judaism. Yiddishism, as Goldsmith points out,
represents one of the most daring attempts by a large sector of
Jewry to confront itself, against the background of the world of
the twentieth century, as a "normal" modern nation. Because the
Yiddish intellectuals were remarkably open to the new intellectual and literary currents that bedazzled Eastern European
intellectuals from the middle of the nineteenth century to the eve
of World War Two, yet remained deeply rooted in Jewish values
and ethical concerns, they could forge a stance that was perhaps
the most hopeful and, for several decades, seemingly the most
reasonable of all Jewish ideologies of Eastern European origin —
an optimistic faith in human progress and in the prospects of a
vigorous secular Jewish culture in a diaspora that had transcended the premodern without losing touch with the classical
heritage of Judaism.

Winning a place for Yiddishism was no easy achievement.
The mystique of a normalized, secular Jewishness through the
medium of the Yiddish language emerged in Eastern Europe
only in the face of considerable opposition from several direc-
tions. After surveying the early history of the Yiddish language

3

and literature, Professor Goldsmith describes the maverick writers, lexicographers, dramatists, and newspaper entrepreneurs who defied the condescending scorn of most nineteenth-century Hebraists for the "jargon," as Yiddish was usually labelled. Eventually modern Yiddish found its special public through a network of periodicals, publishing houses, and theaters, and it found its special sources of political support in the Jewish Workers' Bund of Russia, Poland, and Lithuania, among some Zionist Socialist groups, and in the small non-socialist *Folksparetey* (People's Party). In 1908 Yiddishism came of age at the historic Conference of Yiddish writers and ideologists that was convened at Czernowitz in Bukovina (then a part of the Austro-Hungarian empire) from August 30th to September 4th of that year. After much discussion, the seventy delegates demanded that Yiddish be recognized as "a national language of the Jewish people" (but not as "the national language," which a few extremists had preferred). The Czernowitz Conference itself became a prime emblem of the Yiddish renascence, generating an extensive debate in the Jewish press between Hebraists and Yiddishists of all persuasions. The positive Yiddishist self-consciousness catalyzed by the Conference paved the way for the major achievements of post-World I Yiddishism — the founding of the Yivo Institute in Vilna in 1925, the development of Yiddish school systems in Poland and America, the flourishing of modernist Yiddish writing, and so forth.

There is, however, a paradox in the contrast between the fame of the Conference and the actual historical record. Although the Czernowitz Conference was a landmark in the cultural history of twentieth-century European Jewry, there survived no minutes or contemporary records of the stormy exchange of views expressed there concerning the linguistic future (and therefore the social future) of Eastern European Jewry. Professor Goldsmith has admirably filled this gap by reconstructing the Conference in its larger historical context; he delineates the long-range processes and the immediate

4

circumstances that led to the meeting and the four key personalities who dominated the proceedings: Nathan Birnbaum, Yitzkhok Leybush Peretz, Matisyohu Mieses, and Chaim Zhitlovsky. And the last years and afterthoughts of these four men permit Professor Goldsmith to illuminate further the inherent dilemmas of the Yiddishist movement as it developed in the troubled years between the two world wars.

What remains of the legacy of the Czernowitz Yiddish Conference of 1908? As a result of the Holocaust, the destruction of Yiddish cultural institutions in the Soviet Union, the establishment of the state of Israel, and the linguistic acculturation of Western Jewries, illusions held by the Yiddishists of the earlier generation have been brutally exposed. In his summing up of the strengths and limitations of the Yiddishist movement, Goldsmith judiciously notes that, for all its obsessive concentration on language as the sine qua non of modern Jewish existence and its tendency to dogmatic secularism, there is much to be said for the positive contribution of Yiddishism to ongoing Jewish survival. Modernity is a state of almost continual change. That Yiddishism played a significant role in conserving the vitality of the Jewish tradition during critical decades is no mean attainment: in the last analysis, it is all that any modern Jewish movement can claim for itself. Students of twentieth-century Jewish life are grateful to Emanuel Goldsmith for this book enabling us to admire the industriousness, the passions, and the fortitude of the doughty band of intellectuals, fanatics about Yiddish and Jewishness, that he so lovingly portrays.

ACKNOWLEDGMENTS

I WOULD LIKE TO EXPRESS MY HEARTFELT GRATITUDE TO teachers, colleagues, and friends who, in various ways, have helped make this book possible. Professor Benjamin Halpern of Brandeis University helped me plan the work and organize the material and provided wise counsel. Professor Nahum N. Sarna, Chairman of the Department of Near Eastern and Judaic Studies at Brandeis, was a constant source of cooperation and encouragement. Professors Nahum N. Glatzer, Joshua Rothenberg, and Robert Szulkin of Brandeis and Professor Yosef H. Yerushalmi of Harvard University read the manuscript and made helpful suggestions, as did my good friends, Mrs. Vivienne Silverstein and Rabbi William G. Braude.

My first teacher of both Hebrew and Yiddish was the kindly Mr. Noah Aptekar, Principal of the Wilkins Avenue Talmud Torah in the Bronx, New York. My interest in Yiddish studies was kindled by the late Professor Max Weinreich of the City College of New York and further stimulated by Professor Nathan Susskind of CCNY and by Professor Chaim Gininger and the late Professor Uriel Weinreich of Columbia University. I recall gratefully the friendship of two giants of Yiddish writing, both no longer with us, Jacob Glatstein and Aaron Zeitlin. I also had the privilege of studying Yiddish language and literature with Professor Chaim S. Kazdan and the late Professor Yudel Mark at the Jewish Teachers Seminary in New York, and with Professors Joshua Rothenberg and Joseph C. Landis at Brandeis University.

Without the materials available in the library and archives of the Yivo Institute for Jewish Research and the archives of the Jewish Labor Bund, this book would not have been possible in its present form. My sincere thanks go to Miss Dinah Abramowicz and Mr. Ezekiel Lifschutz of the Yivo library and archives and to Mr. Hillel Kempinski of the Bund archives. I am also grateful to Professors Mordkhe Shaechter of Columbia University, Elias Schulman of Queens College and Zosa Szajkowski of Brandeis University for making me aware of some significant materials.

To Mrs. Mathilde E. Finch of Associated University Presses, Inc., my thanks for her skillful help in preparing the manuscript for publication.

I also wish to thank the following publishers for having given me permission to quote from published works :

East and West Library for permission to quote from *Ahad Haam, Essays, Letters, Memoirs,* translated and edited by Leon Simon.

Jewish Publication Society for permission to quote from *Selected Essays by Ahad Haam,* translated by Leon Simon, and from Simon Dubnow, *Nationalism and History,* edited by Koppel S. Pinson.

Aharon Megged and Theodor Herzl Foundation, Inc., publishers of *Midstream,* for permission to quote from "Reflections on Two Languages" by Aharon Megged.

The Reconstructionist Press, for permission to quote from *Questions Jews Ask: Reconstructionist Answers* by Mordecai M.

Kaplan and from *Jewish Education in Democratic Society* by Jack J. Cohen.

The Spero Foundation, publisher of Jewish Pocket Books, for permission to quote from *Confession* by Nathan Birnbaum. Yivo Institute for Jewish Research for permission to quote from *Peretz*, translated and edited by Sol Liptzin. Thomas Yoseloff, Inc., for permission to quote from *The Way We Think: A Collection of Jewish Essays*, edited and translated by Joseph Leftwich, and from Mendele Mocher Seforim, *The Parasite*, translated from the Yiddish by Gerald Stillman.

E. S. G.

Storrs, Connecticut
Second day of Hanukkah 5736
November 30, 1975

NOTE ON THE
1997 EDITION

In the two decades since this book first appeared, interest in Yiddish studies has continued to grow. It is my hope that the republication of this work will make the story of the rise of Yiddishism familiar to new readers. Since its initial publication, a number of worthwhile books on the social, cultural, and linguistic history of Yiddish have appeared. The most important are:

Otsrot Yidish by Y. H. Biletski, Papyrus Publishing House, Tel Aviv, 1989.

Yiddish: A Survey and a Grammar, by Solomon A. Birnbaum, University of Toronto Press, Toronto, 1979.

Ideology, Society, Language: The Odyssey of Nathan Birnbaum by Joshua A. Fishman, Karoma, Ann Arbor, 1989.

Never Say Die! A Thousand Years of Yiddish in Jewish Life and Letters, edited by Joshua A. Fishman, Mouton Publishers, The Hague, 1981.

11

Yiddish: Turning to Life by Joshua A. Fishman, John Benjamins Publishing Company, Amsterdam, 1991.

The Politics of Interpretation: Alterity and Ideology in Old Yiddish Studies by Jerold C. Frakes, State University of New York Press, Albany, 1989.

Prophecy and Politics: Socialism, Nationalism, and the Russian Jews, 1862–1917, by Jonathan Frankel, Cambridge University Press, Cambridge, 1981.

Mame-Loshn: The Making of Yiddish, by John Geipel, The Journeyman Press, London, 1981.

The Meaning of Yiddish by Benjamin Harshav, University of California Press, Berkeley, 1990.

Origins of the Yiddish Language edited by Dovid Katz, Pergamon Press, Oxford, 1987.

Dos Gerangl far Yidish by Yitzhok Korn, Veltrat far Yidisher Kultur, Tel Aviv, 1982.

The Prime of Yiddish by David Passow, Gefen Publishing House, Jerusalem, 1996.

Tsvishn Yo un Neyn: Yidish un Yidish-Literatur in Erets Yisroel, 1907–1948, by Arie L. Pilovsky, World Council for Yiddish and Yiddish Culture, Tel Aviv, 1986.

Fun a Mol un Haynt by Joshua Rothenberg, Farlag Y. L. Peretz, Tel Aviv, 1990.

Laytish Mame-Loshn by Mordkhe Schaechter, Yidish Lige, New York, 1986.

Portretn un Etyudn, by Elias Schulman, Cyco Bicher Farlag, New York, 1979.

Live and Be Well: A Celebration of Yiddish Culture in America from the Immigrants to the Second World War, by Richard F. Shepard and Vicki Gold Levi, Ballantine Books, New York, 1982.

Prokim fun der Yidisher Literature-Geshikte by Chone Shmeruk, Farlag Y. L. Peretz, Tel Aviv, 1988.

Yiddish Panorama: A Thousand Years of Yiddish Language, Literature, and Culture, edited by Barry Walfish, Jewish Studies Program at the University of Toronto, Toronto, 1995.

History of the Yiddish Language, by Max Weinreich, translated by Shlomo Noble with the assistance of Joshua A. Fishman, The University of Chicago Press, Chicago, 1980.

I. L. Peretz and the Making of Modern Jewish Culture by Ruth R. Wisse, University of Washington Press, Seattle, 1991.

I am most grateful to my esteemed colleague, the noted historian Professor Robert M. Seltzer, for writing the foreword.

E.S.G.

Briarwood, New York
Tishri 13, 5757
September 26, 1996

ADDENDUM TO THE 2000 PRINTING

Classic Yiddish Fiction: Abramovitsh, Sholem Aleichem, and Peretz, by Ken Frieden, State University of New York Press, New York, 1995.

The Politics of Yiddish: Studies in Language, Literature, and Society, edited by Dov-Ber Kerler, Altamira Press, Walnut Creek, CA, 1998.

Yiddish Language and Culture: Then and Now, edited by Leonard Jay Greenspoon, Creighton University Press, Omaha, Nebraska, 1998.

INTRODUCTION

THIS STUDY EXPLORES THE JEWISH CULTURAL IDEOLOGY KNOWN
as Yiddishism through an analysis of the positions of the four
most prominent participants in the First Yiddish Language
Conference in Czernowitz (Cernauti), Bukovina, in 1908. During
this Conference, at which the Yiddish language was proclaimed
to be a "national language" of the Jewish people, Yiddishism
drew attention as a distinct ideological trend in Jewish life. The
book traces the social, political, and literary roots of Yiddishism
up until the Conference, and attempts to clarify what it was
that caused the devotees of Yiddish to develop into a distinct
ideological grouping. It discusses the positions and activities of
Nathan Birnbaum, Yitzkhok Leybush Peretz, Matisyohu Mieses,
and Chaim Zhitlovsky before, during, and following the Conference. It attempts a summation of the chief factors in the
growth and decline of Yiddishism and tries to assay its strengths
and weaknesses in the context of modern Jewish life.

In 1939, eleven million Jews, scattered throughout the
world and comprising some 65 to 70 percent of the world

Jewish population, spoke a language created by, and peculiar to, the Jewish people. Never before in the history of Jewry had any one language been the vernacular of so many Jews. The Yiddish language had served as the spoken language of a major portion of the Jewish people for a period equal to that during which Hebrew had fulfilled a similar purpose. Yiddish had absorbed many of the functions of the earlier Aramaic in the life and faith of the Jewish people. It thus continued the tradition of Jewish bilingualism that began in antiquity. By incorporating a larger number of Hebrew words than any of the other languages created by Jews outside their ancestral home-land, its Jewish character was reinforced. In addition, by keeping a minimum knowledge of Hebrew alive in the daily speech of the masses of the Jewish people, Yiddish contributed inestimably to the renaissance of spoken Hebrew in the twentieth century.

Yiddish had been intimately involved in the evolution of Jewish religious practices and folkways in Europe since the early Middle Ages. In more recent times, it served as the vehicle for the propagation of the ideals of the religious move-ments of Hassidism and Mussar. It helped spread the doctrines of the Jewish enlightenment (Haskalah) and of the Jewish nationalist and socialist movements. In the nineteenth and twentieth centuries, Yiddish literature attained a degree of excellence equal to that of many of the most advanced European literatures. The Yiddish press and theater also achieved a level of sophistication that could rival those of many European nations. Yiddish was becoming a language of modern Jewish education in the growing Yiddish secular school movement at the beginning of the twentieth century even as it continued to be the language of instruction in the traditional *heder* and *yeshiva*. In institutions such as the Yiddish Scientific Institute (YIVO) in Vilna, Yiddish was also becoming a language of modern Jewish scholarship and literary research.

Yiddishism, also known as the Yiddish language movement, the Yiddish culture movement, or Yiddish Culturism, con-sciously attempted to secure a position of primacy for Yiddish and Yiddish culture at the dawn of the century. Yiddishists generally viewed the emergence of Yiddish as the most significant manifestation of Jewish vitality in the modern world. They saw the Yiddish language as the living bond that united Jewry and thwarted the corrosive effects of dispersion, minority status, and assimilation. It was for them the symbol of Jewish "normalcy." They saw it as both a sign of Jewish creativity and a guarantee of Jewish survival. In the course of their efforts to win recognition for Yiddish, Yiddishists were also compelled to consider the multitude of social, political, and cultural issues facing Jews, to develop approaches to these issues and institutions in which to implement them. Thus, although Yiddishism remained essentially an approach to Jewish cultural problems, it had far-ranging social, political, and even economic and religious implications as well. It contributed immensely to the dynamism and fascination of Jewish life in modern times.

Birnbaum, Peretz, Mieses, and Zhitlovsky, the four leading architects of Yiddishism at the beginning of the twentieth century, were the spiritual heirs of such nineteenth-century Yiddishists as Yehoshua Mordecai Lifshitz, Joseph Judah Lerner, and Alexander Zederbaum. They came to Yiddishism in the course of their efforts to understand the nature of Jewish life in the modern world and to fashion a program for the continued development of the Jewish people and its historic civilization. Despite the tremendous changes in the life of the Jewish people in the past several decades, much of what they had to say still possesses relevance and significance.

NOTE: *All translations from Yiddish or Hebrew sources in the text, unless specified otherwise, are by E.S.G.*

MODERN
YIDDISH
CULTURE

The Story of the
Yiddish Language Movement

An empire of scattered, beautifully blossoming islands
Is Yiddish Culture,
Its playful brooks and rivers
Cutting through the great oceans
Of peoples and cultures
And its tongue—the beautiful, tender, mellifluous Yiddish
Resounding proudly in the chorus of tongues.
. . . .
I would raise myself to the highest height
And from the height consider the scattered empire
Of Yiddish Culture
And see it stretch before my eyes
In a thousand colors and countless variations,
In so many throbbing, blossoming islands,
Rivers, gulfs, streams
And bless, bless, bless
With all the love in my soul
This dauntless Culture that cuts its way
Beneath the whips and stones of enemies.

A. Almi, "Yidish," *Far Yidish: A Zamlbukh*, ed.
S. Erdberg (New York, 1930), p. 59.

The Yiddish language has developed a great national
literature which is incomparable both in its vitality, in its
encouragement of Jewish survival, and in its bemoaning the
destruction of our people in the Hitler era, in shattering
expressions of lamentation.

H. Leivick, "The Individual Jew," *The Reconstructionist,* December 27, 1957, p. 10.

Our life as Jews is unthinkable without our cultural and
spiritual heritage. The Yiddish language and culture are an
important part of that heritage. If we will not retain them as
part of that heritage, we will eliminate from it a most valuable
segment. In that literature and culture are preserved the following values produced by centuries of Jewish life in Eastern
Europe : (1) the folk-spirit resulting from the use of Yiddish,
as the vernacular of the principal centers of Jewish life during
that period; (2) the wealth of the pietistic Hasidic lore that has
inspired so much of modern Jewish poetry, fiction and drama,
even beyond Hasidic circles; (3) much of the social idealism
manifest in the literature of Jewish socialism, trade-unionism
and labor Zionism. Jewry can ill afford to consign the culture
embodying these values to oblivion. . . . When we reflect that,
for centuries, Yiddish was the spoken language of East European
Jewry, where Jewish life was largely autonomous and where it
was lived most intensively and most creatively, we can understand the importance to be attached to the Yiddish language
and literature.

Mordecai M. Kaplan, *Questions Jews Ask: Reconstructionist Answers* (New York, 1956), pp. 376–77.

I never spoke Yiddish; I never learned it. The little of it that I
know I picked up as a child in grandfather's house and later
from neighbors, storekeepers and—from Arab peddlers. Nevertheless, it seems to me that I understand it much better than
I know it. I "feel" the language and its qualities; I see into
its heart; I am related to it . . . there are times when I have a
desire to speak Yiddish. It seems to me that were I to do so,
everything would somehow be simpler, more obvious, more
homey. And also that I would then belong to some extensive
Jewish family, one within which relations are intimate and
warm and everyone helps one another. Of course there will also
be quarreling in this family, but blood ties will remain strong.
Around me at the table there will be father and mother, grandpa
and grandma, uncles and aunts and all kinds of in-laws. Naturally, I would not love all of them : one may be greedy and
another quick to anger, one ugly and another a bitch, etc. But
what is more precious than the sense of belonging? For Yiddish
contains within itself so many of the traits of Jews in recent
generations : the humor of "on the other hand," a certain
craftiness and a cunning that goes with a sly wink, and also

wisdom in the ways of life gained from the struggle to survive. All the wrinkles of sorrow and of laughter to be found on Jewish faces are engraved on Yiddish words, sentences and intonations.

Aharon Megged, "Reflections on Two Languages," *Midstream* 12, no. 8 (October 1966) : 36.

The war between Hebrew and Yiddish, to all intents and purposes, is over. The status of Hebrew as the official language in the State of Israel has given it the victory. But it is a pyrrhic triumph, for the total disappearance of Yiddish would be a sad moment in Jewish history . . . for centuries Yiddish possessed a power which Hebrew never had during the entire Exile. It had the vitality of folk usage and expression. Perhaps it can retain that vitality even under the new conditions of freedom. Be that as it may, Jewish educators ought to give some serious thought to a means of retaining Yiddish for the young American Jew. Certainly the richness of Yiddish literature should not be shut off from American Jews, and translation is only a partial and inadequate answer. . . . The time has not yet come when we can afford to close the book on the culture of the six million.

Jack J. Cohen, *Jewish Education in Democratic Society* (New York, 1964), pp. 175–76.

As far as Yiddish is concerned, in a profound historical sense it is not the language itself which is the main thing but our history of a thousand years which was experienced in Yiddish. . . . We absorbed all of our history with the psychological dynamics and emotional reactions which the Yiddish epoch transmitted to us. Approaching Yiddish solely as a language is therefore superficial. Yiddish encompasses everything that the most important and most creative portion of our people produced in recent centuries. It is not literature or music or scholarship or ideas but all of these and something more. Call it culture or civilization. It is throbbing life, Jewish spiritual energy, dream of redemption, consciousness and instinct, idea and fantasy, law and lore, discipline and liberty.

Ephraim Auerbach, *Getrakht mit Ivri-Taytsh* (New York, 1955), pp. 172–73.

In Exile, Jews continued their ethical life. In *Golus,* the Jewish heart was purified and the cultivation of the Jewish spirit, which the prophets in ancient Jerusalem had sought in vain, was achieved. . . . In *Golus,* Jews created for themselves a spiritual Eretz Yisrael. In *Golus,* the modern Jewish nationality was crystallized. The proletarian spiritual aristocracy of Hassidism emerged. The weapons of radicalism were forged. And the greatest philological wonder of modern times, the Yiddish language, took shape. . . . Hatred of *Golus* existence bespeaks profound ingratitude. Of course, we seek liberation from *Golus.* Our forefathers liberated themselves from *Golus* thrice daily. But to spit at the *Golus* experience is to spit at oneself.

> Jacob Glatstein, *Mit Mayne Fartogbikher* (Tel Aviv, 1963), pp. 29f.

Once it was assumed that Yiddish represented the Diaspora and anti-Zionism, while Hebrew represented Israel and Zionism. Leivick was one of those great poets who, while writing in Yiddish, also expressed, felt, and spoke in Hebrew. He lived and identified with the land of Israel, the great work of construction, and the fight for Jewish survival. This house in his name is an expression of the elimination of the partition between Yiddish and Hebrew. There is no longer a battle between the languages. It is a tragedy that Hebrew no longer faces competition from the millions of Yiddish speakers. . . . The task of the Leivick House should be to bring the Jewish youth of Israel and the world closer to Yiddish and the cultural treasures of the Jewish past and present. . . . We have a wonderful youth who do not know the meaning of the word impossible. Every restraint in achieving the tasks and goals set before them is foreign to them. It is our duty to teach them the history and the culture of our millions who are no longer with us, and of the millions who are living and creating Yiddish culture. . . . We must not forget the injustices done to us by our enemies, and we must guard against doing injustice to our own past. The spirit of the murdered millions lives in Yiddish culture. We dare not commit the offense of not having provided our youth with a consciousness of deep attachment to those millions and to the great cultural treasures they created. The spirit of those Jews must continue to live.

> Golda Meir, "Address at the Dedication of the Leivick House in Israel, May 14, 1970," *Yiddish: A Quarterly Journal,* 1 :1 Summer, 1973.

נייע ביבליאטעק יודישע פראגען נו' 1

ד"ר נתן בירנבוים

דער יחום פון יודיש

בערלין 1913

פערלאג ש. ליפשיץ

ס"יי 30 פפ.: 15 קאפ.

Nathan Birnbaum's Yiddishist tract *Der Yikhus fun Yidish* (The Lineage of Yiddish), Berlin, 1913.

1
THE LANGUAGE
OF ASHKENAZ

THE RISE OF YIDDISH IS BUT ONE EXAMPLE OF THE development of Jewish dialects and Diaspora languages, a process that began in the biblical period and continued throughout Jewish history. Wherever Jews lived in large numbers until modern times, they gradually developed their own linguistic media by combining elements of Hebrew with the local veraculars. Of the sixteen or more Jewish Diaspora vernaculars, the most widespread were Aramaic, Judeo-Greek, Judeo-Arabic, Judeo-Latin, Judeo-Italian, Judeo-Provençal, Judeo-French, Yiddish, Judeo-Spanish (Ladino, Romance, Judesmo, or Spaniolit), and Judeo-Persian. The Jews in the Caucasus Mountains still have their own dialect of Judeo-Persian, as do the Jews of Bokhara in the Soviet Union. These languages developed for several reasons. Although Jews were usually fluent in the local non-Jewish vernaculars, their distinctive religious and cultural life required the utilization of terms not found in those tongues. The Jewish dialects also provided the protection and intimacy of private argots. Moreover, when they were expelled from what they believed to be areas of greater to areas of lesser cultural development, Jews tended to preserve and develop their own version of the language of the former. Thus Jews from Germanic lands brought Yiddish to Poland in the fifteenth century and Jews from Spain brought Ladino to Turkey after 1492.

The outstanding features of the Jewish Diaspora tongues may be traced to the distinguishing features of Jewish life—the religious regimen, the Hebrew or Hebrew-Aramaic literary heritage, the Jewish judicial system, the Jewish occupational structure, the international character of Jewry, and so on. The influence of Hebrew on each of them was crucial, although the proportion of Hebrew words in each varies. Under the influence of Hebrew, the morphology and syntax of each of the native tongues was altered. Equally significant was the fact that these vernaculars utilized the Hebrew alphabet. Almost all Jews could read and write Hebrew, whereas knowledge of other alphabets was not so common among them. The Hebrew alphabet also contributed to the protective quality and intimacy of these tongues.[1]

Yiddish is unique among the Diaspora tongues in having been spoken by a larger number of Jews and for a longer period than any of the others. The community that used it achieved one of the highest levels of cultural independence in the annals of Jewry. In its intimate association with Jewish religion, Yiddish may be compared only to Aramaic.[2] Yiddish reached the zenith of its development in Eastern Europe between the sixteenth and twentieth centuries, the golden period in the spiritual history of the Ashkenazim. Moreover, in no other Diaspora tongue did the Jewish people produce both a sacred and secular literature comparable in quantity and quality to

1. Cf. Y. Efroykin, *Oyfkum un Umkum fun Yidishe Golus-Shprakhn un Dialektn* (Paris, 1951), pp. 56, 59–60.
2. Cf. M. Glenn, "Ivrit, Aramit Veidit," *Ahisefer*, ed. S. Niger and M. Ribalow (New York, 1943), pp. 36–45.

Yiddish literature. As we shall see, one of the causes of the bitter language controversy between Hebraists and Yiddishists at the beginning of the twentieth century derived from the fact that Yiddish had reached the point where it was able to rival Hebrew as a literary language as well as a spoken tongue.

The birth and growth of Yiddish is historically coterminous with the development of Ashkenazic Jewry, which in 1939 constituted 92 percent of the world Jewish population of seventeen million.[3] The Jewish communities north of the Alps and Pyrenees emerged as a distinctive sector of Jewry, with traditions, customs, and rituals of their own sometime in the eleventh century. At about the same time, the biblical names Ashkenaz and Sepharad were chosen as Jewish designations for Germany and Spain, respectively, probably because of their similarity in sound to As-Skandz (Saxony) and Hesperia (Spain).[4]

In Roman times, there were Jewish settlements in Cologne and other German towns. The later Jewish settlers in the Rhineland who formed the nucleus of Ashkenazic Jewry were probably exiles from Eastern France following the expulsions of the ninth, tenth and eleventh centuries. These migrations continued until the final expulsion of Jews from France in 1394. The French Jews were joined by Jewish settlers from Northern Italy.[5] Ashkenazic Jewry retained contact with the remaining Jewish centers in Italy and Palestine, whereas Sephardic Jewry, as part of the Muslim empire, was under the influence of the surviving Jewish academies of Babylonia. With Rabbenu Gershom's ban against polygamy at the beginning of the eleventh century, the Ashkenazim achieved spiritual independence from the Sephardim, who tolerated polygamy well into the twentieth century.

The Yiddish language emerged in what Jews called "Loter," the area of the Rhinelands comprising the basin of the Moselle

3. M. Weinreich, "Yidishkayt and Yiddish," *Mordecai M. Kaplan Jubilee Volume,* English Section (New York, 1953), p. 482.
4. S. W. Baron, *A Social and Religious History of the Jews,* (New York, 1954), 4 : 4.
5. M. Weinreich in *Algemeyne Entsiklopedye,* Yidn B. (Paris, 1940), p. 31.

and the left bank of the Rhine, roughly between Cologne and
Speyer. The principal components in the formation of the
language were Rabbinic Hebrew, Loez or Laaz (the Jewish
dialects of Old French and Old Italian), various dialects of
medieval German, and from the sixteenth century, with the
eastward migrations of Ashkenazic Jewry, different forms of
Slavic. Yiddish was from its very inception a fusion language
that absorbs, adapts, and modifies words from other languages
and gives them new meaning.[6]

As Jews migrated into areas in which the various German
dialects were spoken, Yiddish developed, and as they migrated
into other language areas, they took Yiddish with them. Yiddish
soon advanced into South and Central Germany, Bohemia,
Moravia, Poland, and Lithuania. It reached Northern Italy in
the fifteenth century and the Ukraine in the sixteenth. In the
nineteenth and twentieth centuries it spread to North and South
America, to Africa, Australia, and the Middle East.[7] It became
a truly international language rivaling English, German, French
and Spanish in terms of geographic distribution.

The name "Yiddish," meaning "Jewish" in the language
itself and sometimes referring to Hebrew, first appears in texts
of the fifteenth century. It was used unambiguously in the middle
of the seventeenth century and was revived again toward the
end of the nineteenth century. In Hebrew, Yiddish was referred
to as *Leshon Ashkenaz* (the language of Ashkenaz) or *Leshoneynu*
(our language). Perhaps because the bulk of Yiddish speakers
originally lived in Germany and it continued to be regarded as
a variant of German even after the migrations to East Europe,
the language was often called *Taytsh* (German). It appears
clear, however, that almost from its very beginning Jews dis-

6. Cf. M. Weinreich, "Prehistory and Early History of Yiddish: Facts
and Conceptual Framework, *"The Field of Yiddish*, 1, ed. U. Weinreich
(New York, 1954), pp. 78f, and Y. Mark, "The Yiddish Language: Its
Cultural Impact," *American Jewish Historical Quarterly* 59, no. 2 (December 1969): 202.
7. M. Weinreich in *Algemeyne Entsiklopedye*, Yidn B., pp. 29f.

tinguished between their own variety of German and that of their Christian neighbors.[8]

Vestiges of the name *Taytsh* are still to be found in the Yiddish words *fartaytshn* meaning to explain (originally "to render into Taytsh"), *staytsh?*, that is, what does it mean? and *Taytsh-khumesh*, that is, a Yiddish translation of the Pentateuch. Other names for the language among Jews were derived from the practical uses to which it was put, for example, *Ivri-Taytsh* (stylized archaic translation of Hebrew), *Vayber-Taytsh* (old Yiddish typeface) and *Khumesh-Taytsh* (traditional method of translating the Pentateuch). Scholars frequently referred to it as Judeo-German or Hebreo-German.[9]

The role of Yiddish in medieval Jewish life may be compared to that of the earlier Aramaic that was spoken by Jewry in various dialects as far back as biblical times and that became a Jewish literary language toward the end of the Second Commonwealth period.[10] In addition to the vast Aramaic literature created by Jews in the Talmudic period, there is also a large medieval rabbinical and Jewish mystical literature in the language. In medieval Hebrew, Aramaic words, phrases, and grammatical forms were used extensively and Aramaic remained an important element in the Jewish cultural heritage even after it ceased to be used as a vernacular. Hebrew and Aramaic were thus fused in the consciousness of the Jewish people.

With the rise of Islam in the seventh and eighth centuries, Arabic gradually replaced Aramaic as a vernacular among Jewish communities throughout the Muslim world. The Jews created an Arabic language of their own. Judeo-Arabic as spoken by the masses and as written by educated Jews was distinguishable from the local dialects and the classical Arabic.[11]

Unlike their brothers in the East, the Jews of Italy, France, and Germany, in the tenth and eleventh centuries, did not adopt

8. *Ibid.*, p. 26; Weinreich, "Yidishkayt and Yiddish," p. 486.
9. Y. Lewinsky, *Entsiklopedya Shel Havay Umasoret Bayahadut* (Tel Aviv, 1970), 1: 254.
10. See Baron, 2:146.
11. See Baron, 8:59f.

the literary language of their neighbors. Jews referred to Latin as the Christian language or the priests' language and had no desire to make it their own. In the eyes of the Jews, the cultural level of the Christian population was so low as not to be considered worthy of emulation. The literary language of the Jews was a synthesis of Hebrew and Aramaic and their vernaculars were the Jewish dialects of Old French, Italian, or German.

For the ordinary Jew, whose knowledge of the rabbinic literature was limited; the women, who had little if any formal education; and the children in the schools, the vernaculars soon also became literary languages. Some Yiddish literary works were created by bards, jesters, and other Jewish counterparts of medieval troubadors and minstrels. They were based on biblical tales and on medieval stories like those of King Arthur and his knights. The Reformation, Luther's translation of the Bible into German and Guttenberg's invention of movable type contributed to the replacement of Latin by German as the literary language of Germany and to the development of German folk literature. Editions of the anonymous works of early German literature also appeared in the Hebrew alphabet with very minor changes.

The earliest classics of Yiddish literature were products of the fourteenth, fifteenth, and sixteenth centuries. They include verse epics such as those based on the biblical books of Samuel and Kings. The Hebrew grammarian Elijah Levita (Bokher) wrote his famous *Bovo-Bukh* in 1507. The *Mayse-Bukh,* a compilation of Talmudic and medieval folk tales, appeared in 1602.[12] In 1554, the printer Joseph bar Yokor published the first translation of the Prayer Book into Yiddish. In his introduction he described those who worshiped only in Hebrew without understanding the language as "complete fools."[13] More successful than bar Yokor was the Polish rabbi Jacob ben Isaac Ashkenazi (1550-1628). His

12. See Elye Bokher, *Poetishe Shafungen in Yidish,* vol. 1, ed. J. A. Joffe (New York, 1949) and *Ma'aseh Book,* 2 vols., ed. M. Gaster (Philadelphia, 1934).
13. I. Zinberg, *Di Geshikhte fun der Literatur bay Yidn* (Buenos Aires, 1967), 6:95.

Tseno-Ureno (1616), an interpretive, amplified version of the
Pentateuch for women, became the most successful book in the
history of Yiddish literature and contributed immeasurably to
the education and entertainment of Jewish women for more than
three centuries.[14]

The seventeenth-century mystic, Rabbi Yekhiel Mikhl
Epstein, author of liturgical and moralistic works, has been
described as an early champion of Yiddish. He encouraged the
study of Yiddish pietistic tracts and also advocated praying in
the language. He recognized that Yiddish could render an
important service in the development of piety and ethical
conduct. Although he was primarily concerned with the
maintenance of the traditional religious regimen, he unconsciously raised the prestige of Yiddish as a dynamic factor in the
communal life of Ashkenazic Jewry.[15]

The recognition of Yiddish as a literary language came very
slowly. Rabbis frequently opposed not only the secular Yiddish
works that mirrored European literature but even the Yiddish
versions of religious and ethical works. Yet, Chaim ben Nosn of
Prague, author of a Yiddish Bible translation (1674), declared
that there was no shame in reading Yiddish books since even
the sages of old had always interpreted the Talmud in the
vernacular. It was all the same whether one studied sacred
works in Hebrew or Yiddish, for even when the *Halakha* was
studied, Yiddish was employed in explaining it.[16]

In 1709, Aaron ben Samuel, an educational reformer and
precursor of the German Haskalah, published a book of
devotions in Yiddish that was intended to serve as a kind of
vernacular catechism for children and untutored folk. He
explained, in his introduction, that as a young orphan he had
sought comfort in the sacred books but they had remained

14. See N. C. Gore, *Tzeenah U-Reenah: A Jewish Commentary on the
Book of Exodus* (New York, 1965).
15. Cf. M. Pyekazh, "Vegn Yidishizm in Sof Zibetsntn Yorhundert
un der Ershter Helft Akhtsntn Yorhundert," *Di Goldene Keyt*, no. 49 (Tel
Aviv, 1964), p. 176.
16. I. Zinberg, "Der Kamf far Yidish in der Yidisher Literatur,"
Filologishe Shriftn 2 (Vilna, 1928), p. 98.

sealed to him because of his ignorance of Hebrew. In the Yiddish volumes, however, he had found comfort and knowledge, for which he was grateful to the Almighty. That experience prompted him to compose his manual of devotions and to set forth his educational theories in the introduction to his book. His most radical suggestion was that during their early years children be taught religious values and prayers in their mother tongue and only later be introduced to Hebrew. Such a practice was customary among the Portuguese and Italian Jews of his day. It was symptomatic of the times that Aaron ben Samuel's book was confiscated and that he was persecuted and ridiculed for his radical notions.[17]

In 1772, Rabbi Moses Frankfurt challenged the opponents of translations of sacred books into Yiddish. He accused them of seeking to keep the secrets of the sacred literature from the people. In the introduction to his translation of *Menorat Hamaor* by the Sephardic rabbi Issac Aboab, he stated that it was a *mitzvah* to publish sacred books in every language in order that those who knew no Hebrew might study them.[18]

Following the Thirty Years War in Germany and the Chmielnitzky Massacres in the Ukraine in the seventeeth century, Jewry was suffused with ascetic concepts and mystical longings. The Lurianic Kabbalah became the most important influence in Jewish life. The mystics were by and large in favor of translations of the Zohar and other mystical works into Yiddish because of their desire to disseminate Kabbalistic ideas as widely as possible. Such works were read avidly by all classes of the population, including scholars. They helped prepare the ground for the propagation of Hassidism. In the introduction to the Yiddish translation of the Zohar (1711), Rabbi Zvi Hirsh Khotsh wrote that redemption could not be attained except by

17. See A. Shohet, *Im Hilufey Tekufot* (Tel Aviv, 1960), p. 304; S. Stein, "Liebliche Tefilloh: A Judeo-German Prayer-Book Printed in 1709," *Leo Baeck Institute Year Book XV* (London, 1970), pp. 41–72; S. Freehof, "Devotional Literature in the Vernacular," *Yearbook of the Central Conference of American Rabbis*, 1923, pp. 375–424.

18. Cf. S. Niger, *Di Tsveyshprakhikayt fun Undzer Literatur* (Detroit, 1941), p. 54, and Zinberg, "Der Kamf . . . ," p. 100.

means of the Zohar and for that reason it was important that
every Jew study it to the best of his ability.[19]

> The reward for the study of this translation of the Zohar into
> *Leshon Ashkenaz* is very great indeed since Moses interpreted
> the holy Torah in seventy tongues. . . . Let not any intelligent
> person be ashamed of reading books in *Taytsh* since Aramaic is
> just like *Taytsh*.[20]

Sacred and secular works in Yiddish began to multiply in
the packs of the wandering Jewish booksellers, who spread their
wares out on tables in the synagogues and houses of study, as
well as in stalls at public fairs. By the end of the eighteenth
century, one could obtain almost any type of sacred work,
including almost all the Hebrew religious classics, in Yiddish
translation.

> Truth to tell [wrote Gedaliah Teykus, author of *Emunas
> Yisroel*], all the lessons which the child hears from his teacher
> he can read more effectively in *Taytsh* books. In our day,
> veritably the entire Torah and all the laws are available in
> *Taytsh*.[21]

With the spread of Hassidism in the latter half of the
eighteenth century, Yiddish achieved new status and dignity.

19. Zinberg, "Der Kamf . . . ," p. 104.
20. Quoted in M. Erik, *Di Geshikhte fun der Yidisher Literatur* (Warsaw, 1928), pp. 241f.
21. Quoted in Zinberg, "Der Kamf . . . ," p. 99. On Hassidism
see M. Aron, *Ideas and Ideals of the Hassidim* (New York, 1969);
M. Buber, *The Tales of Rabbi Nachman* (New York, 1956); S. Dresner, *Levi
Yitzhak of Berdichev* (New York, 1974); S. Dubnow, *Di Geshikhte fun
Khsidizm*, 3 vols. (Buenos Aires, 1957); G. Fleer, *Rabbi Nachman's Fire*
(New York, 1972); S. A. Horodetsky, *Hahasidut Vehahasidim*, 4 vols. (Tel
Aviv, 1953); A. Kaplan, *Rabbi Nachman's Wisdom* (New York, 1973);
Y. Kuk, *Rabi Nahman Mibraslav: Iyunim Besipurav* (Jerusalem, 1973);
J. S. Minkin, *The Romance of Hassidism* (New York, 1935); S. Niger, *Bleter
Geshikhte fun der Yidisher Literatur* (New York, 1959); I. Rabinovich,
Shorashim Umegamot (Jerusalem, 1967); H. M. Rabinowicz, *The World
of Hasidism* (Hartford, Conn., 1970); S. Rozhanski, ed., *Sipurey Mayses*
(Buenos Aires, 1967); S. H. Setzer, *Sipurey Mayses, Vunder Mayses* (New
York, 1929); N. Shemen, *Dos Gezang fun Khsidus*, 2 vols. (Buenos Aires,
1959); E. Steinman, *Kitvey Rabi Nahman* (Tel Aviv, 1951); E. Wiesel, *Souls
on Fire* (New York, 1972); Y. Yaari, ed., *Sipurey Ma'asiyot* (Jerusalem,
1971); H. Zeitlin, *Reb Nakhmen Braslaver* (New York, 1952).

The hassidic teachers conferred prestige on the tongue of the common folk and openly recommended its use for sincere prayer. The hassidic *rebbes* wrote fables and prayers for the people in Yiddish and, in turn, the wonder tales that the *hassidim* told about the *zaddikim* were published in Yiddish as well as Hebrew. Rabbi Levy Yitzkhok of Berdichev (1740–1809) composed original prayers, poems, and songs in Yiddish and Rabbi Nakhman of Bratzlav (1772–1811), whose fables have become classics of Yiddish literature, urged his followers to worship in Yiddish.

> In the sacred tongue it will be difficult for him (the *hassid*) to say everything that he wishes and he will not be able to be as sincere since we do not speak the sacred tongue. But in *Leshon Ashkenaz* which we always use it will be easy for him to speak his heart. His heart is drawn to *Leshon Ashkenaz* to which he is accustomed.[22]

The Haskalah or Jewish Enlightenment movement in Germany took a completely negative attitude toward Yiddish. The *maskilim* rejected the culture of the Hassidim and of the Polish-born teachers in the Jewish schools of Germany. Many of them discarded Hebrew as well as Yiddish. But they looked upon the disappearance of Yiddish as a special sign of enlightenment and as a precondition of emancipation. One of the motivations behind Moses Mendelssohn's initiation of a German translation of the Bible with Hebrew commentary was undoubtedly his desire to wean his coreligionists away from Yiddish.

> I am afraid [he wrote in 1782] that this Jargon has contributed not a little to the rudeness of the common man and I anticipate good results from the growing usage of the pure German vernacular among my brethren. . . . Pure German or pure Hebrew . . but not a mixture of the languages![23]

To Mendelssohn and his followers, Yiddish symbolized foreignness and illegitimacy. The old speech represented the past

22. Quoted in Niger, p. 92.
23. *Mendelssohns Schriften* (Leipzig, 1844), 5 : 505–6. Cf. Zinberg, *Di Geshikhte . . . , 7 : 47.*

that had to be overcome and the antithesis of the "culture" that they wanted to achieve.[24] Mendelssohn associated Yiddish with what his friend Lessing called the "wretched rabble which roams about at the fairs" and with another friend, the irascible Solomon Maimon, who, in moments of excitement, was wont to revert to the Yiddish of his youth. Maimon, in his autobiography, describes the mother tongue of the Jews as an impoverished language, a patois derived from many tongues, which has somehow managed to retain the specific grammatical errors of each of the languages from which it is derived.[25]

Despite such attitudes, a few German *maskilim* did contribute to the development of Yiddish literature. Isaac Eichel and Aaron Wolfson, for example, wrote Yiddish dramas. Eichel (1756–1804), a distinguished biblical scholar who edited the Haskalah journal *Hameasef*, turned to Yiddish out of despair at the sight of young German Jews at the baptismal font and the sacred Hebrew tongue abandoned. His satire *Reb Henokh* could not be written either in Hebrew, which people no longer understood, or in German, which the enemies of the Jews might read. His associate, Wolfson, turned to Yiddish for similar reasons.

Another contribution to the development of Yiddish was made by Moshe Marcuse, who spent the major part of his life as a physician in Poland, Lithuania, and White Russia. His *Seyfer Refues* (Book of Remedies), written in the spoken Yiddish of his patients and on their behalf, was published in 1789. In addition to its rich and natural vocabulary, it is an important source of ethnographic information and marks the development of the Haskalah from a West European to an East European movement.[26]

The Jewish scholars and historians in Germany associated with the scientific study of Judaism (*Wissenschaft des Judentums*)

24. Cf. M. A. Meyer, *The Origins of the Modern Jew* (Detroit, 1967), p. 44. See also H. Walter, *Moses Mendelssohn: Critic and Philosopher* (New York, 1930), pp. 139ff.
25. Zinberg, *Di Geshikhte* . . . , 7:45.
26. *Ibid.*, pp. 140, 141, 149, 151f.

in the nineteenth century sought to demonstrate for political and psychological reasons that Yiddish was nothing but corrupt German. They viewed it as a deterrent to the realization of emancipation and associated it with everything they viewed as negative in Jewish life. They contended that until the sixteenth century Jewish and Christian Germans spoke the same language. It was the Polish Jews, they claimed, who were responsible for turning the beautiful German language into a detestable dialect.

The distinguished historian Heinrich Graetz referred to Yiddish as a "semi-animal tongue." The bibliographer Moritz Steinschneider confessed that for him Yiddish was "something revolting." Abraham Geiger, biblical scholar and champion of religious reform, described Yiddish as "an example of poor taste." Leopold Zunz, historian and theoretician of the *Wissenschaft des Judentums,* did all he could to prove that Yiddish was a comparatively late phenomenon, having emerged no earlier than the sixteenth century. Steinschneider disputed that point with him, dating the origins of Yiddish in the seventeenth century.

The only German Jewish scholar to take a different view was Graetz's predecessor, the historian Isaac Marcus Jost (1793–1860). Jost believed that Yiddish originated in the thirteenth century, when large numbers of Jews exiled from Provence settled in Southern Germany.[27]

From the beginning of the nineteenth century, the continuous development of proto-Yiddishism is clearly discernible. In 1814, Mendl Lefin (1749–1826) of Satanov, a member of Mendelssohn's circle who had settled in Galicia, published a translation of the Book of Proverbs as the first part of a projected complete translation of the Scriptures into colloquial Yiddish. His work aroused the ire of Galician *maskilim* such as the Hebrew publicist Tuvyah Feder (1760–1816), for whom Yiddish was a corrupt dialect to be replaced by pure German in

27. *Ibid.,* 6:21.

the daily life of the people.[28] Feder launched a vitriolic attack against Lefin in a special brochure (*Kol Mehatsetsim*). In spite of the fact that such illustrious personalities as Isaac Baer Levinsohn, leader of the Haskalah movement in Russia, and Jacob Samuel Bik of Brod, came to Lefin's defense, he was compelled to abandon his project and the other sections of the Bible that he translated were circulated in manuscript only.

Bik (1772–1831), a romantic by nature, was unique among the Galician *maskilim* in his positive appraisals of both the Hassidic movement and Yiddish. His letter to Feder is the earliest complete defense of Yiddish as a language. How did Feder dare compare the language into which Lefin translated the Book of Proverbs to the screeching of birds and the bellowing of cows? asked Bik. The Jews of Poland had been speaking that language for 400 years and the great religious leaders, including the Gaon of Vilna, had thought and preached in it. The scholars of every nation had a duty to educate their peoples in their own vernaculars. French and English were also synthetic languages that had been refined. Even German and Russian had but recently been made suitable for conveying noble thoughts and feelings.

> The masses are the creators of every language and at first each tongue has the same pedigree. No one is better or more refined than the other. In the beginning they all stammer and are unformed and unpolished. It remains for the thinkers to make a wonderful instrument out of the formless mass.[29]

In their battle against the *hassidim*, Galician *maskilim* such as Mendl Lefin and Joseph Perl (1773–1839) gradually appropriated one of the successful tactics of their adversaries and began publishing Yiddish tracts. They were soon followed by their Russian and Polish counterparts, many of whom published anti-Hassidic pamphlets anonymously.

28. Cf. R. Mahler, *Hahasidut Vehahaskalah* (Merhaviah, 1961), p. 55. See also S. Versus, "Yankev Shmuel Bik—Der Blondzhendiker Maskil," *Yivo Bleter* 13 (Vilna, 1938): 505–36.
29. *Kerem Hemed*, 1 : 96–102. Cf. Zinberg, *Di Geshikhte* . . . , 8 : 208.

Isaac Baer Levinsohn (1788-1860) wrote that although he sanctioned prayers in any language, he excluded Yiddish as a language fit for prayer. "Why do you need the crippled Judeo-German?" he wrote. "Speak pure German or the language of of the country, the pure, beautiful and rich Russian tongue!"[30] Nevertheless, Levinsohn wrote a bitter satire on Jewish communal life in Yiddish (*Di Hefker-Velt*), which became the prototype of the militant realistic writing of much of nineteenth century Yiddish literature.

Another leading Haskalah writer, Kalman Shulman of Vilna, epitomized the Russian Haskalah's attitude toward Yiddish when he asked God to keep him from writing in the "Jargon." He forbade translation of his Hebrew works into Yiddish.[31] In 1823, one *maskil*, Anton Eisenbaum of Warsaw, published a German newspaper in Hebrew characters with the express purpose of weaning Jews away from Yiddish. Since people could not understand German, however, the paper closed in less than a year.[32]

Although they despised the language and viewed it solely as a temporary means to enlightenment, many of the propagandistic and didactic works of the Russian *maskilim* possessed literary merit and became foundations upon which modern Yiddish literature was established. As more and more people read these works, the value of Yiddish as a modern cultural vehicle increased and it became more difficult to treat it offhandedly. According to the anti-Yiddish Russian *maskil* Joachim Tarnopol,

> In many cities of our fatherland, including Warsaw, Vilna, Odessa, Mohilev, Berdichev, etc., where there are groups of educated Jews, there exists among these enlightened circles a special kind of literary entertainment. Time is spent reading aloud in the simple Polish-Jewish Jargon stories, plays, and whole pamphlets of poetry or prose. In these booklets, which

30. Y. B. Levinsohn, *Teudah Be-Yisrael* (Vilna, 1828), 2, chap. 8. Cf. Zinberg, *Di Geshikhte* . . . , 10:42.
31. Zinberg, *Di Geshikhte* . . . , 10:138.
32. I. Zinberg, *Kultur-Historishe Shtudyes* (New York, 1949), p. 160.

are read to the entire assembled audience, silly customs, archaic beliefs and false hassidic attitudes are severely ridiculed.[33]

The first Haskalah writers to use Yiddish exclusively as well as regularly and systematically, thereby helping to create a modern literature in the language, were Israel Axenfeld of Russia and Solomon Ettinger of Poland. Axenfeld (1787–1866) laid the foundations of modern Yiddish fiction in some twenty-five stories and novels, which became prototypes for the works of later writers. A fierce opponent of Hassidism, he felt that fiction and drama in Yiddish were the most effective weapons in the war against the movement. Ettinger (1800–1856), the author of *Serkele,* a dramatic comedy, wrote poems, fables, and epigrams as well as plays. He was more interested in aesthetic considerations than in the Haskalah solutions to the problems of Jewry. He wrote in a highly polished style, helped refine the Yiddish language, and coined many new words in his works.

Abraham Baer Gottlober (1811–1899), a poet and dramatist who wrote in both Yiddish and Hebrew, typified the ambivalent attitude toward Yiddish that still prevailed among East European *maskilim* in the middle of the nineteenth century. In an article published in 1865, he urged his fellow enlighteners not to be ashamed of the language. "My friends, do you not know that many languages were at first in the same condition as this tongue? In their works, authors improve the languages and make them fit and proper." At other times, however, he referred to Yiddish as the "tongue of Babel" and a "Godless barbarity."[34]

Russian *maskilim* who wrote in Yiddish did so secretively, circulating their works in manuscript only. The few published works were issued anonymously or under pseudonyms.

Some wrote in Yiddish as a joke [wrote Alexander Zederbaum] and did not think of publishing such writings. Some were ashamed of suddenly becoming writers in the poor Jargon,

33. *Kol Mevaser,* no. 22 (Odessa, 1869). Cf. Zinberg, *Kultur-Historishe Shtudyes,* p. 161.
34. *Hamelitz* (St. Petersburg, 1865), pp. 180–81. Cf. Zinberg, *Di Geshikhte . . . ,* 10:168f.

which would hopefully be forgotten by our Russian brethren as
in Germany, where it has already ceased to exist. Some were
incensed lest the harmful Jargon be improved. Writers in the
language were considered buffoons. Who wanted to play such
a role?. . . It is no great honor to be able to write in that
despicable tongue which requires no study and possesses no
grammar, a language which we ourselves consider a misfortune.[35]

By the 1850s Yiddish books of a secular character began to
be printed in large quantities. The inexpensive pamphlets containing simple stories by Isaac Meyer Dik (1814–1893) of Vilna
and other writers helped create a mass audience for secular
Yiddish literature. Dik, the most popular Yiddish writer of the
time, took an attitude toward Yiddish that was typical of the
East European *maskilim*.

> The old German proverb says that a man without a language
> is not a man. If we consider our Lithuanian Jews from this
> point of view, they are not men. We have no language but
> speak only Jargon, a non-language which is a conglomeration
> of old German with Hebrew, Russian, Polish, English, Spanish
> and French; a language which is not understood or spoken by
> any nation; a language which has no grammar but has gathered
> words and expressions from all languages like a beggar. Now,
> thank God, we dress like true Europeans and are on the way to
> speaking the language of our country since we study the
> Russian language eagerly.[36]

By the middle of the nineteenth century, the language of
Ashkenaz had made remarkable progress. Despite opposition
and ridicule, there were Jews who treasured it and spoke out in
its behalf. They were coming to view it as an integral component
of Jewish cultural life. The Galician writers Hirsh Raytman,
Isaiah Finkelstein, and Isaiah Gutman, for example, were developing respect and a genuine fondness for the language. In
Gutman's plays ordinary Yiddish is spoken by all of the char-

35. *Kol Mevaser,* 48 (Odessa, 1869). Cf. Zinberg, *Kultur-Historishe
Shtudyes,* p. 162.
36. I. M. Dik, *Di Eydele Rakhe* (Vilna, 1875), p. 19, Cf. Y. Elzet,
"Undzer Folks-Oyster," *Yidish Amerike,* ed. N. Steinberg (New York,
1929), pp. 244-45.

actors and there is no resort to other languages in order to identify the characters to the audience. In one play there is a scene in which Jewish students in Budapest agree to speak Yiddish among themselves, and another in which two students demonstrate to one another their expertise in Yiddish idioms and expressions.[37]

37. I. Zinberg, *Di Bli-Tkufe fun der Haskole* (New York, 1966), p. 106.

A popular poem by Morris Rosenfeld defending the status of
Yiddish as a language (*Geveylte Shriftn*, New York, 1912).

2
THE EMERGENCE
OF YIDDISHISM

ALEXANDER ZEDERBAUM (1816–1893), THE PUBLISHER OF THE
first Hebrew newspaper in Russia, was embarrassed at the
thought of publishing a Yiddish newspaper. At first his
Hamelitz, which began appearing in 1860, contained only
articles in Hebrew and in German in Hebrew characters. When
the newspaper failed to sell, however, Zederbaum decided to
issue a newspaper in Yiddish that would be called *Kol Mevaser,*
together with *Hamelitz.* More than any other single factor, *Kol
Mevaser,* which appeared from 1862 to 1871, contributed to
the standardization of Yiddish orthography and the development
of modern Yiddish literary diction. It marked the emergence
of Yiddish as a standard literary tongue.

Kol Mevaser helped establish a mass audience for Yiddish
and a Yiddish writing profession. It paved the way for the
Yiddish newspapers of the seventies in Rumania, Galicia, Eng-

land, America, and Palestine. It introduced the Jewish woman to the outside world and helped prepare the Jewish reader for modern literature. Here the earliest Yiddish literary works of Mendele Mokher Seforim (*Dos Kleyne Mentshele*) and Yitskhok-Yoel Linetsky (*Dos Poylishe Yingl*) appeared in serialized form. Here, too, a conscious awareness of the national and literary values of Yiddish in modern Jewish life gradually developed.

As a *maskil* who wanted Russian Jewry to learn Russian and who viewed Hebrew as the only "pure" Jewish tongue, Zederbaum at first saw no particular significance in Yiddish. "We need not wait until scoffers inquire of us," he wrote in *Kol Mevaser*. "It is better that we state immediately that our common Yiddish is certainly not to be considered a language because it is corrupt German."[1] Only practical considerations and the promptings of two friends, S. J. Abramovitsh (Mendele Mokher Seforim) and Y. M. Lifshitz, persuaded him to publish the newspaper. As a result of the financial success of *Kol Mevaser* and of Lifshitz's arguments on behalf of Yiddish, however, Zederbaum eventually became a defender of the language and wrote that it was idle to believe that Jews would ever be weaned away from it. As an outspoken early Zionist, he even proposed that Yiddish become the national language of the Jews in Palestine.

> We do not consider it impossible for the Jargon to eventually develop itself into an independent Jewish language in the way that all languages developed out of earlier ones. Let us imagine that the plan to settle Jews in colonies in Palestine is realized. What language will they be able to use there? They will be unable to transform Hebrew into a language suitable for all purposes. Arabic, which is spoken there, is not easy either. . . . Therefore the language most suited to their needs is a developed and improved form of the Jargon. Should the Jargon actually

1. *Kol Mevaser*, no. 5 (Odessa, 1862). Cf. A. R. Malachi, "Der Kol-Mevaser un Zayn Redaktor," *Pinkes Far der Forshung fun der Yidisher Literatur un Prese*. ed. S. Bickel (New York, 1965), p. 74. See also M. Mandelman, "Tsum Hundert Yorikn Yubiley fun *Kol Mevaser*," *Di Tsukunft* (January 1963), pp. 24–33.

be accepted as the national language in Palestine, it would certainly not have to be abandoned and betrayed by us.[2]

In 1861, Yehoshua Mordecai Lifshitz (1829–1878), the father of Yiddishism and Yiddish lexicography, circulated an essay among the leading *maskilim* of his day about the significance of Yiddish. Lifshitz was instrumental in getting Mendele as well as Zederbaum to turn to the language. In an essay entitled "The Four Classes," published in an early issue of *Kol Mevaser,* he referred to Yiddish as a "completely separate language" and as "our mother tongue." The education and humanization of Jewry, he contended, could not proceed without Yiddish, and for that reason the refinement and development of the language were necessary.

It is still contested that Yiddish is a corrupt language. I admit to being unable to comprehend how a language in which so many thousands of people live and work can be said to be corrupt. The word "corrupt" applies only to something which was once better and has been spoiled. But where is the proof that other languages were initially better? They all developed, as did our language, from other languages. Why, then, not term them "corrupt"?[3]

In order to popularize his ideas, Lifshitz wrote a poem for *Kol Mevaser* entitled "Yudel and Yehudis" about a married couple who personified the Jewish people and the Yiddish language. Here, too, he explained the importance of Yiddish and defended it from its detractors. Lifshitz published another essay in *Kol Mevaser,* entitled "The German-Jewish Bridge," in which he attacked linguistic assimilation and viewed Yiddish as the bridge linking the Jewish and European cultures.

Lifshitz compiled the first Yiddish-German, German-Yiddish (1867), Russian-Yiddish (1869), and Yiddish-Russian (1876) dictionaries. He eventually became a virulent anti-Hebraist and, in the introduction to his Yiddish-Russian dictionary, bitterly

2. *Kol Mevaser,* no. 19 (1863). Cf. Z. Reisen, *Yidishe Literatur un Yidishe Shprakh,* Buenos Aires, 1965, p. 28.
3. *Kol Mevaser,* no. 21 (1863). Cf. A. R. Malachi, p. 74.

attacked those who sought to revive Hebrew as a modern tongue. His position was symbolic of the conflict between Hebraists and Yiddishists that was emerging at the time and that became more acute in the years that followed.

With the appearance of *Kol Mevaser* and the success of his story *Dos Kleyne Mentshele,* which appeared in it in 1864, Mendele Mokher Seforim (1836–1917), who was destined to become the "grandfather" of modern Jewish literature in both Hebrew and Yiddish, decided to write in Yiddish. His motives were shared by many Yiddish writers of the day.

> I observed the life of my people and I wished to impart to them Jewish tales in the holy tongue. The bulk of them, however, did not understand this language, but rather spoke Yiddish. What profit accrues to the writer for all his thoughts and all his labors if he does not thereby serve his people? This question . . . placed me on the horns of a dilemma. In my time, the Yiddish language was a hollow vessel, the work of fools who couldn't talk like human beings. . . . Our writers, the possessors of the gift of expression, were interested only in the holy tongue and did not care about the people; they looked down their noses contemptuously at Yiddish. If one in ten ever reminded himself of the "accursed tongue" and dared to write something in it, he would hide it behind seven locked doors, he would hide it beneath his holy prayershawl, so that his shame might not be discovered to damage his good name. . . . How great then was my dilemma when I considered that if I were to embark upon writing in the "shameful!" tongue, my honorable name would be besmirched! . . . My love for utility, however, conquered my hollow pride and I decided : come what may, I will write in Yiddish, that cast-off daughter—it is time to work for my people. One of my good friends, Yehoshua Mordecai Lifshitz, stood by me and we both began to convince the editor of *Hamelitz* [the leading Hebrew literary journal of the time] to issue a journal in the language of our people. . . . Then the peace of God descended upon me and I wrote my first story *Dos Kleyne Mentshele.*[4]

4. Mendele Mokher Seforim, "Shtrikhn tsu Mayn Biografye," *Ale Verk* 19 (Warsaw, 1928). p. 164f. Translated in "Introduction" to *The Parasite*

With the publication of *Kol Mevaser,* the language controversy between assimilationists, Yiddishists, and Hebraists emerged as an important issue in modern Jewish life. Russian and Polish Jewish assimilationists and their counterparts in other countries actively furthered linguistic assimilation by Jews as a necessary prerequisite to civic and political emancipation. They were also opposed to Hebrew because of its association with Jewish nationalism and to Yiddish because of its low status among non-Jews. Hebraists and Yiddishists, on the other hand, viewed linguistic assimilation as a serious threat to the integrity and continuity of Jewish life. The press and literature of the two languages developed concurrently and the outstanding Hebrew and Yiddish writers were bilingual. Despite differences, Yiddishists and Hebraists stood together against assimilationists and many of them were even sympathetic to each other's aspirations.

An intensive battle against Yiddish in the 1860s was waged by the Polish-Jewish journal *Yutshenka,* which, in addition to the general ideals of the Haskalah, sought to propagate Polish nationalism and the Polish language among Jews. While discussing the achievements of *Yutshenka* in the pages of the Hebrew journal *Hatsefirah,* Hillary Nusbaum, an important contributor to the Polish journal, savagely attacked those who sought to educate the people in Yiddish. It was imperative, he felt, that Polish Jews learn Polish and translate the Bible and Prayer Book into that language. He deplored the fact that Polish Jews spoke what he called "an unfortunate, abandoned and crippled dialect which lacks all structure and represents a mixture of all kinds of tongues."[5]

Simon Dankovitsh, one of the first modern Jewish nationalists in Warsaw, published an item in *Yutshenka* in 1862 about the need to collect Jewish proverbs and other folklore, since they reflect the national philosophy of Jewry. He was summarily rebuffed by H. Glatstern, a frequent contributor to the journal.

by Mendele Mocher Seforim, trans. from the Yiddish by Gerald Stillman (New York, 1956), pp. 10-11.

5. *Hatsefirah,* no. 5 (1862). Cf. Zinberg, *Di Bli-Tkufe fun der Haskole* (New York, 1966), p. 93.

According to Glatstern, the Jews no longer constituted a nation but a religious union. The idea of gathering Jewish proverbs was mere propaganda aimed at strengthening the despised Jargon. When the enlightenment of the masses called for the uprooting of Jargon, Dankovitsh sought to develop its literature. The requirements of archaeological research, he felt, were not worth the damage that buttressing the despised dialect would entail.

When Daniel Nayfeld, editor of *Yutshenka*, heard of plans to publish a Yiddish weekly in Johannesberg, Prussia, as well as Zederbaum's plans to issue a Yiddish supplement to the Hebrew journal *Hamelitz* in Odessa, he wrote a vitriolic editorial attacking Yiddish and impugning the motives of those behind the new publications. Unless the new trend were countered, he felt, a Yiddish grammar and dictionary would eventually be published. These would be followed by poetry, drama, and history in the language. The true intent of these publications would not be the enlightenment of the people but the profits of the publishers. "And then our Christian fellow citizens will also be compelled to learn this babble because several hundred thousand people will speak it."

> Would that our words find a response in all hearts which love our homeland, would that our Christian fellow citizens stand on guard and protest every time the sound of this dialect rings in their ears. Would that the public press punish the authors, publishers, distributors and propagandists of books and newspapers of this type because we feel that our efforts will not be realized soon enough without the assistance of our Christian brothers.[6]

The Emancipation Act granting Polish Jews civic equality was promulgated on June 5, 1862. The seventh point of that Act, which forbade Jews to use Hebrew or Yiddish in legal documents, was hailed in *Yutshenka* as an opportunity for Jews to learn to speak and write Polish. Zederbaum attacked the point as an insult to his people but Nayfeld took the opportunity to berate Yiddish once again. "Down with filth, spiderwebs,

6. Quoted from *Yutshenka*, no. 37 (Warsaw, 1862), pp. 291–95 in Zinberg, pp. 97, 99.

Jargon and every kind of refuse!" he wrote. "We need a broom,
a broom!"[7]

The appearance of *Kol Mevaser* signaled a new turning
inward among Russian and, later, Polish *maskilim,* which in
turn drew strength from the success of the paper, the theoretical
arguments of Lifshitz, and the artistic accomplishments of
Mendele. The growth of populism among Russian students and
intellectuals (*Narodniki*) in the 1870s also influenced Jewish
students and *maskilim* to acquaint themselves more intimately
with their own people and its language and culture.

During the period of political reaction, persecution, and
pogroms in the early 1880s, assimilationist ideology was completely shattered.

> How long is it [wrote the Russian-Jewish writer, B. Brandt, in
> 1881] since we did everything we could when walking in the
> street, riding on a train or sitting in our homes, not to be
> recognized as Jews. Now we have at last cast off that false
> shame. We are not even ashamed to speak Jargon because it
> is the language of the people. Our finest writers in the Russian
> and Hebrew tongues have even begun to write Jargon of late,
> in order to be closer to the people and so that the people
> understand them and derive some benefit from them.[8]

Modern nationalist, populist, and romantic trends emerged in
Jewish life and letters toward the end of the decade. Yiddish
writers turned to Jewish historical and national themes and
many Hebrew and Russian Jewish authors turned to Yiddish.
The prestige of Yiddish rose together with the growth of Jewish
national sentiment and self-respect. Yiddishist theory evolved
together with the developing Yiddish press and literature and
with the Jewish political movements that employed Yiddish in
order to reach the Jewish masses.

With Sholom Aleichem's literary anthologies, *Yidishe Folks-
Bibliotek* (1888, 1889), and Mordecai Spektor's *Hoyz-Fraynd*

7. Quoted from Yutshenka, no. 50 (1862) p. 428 in Zinberg, p. 101.
Cf. J. Shatzky, *Geshikhte fun Yidn in Varshe* (New York, 1948), 2:222f.
8. *Yidishe Folks-Bibliotek* (Kiev, 1899), 2:18. Cf. S. Niger in *Algemeyne
Entsiklopedye,* Yidn G. (New York, 1942), p. 115.

(1888, 1889, 1891, 1895, 1896), the flowering of Yiddish and the renaissance of Yiddish literature in the modern period begin. These literary annuals, edited by two outstanding Yiddish writers, represent the culmination of a process that began with the pogroms in the early 1880s. The growth of the Russian populist movement, the mass emigration to the United States and Argentina, and the rapidly emerging Jewish national consciousness were other factors contributing to this development.

Gradually, the feeling that Yiddish was not a temporary phenomenon, that it had roots in the past as well as the present, began to take hold. Sholom Aleichem and Spektor published works of deceased Yiddish writers that had hitherto been available only in old manuscripts. They brought writers of the older and younger generations together in their annuals, including many who had not written Yiddish for many years. Many Hebrew and Russian-Jewish writers contributed to the anthologies. A new awareness of the possibilities and significance of Yiddish was emerging from these annuals and from the literary creativity that they were stimulating.

Many Jewish intellectuals, however, were appalled by these developments, which smacked of antiquarianism and reaction. In 1889, the celebrated Hebrew poet Y. L. Gordon responded to Sholom Aleichem's invitation to contribute to his Yiddish journal as follows:

> You ask for my opinion of the Jargon? If you promise me to distinguish between this question and personalities and between the Jargon literature and its writers, I will openly declare that I have always considered the survival of this dialect in the mouths of our people as the most unfortunate phenomenon of its historic existence. It is the badge of shame of the hounded wanderer and I consider it the duty of every educated Jew to do what he can to see to it that it is gradually erased and vanishes from our midst. It may be tolerated as a necessary evil. It may be used as a means with which to realize the best ideas among our benighted masses. But under no circumstances should one concern himself with its strengthening or flowering. Truth to tell, I am surprised at you. You write Russian well and have a beautiful command of our literary tongue (Hebrew).

How then can you devote yourself to the Jargon culture? There is no doubt that you possess a magnificent writing talent. I know that our benighted brothers take delight in your works and it is your right to write in Jargon as much as your heart desires. But it would be a sin for you to educate your children in that language. It would be like compelling them to march down Nevsky Boulevard in undershirts and with their boots sticking out.[9]

The theoretical underpinning of the new Yiddishist trend was supplied by the literary critic, dramatist, and folklorist Joseph Judah Lerner (1847–1907), who wrote extensively in Russian and Hebrew as well as Yiddish. Lerner was a radical Yiddishist who defended the language as a tool of enlightenment and as an essential aspect of the Jewish nationality. He praised the language for its originality and for having absorbed the precision of French, the depth of German, and the rigorousness of English. He believed that only in Yiddish would the Jew be willing to listen to new ideas that would enable him to improve his life. In the renaissance of the language and its literature he perceived the rebirth of Jewry. Yiddish, he said, would endure as long as the Jewish people. In an address delivered in 1889 he said the following:

Three generations back our parents linked the fortune of the Jewish people with the language. They bound both their nationality and their sad experiences to Yiddish so that this threefold cord will never be broken. Our children and the younger generation may be fluent in the language of the country and not even understand Yiddish. Nevertheless, our language will continue to live because it is called Yiddish and is indeed Jewish! It is in the Jargon that one meets the Jewish proverb, the ingenious Jewish stratagem, the clever Jewish notion, the striking Jewish argument, the Jewish sigh. Here one finds the essential Jew. No matter how estranged one may be from the externalities of Judaism, no matter how far his education takes him from Jewish concerns, he remains bound to that which we call the spark of Jewishness. . . . As long as he loves Jews

9. Quoted in *Dos Sholom Aleichem Bukh*, ed. Y. D. Berkovits (New York, 1926), p. 183.

he will love Yiddish. . . . If his brethren are close to him,
he will not withdraw himself from their language. Who can
remove himself from his own unfortunate, powerless people?
Who can reject that which his people call "Yiddish" and which
they exhibit proudly on the banner of their nationality? . . .
The language has been transformed into the tablets of stone
upon which the Jew has engraved his hopes and his national
feelings, his very life. . . . As long as there are Jews they will
speak Yiddish. In other words, Jargon will live as long as the
Jewish nationality.[10]

In attacking those who saw nothing of literary value in
Yiddish poetry, Lerner advanced the concept of Yiddish literature as the national literature of Jewry instead of merely
a temporary concession to Jewish women and uneducated men.
The Yiddish muse, he believed, was endowed with its fair share
of God's gracious blessings.

On the green hill where all the muses stand before the throne
of glory, the Yiddish muse has an honored place and has been
graced with an equal measure of loveliness and beauty. She is
not a withered limb but a stream of the source which refreshes
the thirsty human heart. She is part of the flame which will
burn forever and never be extinguished.[11]

Yehoshua Hona Ravnitsky (1859–1944), a Hebrew and
Yiddish literary critic, was also extremely sympathetic to the
new developments. In 1882, Ravnitsky wrote that the Jewish
people and the Yiddish language shared the same fate. While
the nations refused to recognize the Jews as a nation, the Jews
refused to recognize Yiddish as a language.[12] As we shall see,
this idea was later developed by Chaim Zhitlovsky, the principal
exponent of Yiddishism. Ravnitsky's viewpoint was that Yiddish

10. Quoted in N. B. Minkov, *Zeks Yidishe Kritiker* (Buenos Aires, 1954),
pp. 97–98.
11. Y. Lerner, "Di Yidishe Muze," *Hoyzfraynd* (St. Petersburg, 1889),
2:182–98. Cf. Minkov, p. 99.
12. *Yidishe Folks-Bibliotek,* 2:330. Cf. S. Niger, *Bleter Geshikhte fun
der Yidisher Literatur* (New York, 1959), p. 394.

literature was primarily a means of raising the cultural level of the masses. He attacked his fellow Hebraists who refused to acknowledge that fact.

> Hebrew is precious and ever so sacred. But what should the thousands of our poor brethren and the hundreds of thousands of our sisters, the mothers of our children, who do not understand that language, do? Why is it that when Hebrew writers sometimes write in Russian, German, etc., no interpretations are attached to their actions, while the unfortunate stepchild, the Jargon, arouses the envy of all. When it opens its mouth to speak, it is accused of wanting to swallow the world![13]

Ravnitsky also wrote that, in addition to the functional desirability of Yiddish, "Jewish life can in no language be depicted as correctly as in the Jewish folk tongue, in Jargon which is spoken by several million Jews."[14]

Ravnitsky viewed Hebrew as the only national language of Jewry and took issue with the militant Yiddishists among his colleagues in the Zionist camp, whom he considered "folkists" rather than true nationalists. But he also opposed the anti-Yiddishists, whom he accused of being blind to the historical and practical significance of the folk tongue that they jeered at as the "language of the exile."

> There is nothing [he wrote in 1903] which angers me more than this epithet which is used by so many and particularly by our young nationalist and Zionist *maskilim* who know Hebrew. Consider how this language which our parents and ancestors spoke for several hundred years (not just one party or Jewish sect but all sections of the people from the smallest to the greatest, the masses as well as the great rabbis, the poor and the wealthy) —this language in which the people thought, laughed, sighed and cried for such a long time, which comprises part of its soul and clearly bears the stamp of its unique spirit; consider how they frivolously come to abolish it, degrade it, defame it and turn it into a rag which the Hebrews wore during medieval times. Such a language they seek to consciously erase and

---

13. *Yidishe Folks-Bibliotek*, 2 : 272. Cf. Niger, p. 395.
14. Y. Ravnitsky, "Hebreyish un Yidish (Zhargon)," *Hoyzfraynd*, vol. 5 (St. Petersburg, 1896). Cf. Minkov, p. 141.

destroy? . . . The language of the Exile! But what are we and
what is our life? Are not our people in the Diaspora children
of the Exile and is not their life the life of the Exile? I am
unable to comprehend what is meant by an ugly and disgusting
language. If an untalented writer writes Jargon and what he
writes is unacceptable, it would be just as unacceptable if he
wrote Hebrew. . . . But that is not the case when a writer like
Mendele or even a writer of modest talent writes Jargon.
Jargon—corrupt German! But English, too, was once like this
corrupt language, this patois. . . . If we carefully dissect and
analyze this animosity to Jargon we find that it contains a
variety of elements: elements of the old Haskalah spirit which,
because it sought to accommodate itself to European tongues,
detested the language as a symbol of ignorance; elements of the
aristocratic spirit which snubbed the language and attempted to
retreat from the "ugliness" and separate itself from the small
oppressed community with its hovels and cellars of benighted
masses with faltering, earthy speech . . . and other such alien
elements. All of this is unconscious, of course. Consciously they
try to justify their opposition on flimsy "nationalist" grounds.
On the basis of such noble considerations they proclaim: Rid
yourselves of the Jargon! It is a disgusting, contemptible, revolting abomination which must be destroyed. . . ![15]

The Jewish historian Simon Dubnow (1860–1941), who
also wrote literary criticism in Russian for the Russian Jewish
journal *Voskhod,* became another defender of Yiddish during
this period. Dubnow's attitude toward Yiddish was of particular
significance because of the influence of his ideas of Jewish
national and cultural autonomy in the Diaspora. Dubnow
believed that despite emancipation, the national characteristics
of Jewry could be preserved in the Diaspora by means of
democratic Jewish self-government within the framework of
multinational states. These ideas, which influenced all shades
of Jewish nationalist thought, served as the basis of the Russian
Jewish *Folkspartey,* which was formed in 1906, and of the
Polish Jewish *Folkspartey,* organized during the First World War.

As late as 1886, in the course of a review of a book of
Yiddish poems (*Sikhas Khulin*) that the anti-Yiddish Hebrew

15. Y. H. Ravnitsky, *Dor Vesofrav* (Tel Aviv, 1937), 2:188–90.

poet, Y. L. Gordon, had grudgingly consented to have published, Dubnow wrote:

> The right of the Jewish Jargon to literature and to poetry in particular has always appeared questionable to me. In order to be a literary language, Jargon must first of all become a language with an established grammar and phraseology which are not in dispute. Jargon does not fulfill these requirements. There is something awkward and laughable about the Jargon language. It is suited to a very limited group of concepts.[16]

Only two years later, however, as a result of the literary renaissance engendered by the publications of Mordecai Spektor and Sholom Aleichem, Dubnow radically altered his position.

> Before our eyes a transition which makes us rejoice is taking place in the Jargon literature from flimsy primitive works which the masses were given of necessity, to serious works which stimulate thought and convey a fertile refreshing stream to the popular mind. We see very promising beginnings in the Jargon literature of serious period fiction. We see talented authors who are coming forth with spirit. We notice the rise of a periodical press which satisfies the needs of a specific section of the reading public. We are witnesses to a folk literature in the process of organization which is filled with a variety of sincere efforts and which appreciates the responsibilities and needs of the modern age. What makes Yiddish worse than Bulgarian or than the minor Slavic, Germanic or Romance dialects which no one denies the right to possess literatures? Is the number of Jews who speak Jargon smaller than the number of Czechs and Bulgarians who have their own literatures (there are about 3 million Czechs and 2 million Bulgarians)? . . . Jargon is more suited to the depiction of Jewish life than Russian or Hebrew.[17]

In his influential *Letters on Old and New Judaism,* which originally appeared in *Voskhod* between 1897 and 1907, Dubnow compared the Jewish people to a cripple with one natural

16. (*Voskhod,* 1886). Cf. N. Mayzel, *Tsurikblikn un Perspektivn* (Tel Aviv, 1962), pp. 11f, and his *Tsum Hundertstn Geboyrnyor fun Shimon Dubnow* (New York, 1961), p. 21.
17. (*Voskhod,* 1888). Cf. Mayzel, *Tsurikblikn un Perspektivn,* p. 10 and *Tsum Hundertstn Geboyrnyor fun Shimon Dubnow,* pp. 22–23.

leg (Hebrew) and one artificial leg ((Yiddish). The Jewish people had stood and survived on those two legs for many generations. The linguistic dualism of Hebrew and Yiddish was similar to that of Hebrew and Aramaic in former generations. "Do those nationalists who affirm the Diaspora wish to remove the artificial leg, which for some time now, has gained the strength of a natural leg? Do they not wish to use it in order to gain a firmer foothold in our national life?"

> Among the forces which are the basis of our autonomy in the Diaspora, I also set aside a place for the powerful force of the folk language used by seven million Jews in Russia and Galicia which, for several generations, now fulfills the function of a spoken language of instruction in the school (the *heder* and *yeshiva*), and to an appreciable degree also a language of literature. . . . Let our relation to the "Jargon" or, more correctly to Yiddish, be what it may, we dare not abandon one of the foundations of our national unity in the very hour that the languages of the peoples around us rob our people of thousands and tens of thousands of its sons, so that they no longer understand the language used by their parents. We must not destroy with our hands the power of our folk language to compete with the foreign languages, which lead to assimilation. Such destruction would amount to suicide. There being no hope of converting our ancient national tongue into the living and daily spoken language in the Diaspora, we would be committing a transgression against our national soul if we did not make use in our war against assimilation of the great counterforce stored up in the language of the people. . . . When the language problem is posed in all its ramifications and when it is clarified not from the viewpoint of one party or of one literary clique or another, but from the general national viewpoint, then there will be no place for errors in this matter. Insofar as we recognize the merit of national existence in the Diaspora, we must also recognize the merit of Yiddish as one of the instruments of autonomy, together with Hebrew and the other factors of our culture.[18]

18. S. Dubnow, *Nationalism and History* (Philadelphia, 1958), pp. 190–91. See also N. Mayzel, *Tsum Hundertstn Geboyrntog fun Shimon Dubnow* (New York, 1961); Y. Mark, *Shimon Dubnow* (New York, 1962); J. Rothenberg, *Shimon Dubnow tsu Zayn Hundert Yorikn Geeboyrntog*

The appearance of Sholom Aleichem's *Folks-Bibliotek* gave rise to a significant series of articles on the language question in the Hebrew journal *Hamelitz* in 1889.[19] E. L. Levinsky, a leading Zionist publicist, wrote that the revival of Yiddish was artificial and misleading. The days of the language were numbered. He recognized that the language had fulfilled an important function for hundreds of years and had been hallowed in the eyes of the people. But with the growth of a significant literature in the language, the danger that it might supplant Hebrew was very real. Levinsky attacked the contributors to the *Folks-Bibliotek*, most of whom were Hebrew writers, as traitors to Hebrew. They had gone over to Yiddish solely for the substantial fees that Sholom Aleichem was paying for contributions to his journal. Hebrew, on the other hand, was in a sorrowful plight, abandoned by its erstwhile devotees.[20]

The deep affection of the genial Yiddish humorist Solomon Rabinovich (Sholom Aleichem, 1859–1916) for both Yiddish and Hebrew remained constant throughout his life.[21] He responded sympathetically to Levinsky, for he too was moved by the plight of Hebrew. He assured Levinsky, however, that the bond that existed between the editor of the *Folks-Bibliotek* and its contributors was deeper and nobler than Levinsky had realized. What Levinsky termed an artificially induced renaissance of Yiddish was actually, according to Sholom Aleichem, an expression of the awakening of the Jewish national spirit. The Yiddish writers were serving the best interests of the Jewish people as a whole. The future of Yiddish was not neces-

(New York, 1961); S. Goodman, "Simon Dubnow—A Reevaluation," *Commentary* (December 1960); R. Mahler, *Historiker un Vegvayzer* (Tel Aviv, 1967), pp. 68–99; S. Rawidowicz, ed., *Sefer Shimon Dubnow* (London, 1954); A. Steinberg, ed., *Simon Dubnow—The Man and His Work* (London, 1961).

19. See G. Kresel, "A Historisher Polemik Vegn der Yidisher Literatur," *Di Goldene Keyt*, no. 20 (Tel Aviv, 1954), pp. 338–55.

20. E. L. Levinsky, "Sefat Ever Usefat Yehudit Hameduberet," *Hamelitz*, nos. 58, 59 (St. Petersburg, 1889). Cf. Kresel, p. 339.

21. Cf. A. Novershtern, "Sholem Aleichem un Zayn Shtelung tsu der Shprakhn-Frage," *Di Goldene Keyt*, no. 74 (Tel Aviv, 1971), pp. 164–88.

sarily bleak and, in any event, the needs of the present indicated its usage.

> Every objective person will have to admit that the revival of Jargon is the best proof of the fact that the self-awareness of the Jewish people is growing. The success of Yiddish attests to our writing not for a handful of elite individuals but for an entire people. The people understands us. Our ideas and opinions penetrate the hearts of our brothers. What more need we ask?[22]

Ravnitsky added his voice to the discussion. Levinsky, he believed, had misunderstood the intentions of the "handmaid" that was Yiddish. She sought not to replace her "mistress," but to serve her. Yiddish would bring the masses closer to their writers, educate them, and make them more receptive to Hebrew as well.[23]

Levinsky renewed his attack in several additional articles in *Hamelitz*. He impugned the motives of the Yiddish writers, pointing out that most of the contributions to the *Folks-Bibliotek* were beyond the comprehension and appreciation of the masses. The Yiddish literati were, in fact, interested not in the common man but in his language, in Yiddish itself. In the past, even the masses had used Hebrew in their letters and for business purposes. Hebrew usage was the true yardstick of Jewish independence and its replacement by Yiddish was a sign of the weakening of that independence. The notion that Yiddish would inspire Jewish national consciousness was false. It was the reverse of that proposition that was nearer to the truth.[24]

The publicist Yehuda Leyb Gamzu took issue with another contention of Levinsky, namely, that modern Yiddish literature

22. Sholom Aleichem, "Lisheelat Hasafah," *Hamelitz*, no. 80 (1889). Cf. Kresel, pp. 340f.
23. Y. H. Ravnitsky, "Hayesh Tsorekh Basifrut Hazhargohit?" *Hamelitz*, nos. 96–98 (1889). Cf. Kresel, pp. 342f.
24. E. L. Levinsky, "Hayey Olam Vehayey Shaa," *Hamelitz*, nos. 104–6 (1889), and "Yohanan Hasandlar Lefanim Veata," *Hamelitz*, no. 113 (1889). Cf. Kresel, pp. 345f.

sought to replace the traditional religious literature in Yiddish
that was still read by the masses. According to Gamzu, the
traditional ethical tracts and the collections of talmudic legends
had long been abandoned for the sentimental pulp novels that
were primarily historical romances bereft of aesthetic taste,
ethical value, and Jewish content. It was the latter that Sholom
Aleichem's *Folks-Bibliotek* sought to replace with good literature
that could offer the people authentic knowledge of its own past.[25]
In 1888 Sholom Aleichem had actually published a ferocious
attack against the leading Yiddish pulp novelist, Nakhum-Meyer
Shaykevitsh (Shomer).[26]

Ravnitsky supported Sholom Aleichem in still another
article. He argued that it was not language but the purposes
and goals that writers took upon themselves that were of primary
importance in a literature. The future belonged not to the
writers of one or the other language, but to those who wrote
well. The demise of Yiddish would not benefit Hebrew and
could only harm those Jews who knew no other language.[27]

Sholom Aleichem had planned to publish a Yiddish translation of Heinrich Graetz's *History of the Jews*. Shlomo Skomorovsky, one of Sholom Aleichem's colleagues, wrote to Graetz for
permision but was refused. In his reply Graetz gave expression
to his negative feelings toward Yiddish and Yiddish literature.
Skomorovsky presented his own views of the matter in an article
in *Hamelitz* reviewing the correspondence.

> Yiddish is the language of 3,000,000 Jews, writing for whom
> is a privilege for any author. Yiddish is an instrument with
> which knowledge may be spread among the masses in order to
> raise their cultural level. Graetz's opposition to Yiddish is
> attributable to his having been raised in Western Europe where
> Yiddish has lost its significance for the Jewish community. If
> he saw what great success Sholom Aleichem's publication is

25. Y. L. Gamzu, "Teshuva Kahalakha," *Hamelitz*, no. 119. (1889). Cf.
Kresel, pp. 348f.
26. Sholom Aleichem, *Shomers Mishpet*, Berdichev (1888). See also
R. Shomer-Batshelis, *Undzer Foter Shomer* (New York, 1950).
27. Y. H. Ravnitsky, "Od Bizehut Sifrut Haam," *Hamelitz*, nos. 130–31
(1889). Cf. Kresel, pp 350f.

having among the Jewish masses in Eastern Europe, he would
certainly alter his opinion and say : Congratulations, wonderful
author, on your works in the field of Jargon![28]

In 1899, *Der Yid,* a Zionist bi-weekly in Yiddish edited by
Ravnitsky, was published in Cracow. With its twenty-first issue,
the journal became a weekly under the editorship of Joseph
Luria (1871–1937), who made it the outstanding Yiddish
publication in the world. The leading Yiddish writers contributed
to it and Sholem Asch made his debut in it. Luria was one of
several leading Zionists who may be considered militant Yiddishists, although he later turned to Hebrew exclusively. On several
occasions he opposed the official negative attitude of the movement toward the language. "The people," he once said, "is
more nationalistic in Jargon than in Hebrew."[29] Luria believed
that both from the standpoint of Jewish nationhood and Jewish
culture, Yiddish was valuable in its own right. He felt that it
merited being treated as more than merely a means of propaganda and argued on behalf of its literary development. He
even proposed that Yiddish be used as the language of instruction
in modern Jewish elementary and secondary schools.[30]

> In the Jargon, the Jewish people has invested part of its soul.
> It is not without reason that the Jewish people considers the
> language its own, loves it and feels insulted when true and false
> intellectuals are ashamed of it and estrange themselves from it.[31]

In 1900 Simon Bernfeld, a well-known Hebrew scholar and
author, published an article in *Der Yid* entitled "The People
and Its Intelligentsia," in which he advocated closer ties between
the two groups through the medium of the Yiddish language.
Yiddish, he believed, could be of great assistance to the national

28. S. Skomorovsky, "Eeneh Af Ani Helki," *Hamelitz,* no. 133 (1889).
Cf. Kresel, p. 352.
29. Quoted by J. Shatzky in *Algemeyne Entsiklopedye,* Yidn G, p. 229.
30. Y. Luria, "Yidish un Zayn Natsyonaler Batayt," *Fraynd* (St. Petersburg, 1906). Cf. S. Rozenhek, "Hebreyish-Yidish," *Di Goldene Keyt,* no. 66
(Tel. Aviv. 1969). p. 160.
31. Y. Luria. Cf. *Leksikon fun der Nayer Yidisher Literatur* (New York,
1963), 5:26.

movement.[32] Bernfeld's article was an indirect response to an anti-Yiddish article by Ahad Haam that had appeared earlier in the same publication. As we shall see, Ahad Haam's attack was countered directly in the Hebrew periodical *Healid* by the young scholar Matisyohu Mieses, who was to play an important role in the Czernowitz Conference. A number of important articles exploring the language controversy from a variety of viewpoints were published in *Di Velt,* an official Zionist weekly in Yiddish founded by Theodor Herzl in Vienna in 1900. One of the participants in the discussion was the Hebrew writer Yitzhak Lubetsky, who, in a series of articles entitled "Concerning a Museum," attacked the attitude of the *maskilim* and the Zionists, Ahad Haam included, toward the language of the folk.

In spite of all that has happened, the enlightened and awakened Jews are still up to their necks in the period of self-deprecation. They hate and despise everything obviously Jewish that lacks an archaic mark of mummification, or the scent of the graveyard. An example of this is the attitude of our so-called *maskilim* to the Jargon. . . . Its spirit makes it even closer to us than the sacred tongue. The little that has remained with us of the ancient Hebraic and Talmudic spirit we have incorporated in Jargon. That which was not included has been lost to us in spite of our having received a basically Hebraic-Talmudic education. From the point of view of habit and experience, it is clear that ninety per cent of the Jewish masses have ever since childhood become accustomed to the sounds of Jargon which rouse every Jewish heart that has been uprooted and estranged from Jewry. Jargon is an aspect of the life and soul f the Jewish people.[33]

A significant statement explaining Zionist and Hebraist sympathy to Yiddish was made by the Hebrew writer Mordecai ben Hillel Hakohen in 1903 :

32. S. Bernfeld, "Dos Folk un di Inteligents," *Der Yid,* no. 2 (Cracow, 1900). Cf. Z. Reisen, p. 32.
33. Y. Lubetsky, "Vegn a Muzeum," *Di Velt* (Vienna, 1900). Cf. Reisen, pp. 33-34.

Without being convinced of the great value of Jargon, we cannot deny that our people created this language and imbued it with both the spirit of its ancient language and their own spirit. Within this language which is basically alien we find many sparks of the light of Israel and rays of its national soul. . . . There is therefore no ground for prophetic writers in the Jewish camp to avoid Jargon which is spoken by most of our people. Only by means of the Jargon can we understand the internal life of the Jewish masses which are hidden from the eyes of foreigners. As long as we do not understand Jargon, we will not feel the pulsebeat of the masses or train our ears to hear the whisper of the strings and the tunes which quietly waft towards us from the lips of the masses when they address us or each other. Nor will we have the real key to the sealed garden, to the people's heart.[34]

Max Nordau, Herzl's colleague and an outstanding figure in the history of Zionism, was also a sincere devotee of Yiddish. "To feel ashamed of the Yiddish language," he once wrote, "is to be guilty of anti-Semitism."[35]

The distinguished Hebrew writer Mikha Yosef Berdichevsky (1865-1921) was the most eloquent expositor in both Hebrew and Yiddish about the respective functions of the two languages and their literatures in Jewish life. He saw Hebrew as the language of the book and of the traditional heritage and Yiddish as the language of daily life and ordinary experience in the present. In Hebrew were contained the values of the Jewish past and the products of the great geniuses of Jewish thought, whereas in Yiddish the common people had created a vessel for their own spirit.

The Yiddish language is indeed taken from foreign soil and drawn from another spring. But it is ours, it has become part of us. It became ours when it ceased being German and became Jewish. It is not roots and words or nouns and verbs which create a language but declensions and usages, conjugations and compound forms, and the way Jews use them orally and

34. M. Hakohen, "Sefat Hagalut," *Luah Ahiasaf* (5663) (1903). Cf. *Kitvey M. Y. Berdichevsky* (Tel Aviv, 1960), 2:188.
35. Quoted in J. L. Baron, ed. *A Treasury of Jewish Quotations* (New York, 1956), p. 558.

psychologically. The Yiddish language, attached as it is to the soul of the simple masses and delimiting as it does their national and intellectual boundaries, is purely Jewish. In it is expressed and revealed the soul of a people which although removed from books was nevertheless raised in an atmosphere of books, of Torah and of *mitzvot*. Yiddish is a hybrid, a combination of parts, and yet a single creation. Its grammar book consists of the winding corridors and rooms of the folk spirit. The Hebrew portion of the Yiddish language, too, is no longer purely Hebraic but has become part and parcel of Yiddish. . . . If we lacked the popular stories of the leading Yiddish folk writers (a portion of Mendele and all of Sholom Aleichem) we would be missing a whole world, a *Mishneh Torah* of the soul of the common people in their own language and their own spirit.[36]

With the mass immigration of Jews to England and the United States in the eighties and nineties, came the flourishing of Yiddish literature, press, and theater. For the first time, modern Yiddish culture was able to develop without religious or governmental restrictions. Yiddish became the vehicle for the propagation of various shades of socialism, anarchism, and nationalism among the immigrants.[37] The first document of Yiddishism in the United States was *Di Yidish-Daytshe Shprakh,* which appeared in a New York Yiddish newspaper in 1886 and as a separate brochure in 1887. Written by the distinguished linguist and lexicographer Alexander Harkavy (1863–1939), it attempted to prove that Yiddish was a language like all others by describing its principal characteristics.[38]. In 1889, a group of Yiddish writers in New York attempted to establish a Society of Literati (*Literatn-Fareyn*) for "the improvement of the Jargon literature in spiritual attitude and external form."[39] In 1899,

36. M. Y. Berdichevsky, pp. 185, 187: See also N. Mayzel, "Der Yidisher Mikha Yosef Berdichevsky," *Yidishe Kultur* (November 1965), pp. 18-21; W. Glicksman, "M. Y. Berdichevsky," *Di Tsukunft* (February 1966), pp. 60-61; S. Bickel, *Shrayber fun Mayn Dor* (Tel Aviv, 1970) 3:403-5.

37. See M. Doroshkin, *Yiddish in America: Social and Cultural Foundations* (Rutherford, N.J., 1969); E. Schulman, *Di Geshikhte fun der Yidisher Literatur in Amerike* (New York, 1943); K. Marmor, *Der Onhoyb fun der Yidisher Literatur in Amerike* (New York, 1944).

38. *Leksikon fun der Nayer Yidisher Literatur* (New York, 1960), 3:82.

39. Reisen, p. 39.

Professor Leo Wiener of Harvard University, who had translated a volume of Yiddish poems by Morris Rosenfeld that became a best seller, published *Yiddish Literature in the Nineteenth Century,* the first history of Yiddish literature in any language.

The 1890s also saw an upsurge of Yiddish literary creativity in Europe as well as a deepening interest in the gathering and publication of Yiddish folklore materials. Both trends, as we shall see, were associated with the figure of Y. L. Peretz, the "father" of modern Yiddish literature.[40]

The phenomenal growth of Yiddish journalism in Europe in the first decade of the twentieth century was spearheaded by the first European Yiddish daily, *Der Fraynd,* which commenced publication in St. Petersburg in 1903. This newspaper, which was originally pro-Zionist and neutral with regard to Yiddish, gradually veered toward the radical and revolutionary movements and an outspoken Yiddishism. In the United States, where Yiddish dailies had been published since the 1880s, Yiddish journalism had developed into a tremendous social and cultural force.[41] Yiddish newspapers and magazines representing the full gamut of Jewish life were appearing in almost every Jewish settlement on both sides of the Atlantic at the beginning of the century.

A number of outstanding Yiddish writers championed the cause of the language at the beginning of the twentieth century. Abraham Reisen (1876–1953), who was active as an editor and publisher as well as a poet and short story writer, launched a campaign for the recognition of Yiddish as a "national language" of Jewry as early as 1900.[42]

40. Cf. S. Niger, *Dertseylers un Romanistn* (New York, 1946), pp. 106f.
41. See M. Soltes, *The Yiddish Press: An Americanizing Agency* (Philadelphia, 1925).
42. Z. Reisen, pp. 35f. On Abraham Reisen see also S. Slutsky, *Abraham Reisen—Bibliografye* (New York, 1956); A. Reisen, *Lider, Dertseylungen, Zikhroynes,* ed., S. Rozhanski (Buenos Aires, 1966); J. Botoshansky, *Ophandlungen yn Rayze Ayndrukn* (Buenos Aires, 1967); S. Bickel, *Shrayber fun Mayn Dor,* vol. 1 (New York, 1958); L. Domankevitsh, *Fun Aktueln un Eybikin* (Paris, 1954); J. Glatstein, *In Tokh Genumen,* vol. 1 (New York, 1947), vol. 2 (New York, 1956); M. Joffe, *Ringen in der Keyt* (New York, 1939); N. B. Minkov, *Yidishe Klasiker Poetn* (New York, 1937); S. Niger,

Baal Makhshoves (Isadore Elyashev, 1873–1924), the most important Yiddish literary critic of the period and an outstanding Zionist publicist, contributed greatly to the growing awareness of the significance of the language. He stressed the value of Yiddish in transmitting new concepts and ideas to the people and in reflecting their inner life and thus enabling them to better understand themselves. Yiddish had become important in effecting a reconciliation between the masses and the intellectuals who had become estranged from the life of their people and were unable to truly comprehend its life.

Those who comfort themselves with the thought that the Jargon is only a temporary means to an end, and one which we will some day rid ourselves of, are in error. A language is not something one bandies about like a shoemaker's awl. History demonstrates more than once how a means may eventually become a primary end. . . .

A language is a living thing which grows together with the soul of a people. It is enriched when the souls of the people who speak it are enriched. It is a vessel which protects each drop. Everything which previous generations invested in it is protected as if in a lime-pit or a well which rainwater cannot penetrate. It is like a balloon which can be constantly stretched to contain new treasures of human art and thought, and nuances of color, sound and feeling. It is like a layer of skin which surrounds the soul of people who speak it and think in it. It is completely saturated with the spirit of its people from whom it cannot be parted.

The opponents of Jargon who use it temporarily in order to educate the people argue that it is not a language, that it is a horrible misfortune, a demon, a plague foisted upon us by the Exile. It is difficult to debate such opponents. Let them argue as they will. One can only advise them to leaf through the works of Mendele, Peretz, Sholom Aleichem and others; and to penetrate the spirit of Jargon which resounds in the streets and

Yidishe Shrayber in Tsvantsikstn Yorhundert, vol. 1 (New York, 1972); M. Olgin, *In der Velt fun Gezangen* (New York, 1919); J. Pat, *Shmuesn mit Yidishe Shrayber* (New York, 1954); B. Rivkin, *Yidishe Dikhter in Amerike,* vol. 1 (New York, 1947); B. Green, *Fun Dor tsu Dor; Literarishe Eseyen* (New York, 1971); D. Leybl, "Der Dikhter fun Mentshlekhn Leyd," *Di Goldene Keyt,* no. 9 (1951); Y. Paner, "Abraham Reisen," *Di Goldene Keyt,* no. 9 (1951).

synagogues, in the factories and shops, at weddings, births, parties and funerals, in times of difficulty and sorrow, in minutes of anger, fear, worry and tragedy. Then perhaps the debate may be ended and in the manner to which we alluded above.

The Jargon is a language. Although it is the language of a people driven from its home, it is still a language. As long as we are a people in Exile, we will not divest ourselves of it for it is perfectly suited to our needs.[43]

At the turn of the century Yiddishism also found eloquent expression in writings by Jews in other languages. In England, for example, the successful Anglo-Jewish writer, Israel Zangwill, was doing much to improve the attitude of British Jewry to Yiddish.[44] In Germany, Richard Loewe, a Germanics scholar, published an important article in a German Jewish journal in 1904 in which he analyzed the hostility toward Yiddish of his fellow German Jews. In it he wrote:

The antipathy of the Christian European environment to the Jews evoked anti-Semitism on the part of the Jews themselves and the detestation which this environment cultivated towards the language of the Jews also became part of the Jews. It is noteworthy that even in the circles where Jewish identity has been reawakened, this hatred toward the Jargon (as the East European Jew himself refers to the language) continues. Even good Jewish nationalists hold their education responsible for their exchanging their "corrupt" language (so they view their Yiddish) for Russian, Polish, Hungarian or Romanian. It is obvious that this is against the interests of the Jewish people. For as long as Hebrew is unable to replace Yiddish, the latter represents our national tongue. The adoption of the vernaculars of our environments which become our family tongues as we abandon Yiddish betokens the complete triumph of assimilation which may place our future generations in a most difficult national situation.[45]

Concurrent with these stirrings among the scholars and

43. Baal Makhshoves. *Geklibene Shriftn* (Vilna, 1910), 1 : 11–13.
44. See I. Zangwill, *The Voice of Jerusalem* (New York, 1921), pp. 254–62: J. Leftwich, *Israel Zangwill* (New York, 1957); and M. Wohlgelernter, *Israel Zangwill: A Study* (New York, 1964).
45. Quoted in Z. Reisen, pp. 36f.

literati, a number of political developments in Jewish life furthered the evolution of Yiddishist sentiment. The Jewish socialist movement, Zionism, and the rebirth of modern Hebrew language and culture that attended it, as well as the struggle for Jewish national rights in Eastern Europe, were all important factors in the development of the Yiddish language and culture in modern times. Consequently, they also contributed to the emergence of Yiddishism. It is to these significant developments that we now turn.

„איך קום ניט צו דיר פון גאַטס־וואַרט אַ
באַשטראַלטע,
אַזוי ווי מיין זשוועסטער פלעגט קומען אַמאָל —
פאַרהייליקט פון ציַיטן פון גרױסע, פון אַלטע,
מיט בליצן און דונערן־אָפּקלאַנג אין קול.

„איך קום ניט, ווי זי, פון אַ זוניקער הױכקייט,
אין הימל אין בלױסטן זיך שפּיגלענדיק ריַין;
איך האָב ניט פון הױגלען פון גרינע די וויַיכקייט,
פון פעלזן־בערג שטאָלצע — דעם וויסט־
ווילדן חן.

„איך קום צו דיר, קינד מיין, פון גלותן שטומע,
פון געטאָס פאַרפּאַקטע, פאַרהאַקטע אין קלעם;
איך האָב נאָר די חנען פון תחינות פון פרומע,
איך האָב נאָר די שיינקייט פון קידוש־השם.

„און טראָג איך אין זיך ניט די בליצן, וואָס
בלענדן,
דעם שלאַמיקן זונ־יואַרט, וואָס וואָנדער באַוויַיזט,
טאָ האָב איך דעם שימער פון שטערן־לעגענדן,
די ליבע לבנה־באַלויכטונג פון גייסט.

„פון וואָרמס, פון מיינץ און פון שפּייער,
דורך פּראַג, און לובלין, ביז אָדעס,
האָט אַלץ זיך געצויגן איין פייער,
האָט אַלץ זיך געצויגן איין נם.
האָט שטענדיק דער בלוט־פיינט געהוועַרט,
געלויערט פיל־אויגיק דער טויט —
אָט דאָרט האָב איך, וויסט און פאַרטרויערט,
די עלטערן דיינע באַגלײב.

„איך בין מיט זיי הונדערטער יאָרן
געזאַנגען דורך יעדער געפאַר,
און איינגעזאַפט האָב איך דעם צאָרן,
און איינגעזאַפט האָב איך דעם צער.
און אויסגעשמידט האָב איך דורך דורות
דעם וואָנדער פון ווילן און וויי,
צו לעבן פאַר הייליקע תורות
און שטאַרבן מיט פעסטקייט פאַר זיי.
און אויב נאָר די קדושה די ריינע
שיינט אָפּ פון ענוויים און פיַין,
טאָ בין איך דיר, קינד מיין, די איינע,
טאָ בין איך די הייליקסטע דיַין.

A fragment of the poem "Yiddish" by Abraham Walt-Lyessin
(New York, 1922).

3
THE POLITICAL IMPETUS

THE EARLIEST ROOTS OF THE JEWISH SOCIALIST MOVEMENT IN Russia can be traced to the anti-governmental activities and the general rebelliousness that characterized the Russian Empire during the reign of Alexander II. The Czar's refusal to establish a constitutional government and solve the land needs of the peasantry sparked the formation of radical groups among university students and intellectuals. In the early seventies, some Jewish students joined these Narodniki groups, which set out to convert the peasants to the ideal of revolution by living among them and teaching them.

The Jewish communities, generally speaking, were loyal to the Czar and grateful for his moderate reforms.[1] But the revolutionary mood also had an impact upon them. Small groups of young Jews in Vilna, Kovno, Grodno, Minsk, and

1. Cf. L. Greenberg, *The Jews in Russia* (New Haven, 1944), 1:146f.

Ycletz established socialist study circles in the seventies in which they read and discussed illegal literature.[2]

The young Jews who were swept into the revolutionary tide generally abandoned their ties to the Jewish people and Judaism. As Russians, they abandoned Hebrew, which they considered a dead language, and Yiddish, which was for them a "jargon" destined to disappear with time. As socialists, they had no use for religion. A few even converted to Christianity in order to dissolve any barriers that might make them unacceptable both to the Russian *muzhiks* whom they sought to propagandize and to their fellow revolutionaries. Jewry, they felt, would vanish with the revolution and with the new world that would inevitably emerge from it. According to one such revolutionary, Vladimir Jochelson,

> We maintained a negative attitude toward the Jewish religion as to all religions. The [Yiddish] jargon we considered to be an artificial language, and Hebrew a dead language of interest only to scholars. National beliefs, traditions and language in general did not seem valuable to us from the common standpoint of humanity. But we were sincere assimilationists, and it was to the Russian enlightenment that we looked for salvation for Jews.[3]

Aaron Samuel Lieberman (1845–1880), a student at the government-sponsored Vilna Teachers Seminary and a member of its socialist study circle, was the first Jewish socialist to conceive the idea of a Jewish wing of the international socialist movement. Torn between cosmopolitan socialist ideals and strong Jewish sentiments, Lieberman attempted to organize Jewish socialist organizations wherever he went. While members of the Vilna Circle were generally opposed to socialist work among Jews, they felt that if such work were carried out its linguistic medium should be Yiddish. Lieberman, however, argued for

2. *Di Geshikte fun Bund* (New York, 1960), 1:48.
3. Quoted in A. Litvak, *Vos Geven* (Vilna, 1925), p. 9. Cf. Koppel S. Pinson, "Arkady Kremer, Vladimir Medem, and the Ideology of the Jewish 'Bund'," *Jewish Social Studies* 7 (1945): 235.

Hebrew, on the grounds that propaganda in that language would be more appealing to the *yeshiva* students whom he hoped to enlist in the movement.[4]

The by-laws of the Hebrew Socialist Union, which Lieberman organized in London in 1876, were issued in both Hebrew and Yiddish and only lack of means prevented him from publishing *The Hammer*, a projected socialist journal, in both languages.[5] Only three issues of *Ha-emet*, the first Hebrew socialist periodical, which Lieberman published in Vienna in 1876, appeared, and he apparently intended to issue propagandistic brochures in Yiddish along with the journal.[6] In a letter to V. Smirnov he rationalized his choice of Hebrew over Yiddish for *Ha-emet* in terms of Russia's persecution of the latter, the widespread knowledge of Hebrew among Jews in general and *yeshiva* students in particular, and the censor's poor knowledge of Hebrew, which would make it easier to have the journal approved.[7]

Lieberman actually had a deep love for Hebrew and a negative attitude toward Yiddish typical of the *maskil*. This attitude, combined with his negative feelings toward religion, hindered his effectiveness as a leader of the Jewish masses in London.[8] Morris Winchevsky (1856–1933), Lieberman's spiritual heir in England and the United States, was much more successful. When he turned from Hebrew to Yiddish, Winchevsky's prose and poetry, particularly the latter, did much to arouse the Jewish working masses on both sides of the Atlantic. *Dos Poylishe Yidl*, which he published in London in 1884, was the first printed socialist newspaper to be issued in Yiddish.[9]

4. Cf. A. Tartakover, *Toldot Tenuat Ha-ovdim Hayehudit* (Warsaw, 1929), 1 : 17.
5. J. Klausner, *Hisitoryah Shel Hasifrut Ha-ivrit Hahadasha* (Jerusalem, 1958), 6 : 229, 232.
6. K. Marmor, *Arn Liebermans Briv* (New York, 1951), p. 136.
7. *Ibid.*, pp. 146f. and G. Kresel, "A. S. Lieberman in Likht fun Zayne Briv," *Di Goldene Keyt*, no. 13 (Tel Aviv, 1952), p. 233.
8. Cf. Klausner, p. 250.
9. Cf. N. B. Minkov, *Pyonern fun Yidisher Poezye in Amerike* (New York, 1956), 1 : 19f., Tartakover, p. 26; M. Epstein, *Profiles of Eleven* (Detroit, 1965), pp. 11–48. See also B. J. Bialostotzky, *Kholem in Vor* (New

In the second socialist circle in Vilna, organized after Lieberman's forced emigration in 1875, the significance of the Yiddish language as a vehicle of socialist propaganda among Jews was taken up again. Practical steps were taken to spread propaganda in Yiddish, but the group was forced to disband shortly thereafter.[10]

As ever-growing numbers of revolutionaries were expelled from Russia, socialist circles developed in centers of immigration. In London, Berlin, Vienna, Koenigsberg, Paris, and Geneva, socialists gradually discovered that Yiddish was a more effective medium of oral as well as written propaganda among Jewish immigrants than Russian.[11] In Geneva, for example, a member of the Vilna Circle, Rachmiel Zuckerman, joined hands in 1880 with M. P. Dragomanov, a leading non-Jewish Ukranian nationalist leader of the day, in issuing a call to members of the Jewish socialist intelligentsia who had become estranged from their own people. The proclamation, urging the publication of socialist propaganda in Yiddish, explained the history and significance of the language, the growth of Yiddish literature and drama in recent times, and the powerful effect of the language on the Jew.

> The rise of modern Yiddish literature and the attitude of the Jewish masses toward it is in full accord with the fact that literatures in common folk tongues are born and flower everywhere. This has been demonstrated recently throughout Europe. It points to the absolute necessity for socialists to also avail themselves of so powerful a tool as the living tongue of the folk masses in order to penetrate the very depths of their life and emotions.[12]

York, 1956); M. Epstein, *Jewish Labor in U.S.A.*, vol. 1 (New York, 1950); B. Green, *Yidishe Shrayber in Amerike* (New York, 1963); J. Klausner, *Historya shel Hasifrut Haivrit Hahadasha,* vol. 5 (Tel Aviv, 1950); A. Litvak, *Literatur un Kamf* (New York, 1930); K. Marmor, *Der Onhoyb fun der Yidisher Literatur in Amerike* (New York, 1944); R. Sanders, *The Downtown Jews* (New York, 1970); F. Schulman, *Geshikhte fun der Yidisher Literatur in Amerike, 1870-1900* (New York, 1943).

10. N. Bukhbinder, *Di Geshikhte fun der Yidisher Arbeter Bavegung in Rusland* (Vilna, 1930), p. 27, and *Historishe Shriftn* (Vilna, 1939), 3 : 256f.

11. H. Burgin, *Di Geshkihte fun der Yidisher Arbeter Bavegung,* (New York, 1915), p. 30.

12. *Historishe Shriftn,* 3 : 570.

The proclamation announced the establishment of a "free Yiddish printing press" to publish socialist brochures and pamphlets. Nothing came of the plan, however, principally because of the opposition of Jewish socialists who were thoroughly cosmopolitan in outlook and imbued with Jewish self-hatred.[13]

In the early 1880s changes occurred in the thinking of the so-called socialists of Jewish extraction, who were frequently university students expelled for revolutionary activities. The growth of the Jewish proletariat and the pogroms at the beginning of the decade forced them to confront the existence of a special "Jewish problem," while the development of Russian industry and the gradual dissemination of Marxist ideas turned their minds from the peasants to the factory workers. Now propaganda among Jewish workers seemed reasonable and acceptable. Small socialist study circles for workers sprang up in towns throughout the Pale, the most important being established in Minsk and Vilna. Here workers were taught Russian, natural science, and socialist theory.

In Vilna, where the circles were most successful, the socialists were confronted with a serious language problem. The Jewish worker knew no language but Yiddish, with which the Russified propagandists were usually unfamiliar. Scientific literature and socialist propaganda in Yiddish were practically non-existent at the time. The intellectuals therefore considered the teaching of Russian to the Jewish workers their primary responsibility.

We did not have even the smallest Yiddish pamphlets at the time. The legal Yiddish language movement began a few years later. We intellectuals read Russian books exclusively and our entire sustenance, our cultural and socialist education, was attained in Russian. Mendele, Peretz and other Yiddish writers were almost unknown to us. We understood Yiddish and often spoke it among ourselves. But in all intellectual circles, discussions and debates were conducted solely in Russian. At the time the Jewish masses in Russia understood less Russian than now. There was a huge contradiction here but we had to use

13. *Ibid.*, pp.557f.; Bukhbinder, pp. 47f.; Burgin, pp. 31f.; *Di Geshikhte fun Bund*, pp. 53f.

only Russian books and brochures because there were no others. We used Russian books and manuals but almost always spoke to each other and interpreted texts in Yiddish. It was a wonderful mixture of Russian and Yiddish. Yiddish was nevertheless the more important language which we used in the workers' circles. Only in the higher circles consisting of boys and girls who understood Russian did we teach in Russian. With oral Yiddish translations and interpretations we overcame the contradiction between the Russian language of our books and the Yiddish language which was the everyday language of the masses and of the members of our workers' circles.[14]

Gradually, the idea of propagandizing the Jewish workers in their own tongue began to take shape. One reason for this was the fact that workers who learned Russian well frequently abandoned both the socialist groups and their trades and became estranged from their own people and their class. Another was that the economic upswing and the success of the twelve-hour-day strike movement in Russia in the early 1890s made feasible the propagandizing of large masses of workers instead of small groups. Still another reason was the growing awareness among the socialist intellectuals of the strong ethnic feelings of Jewish workers and their susceptibility to early Zionist propaganda in Yiddish.

In 1893, a highly influential pamphlet in Russian by Arkady Kremer (1865–1935), a Jewish socialist, stressed the importance of "agitation," that is, mass propaganda integrating political and economic problems in terms that workers could understand. Kremer's seminal pamphlet altered the nature of revolutionary activity throughout Russia. Its immediate objective, however, was the justification of socialist activity among the Jewish working masses of the Pale in the Yiddish language. A simpler pamphlet by Samuel Gozhansky, also urging mass agitation rather than theoretical study by small groups, was written in Yiddish. It was even more popular among Vilna workers.

In 1895, Julius Martov (1873–1923), who was aware of the

14. *Di Geshikhte fun Bund,* 1 : 360.

ethnic sentiments of Jewish workers, proposed the establishment of a special Jewish workers' movement in which Yiddish would be utilized for both oral and written propaganda. He believed that the struggle for Jewish rights necessitated such a movement and he provided an ideological basis and theoretical justification for it.[15]

The transition from study circles to mass agitation and from Russian to Yiddish aroused opposition and created problems. Some workers opposed the switch to Yiddish on the grounds that without a knowledge of Russian the intellectual and political development of the workers would be hampered, since there was very little socialist literature available in the language.[16]

The assimilated intellectuals had to learn Yiddish and struggle with the problem of creating a socialist literature in it. The ranks of the socialist clubs were being swelled by large numbers of former *yeshiva* students who came to Vilna in search of both secular education and work. They were known as "semi-intellectuals" because, despite their wealth of Jewish knowledge, they knew no Russian. They sought books in Yiddish for education and entertainment. The workers, too, had more time to read as a result of the shorter working day won by the strike movement.[17]

A lending library of Yiddish books for workers was established in Vilna in 1893, and two years later, a "Jargon Committee" was formed to disseminate literature, establish workers' libraries throughout the Pale, and publish socialist propaganda in Yiddish. Branches of the committee were set up in Minsk, Bialystok, and smaller towns. The committee functioned until 1898. Its members were mostly Russified intellectuals who spoke Yiddish haltingly and could not read it at all. Nevertheless, they made strenuous efforts to learn the language. Their interest in Yiddish literature was solely political and they were strongly opposed to Zionism and to the Hebrew revival that was taking

15. Cf. Pinson, pp. 146, 244.
16. *Di Geshikhte fun Bund,* 1 : 70.
17. *Ibid.,* pp. 93–94.

place at the time.[18] Their use of the term Jargon, however, was not derogatory, for at the time all intellectuals used it. Only the masses referred to the language as "Yiddish." The Committee published Yiddish stories by Y. L. Peretz and David Pinski (1872-1959) as well as popularized versions of scientific, political, and economic works. It also helped disseminate the publications of the Tsayt-gayst Publishing House established by Pinski and a Jewish student group in Berlin.[19]

This period saw a flowering of Yiddish literature and of Yiddish translations of scientific and belletristic works from other languages. Of special interest to workers were the social tales and satires of Peretz and Pinski and the anthologies published by Peretz, especially his *Yontev Bletlekh* (Holiday Leaves), which began to appear in 1894.

The publications of the Jargon Committee were also supplemented by an illegal socialist press in Yiddish, which gradually developed from handwritten and hectographed newspapers and leaflets to printed materials. Many of these were smuggled into Russia from abroad. The most significant were the periodicals *Der Yidisher Arbeter* (1896) and *Arbeter Shtime* (1897-1905).[20]

In Minsk, Abraham Walt Lyessin (1872-1938), who eventually became one of the truly outstanding Yiddish poets, became a protégé of Pinski and was actively involved in the Jargon Committees.

> When the Russian *intelligent* went to the people [wrote Lyessin], he first learned to speak the language of the Russian peasant, but the Jewish *intelligent* expected his people to speak not their own language but his—Russian. I believed that the language of the masses had to be the language of socialist propaganda, and for me, revolutionary poetry became an important part of socialist propaganda. In "Jargonism," whose purpose was also to fight capitalism, I saw something new, an overturn in Jewish

18. See A. Litvak, "Di Zhargonishe Komitetn," *Royter Pinkes* (Warsaw, 1929), p. 14.
19. Ibid., pp. 5-30; · Ezra Mendelsohnn, *Class Struggle in the Pale* (Cambridge, 1970). pp. 117-18.
20. Cf. *Historishe Shriftn*, 3:577-603.

society, an intimation that the common man would come to demand his share in intellectual life. . . . I was always aware that in Warsaw, where Peretz and Pinski were, the mansion of Yiddish literature was being built from foundation to roof. The more the Jewish masses awakened, all the more would builders of our literature emerge.[21]

Lyessin successfully combined devotion to the struggle of the Jewish working class with loyalty to the Jewish nationalist cause. His Yiddish poems of socialist and Jewish national content utilized an emphasis on the Jewish national heritage and the struggle for Jewish rights as a means of winning Jews for socialism.[22]

In October 1897, thirteen workers—artisans and intellectuals of several cities representing socialist circles, trade groups, and the two illegal Yiddish periodicals—met in Vilna to establish the Jewish Labor Bund of Russia and Poland. The primary reasons for its founding were (a) the need to propagandize the Jewish worker in his own language and (b) the need to defend his civil and political rights. The Bund grew rapidly, largely as a result of the *kasses* or trade groups that became the backbone of the organization. It was successful in organizing strikes and boycotts and in improving the economic position of the Jewish worker generally. In the political sphere, it disseminated revolutionary propaganda and organized demonstrations, quickly achieving a reputation as the most active and best-organized section of the Russian revolutionary movement. It inspired such responses to governmental intimidation of Jewish workers as the

21. Quoted in L. S. Dawidowicz, *The Golden Tradition* (New York, 1967), p. 425.
22. Cf. F. Kursky, *Gezamlte Shriftn* (New York, 1952), pp. 323–41. On Lyessin see also B. J. Bialostotzky, *Kholem in Vor* (New York, 1956), pp. 214–95; S. Niger, *Yidishe Shrayber fun Tsvantsikstn Yorhundert*, vol. 1 (New York, 1972), pp. 299–322; J. Glatstein, *In Tokh Genumen* (New York, 1956), pp. 42–47; N. B. Minkov, *Yidishe Klasiker Poetn* (New York, 1937), pp. 147–80; B. Rivkin, *Yidishe Dikhter in Amerike*, vol. 1 (New York, 1947), pp. 69–107; vol. 2 (Buenos Aires, 1959), pp. 72–79; A. Gordin, *Denker un Dikhter* (New York, 1949), pp. 141–214; A. Tabachnick, *Dikhter un Dikhtung* (New York, 1965), pp. 75–100; Y. Mark, ed., *A. Lyessin Tsum Dritn Yortsayt* (New York, 1941).

attempted assassination of the governor of Vilna by the Jewish shoemaker Hersh Lekert in 1902. It successfully defeated the government-sponsored Independent Jewish Labor Party (Zubatov movement), which sought to curb its influence (1901–1905).

At first, true to its name, the Bund considered itself solely a union or organization of Jewish workers in Russia, Poland, and Lithuania. It was neither a political party nor a Jewish organization in any national or international sense. In 1898 it played an important role in the founding of the Russian Social Democratic Party, which it joined as an autonomous unit. The Bund viewed its constituents primarily as members of the international proletariat and only secondarily as part of the Jewish populations of their respective countries. Its Jewish program was at first limited exclusively to the struggle for equal civil and political rights.

The Bund could not, however, remain oblivious to the rising tide of nationalism that was sweeping Europe and commanding more and more of the attention of the Jewish masses in the form of Zionism. National minorities were asserting their rights in Austria-Hungary, Germany, and the Balkans. Poles, Ukranians, and Finns, among others, were rising up against their Russian overlords and the language question was threatening the very foundations of the Austro-Hungarian Empire.[23] The struggle for the language and cultural rights of minorities was especially acute in Galicia, where Poles and Ukranians were recognized as national minorities with national rights. Jewish citizens of the Hapsburg empire, which included Galicia, were, on the other hand, considered only a religious community. As we shall see, the struggle for Jewish national rights in Austria reached its zenith with the attempt to have Yiddish added to the nine legally recognized languages that appeared in the Austrian census of 1910.

The concept of extraterritorial national autonomy, as

23. Cf. C. A. Macartney, *National States and National Minorities* (London, 1934), pp. 113–51: R. A. Kann. *The Multinational Empire.* 2 vols. (New York, 1950), and his *The Hapsburg Empire* (New York, 1957).

expressed in the writings of the Austrian socialists Karl Renner and Otto Bauer and adopted at the Congress of the Austrian Social Democratic Party in Brno in 1899, had a lightning effect on the intellectual leaders of the Bund, many of whom were émigrés in Austria and Switzerland. They were also highly impressed with the ideas of Jewish cultural autonomy that were formulated at the time by Simon Dubnow and Chaim Zhitlovsky. At the third convention of the Bund at the end of 1899, John Mill (1870–1952) urged that the struggle for equal national rights be adopted as part of the program of the Bund. Mill's principal argument was that victory in the struggle for civil rights would be pointless without national rights. The right of assembly without the right to conduct meetings in Yiddish, he argued, would be of little avail to the Jewish worker who was unable to speak Russian. The convention, however, defeated Mill's proposal because of its fear that a national program would weaken the class consciousness of its members.[24]

At the fourth convention in 1901 the issue was raised again. This time a resolution projecting the future of Russia as a federation of autonomous nationalities and proclaiming the Jews as a national group was passed. But the resolution also stated that it was too early to demand national autonomy for Jews since the inflation of national feelings might reduce class consciousness and lead to chauvinism. The Bund's timidity can be explained in terms of its sensitive position vis-à-vis other Social Democrats in Russia. The Russian Social Democratic Party was hostile to the Bund's Jewish nationalism and to its insistence that it be recognized as the sole representative of the Jewish proletariat. The Bund left the Social Democratic Party and declared itself an independent party in 1903. It retained its autonomy when it rejoined the Social Democrats in 1906.

The nationalistic mood of Russian Jewry grew more intense following the Kishinev and Gomel pogroms of 1903. The organization of Jewish self-defense units by Bundists and Labor Zionists alike quickened Jewish solidarity and stimulated

24. *Di Geshikhte fun Bund,* 1:153f

national sentiments throughout the Pale. In 1904, the Central Committee of the Bund felt compelled to introduce the slogan of national autonomy into its work, even though such a step had not been legally authorized at a convention. However, since the Bund continued to fear the diminution of class consciousness among Jewish workers that might result from the struggle for national political autonomy, it limited its demands to cultural autonomy. This was another reason why the Yiddish language and culture came to play so important a part in its program. At the sixth conference of the Bund in 1905, the demand for national cultural autonomy was officially adopted.[25]

The Bund's overall approach to the Jewish national question throughout its history is best expressed in the writings of Vladimir Medem (1879-1923), its chief theoretician. Despite theoretical and practical changes in his views over the years, Medem remained a Marxist and continued to perceive Jewish problems in terms of the international class struggle. Unlike most Russian Social Democrats, however, he saw nationalism as a major factor in the modern world. He followed the lead of such Austrian Socialists as Karl Renner and Otto Bauer in this respect, although the latter were both specifically opposed to national autonomy for Jews. Medem's basic theory, which came to be known as "neutralism," acknowledged the existence of a Jewish nation with a culture of its own but remained "neutral" as to its future national development. It sought to restrict the national program of the Bund to combating oppression and furthering the interests of the Jewish proletariat.[26]

A similar ambivalence was evinced by the Bund with regard to Yiddish. Despite the fact that the right to organize, propagandize, and struggle for the rights of the Jewish worker in his own language was its chief raison d'être, it took the Bund a long time to view the language as anything more than a temporary vehicle. Since Yiddish had been adopted only with reluctance and solely

25. Cf. G. Aronson, "Ideological Trends Among Russian Jews," *Russian Jewry: 1860-1917*, ed. J. Frumkin, G. Aronson, A. Goldenweiser, *et al.*, (New York, 1966), p. 164.
26. See *Vladimir Medem: Tsum Tsvantsikstn Yortsayt* (New York, 1943).

as a medium of socialist propaganda, no claims for its recognition were made during the first few years in the history of the Bund. Recognition of the language of the Jewish proletariat as a major instrument of Jewish national culture came only hesitatingly after the adoption of the demand for national cultural autonomy in 1905. At that time, the Bund urged that the rights of the Jewish population to use Yiddish in courts and other public institutions be legally guaranteed.[27] Even then, however, the policy of "neutralism" with regard to Jewish national and cultural interests prevented the Bund from viewing Yiddish as more than a tool of the Jewish working class.

Medem's formulation was essentially an attempt to mediate between the assimilationists and nationalists in the party, and to counter the accusations of nationalistic chauvinism leveled against the Bund by the *Iskra* faction of the Russian Social Democratic party. The *Iskra* group, which was attempting to gain control of the Social Democrats, was led by a number of Jewish assimilationist intellectuals such as Leon Trotsky, Julius Martov, Pavel Axelrod, and Feodor Dan. They were militantly opposed to the Bund's national program and to its autonomous status within the larger party.

It was not until 1910, two years after the Czernowitz Conference, that deliberations at a conference of the Bund were held exclusively in Yiddish, the first resolution on the language passed, and a program calling for the organization of Jewish cultural groups and agencies adopted.[28]

Nevertheless, the achievements of the Bund in the development and recognition of the Yiddish language and in the flowering of the Yiddish press and literature were formidable, even if lacking in theoretical confirmation by the ideologues. Between 1897 and 1904 alone, the Bund published some seventy-three brochures in Yiddish, as well as newspapers and magazines.[29] In making Yiddish the language of a modern political

27. Cf. A. Menes, ed., *Der Yidisher Gedank in der Nayer Tsayt* (New York, 1957), p. 115.
28. Pinson, p. 249.
29. *Di Geshikhte fun Bund*, 1 : 258-60.

party and stimulating the production of literature in the language, the Bund was instrumental in increasing the prestige of Yiddish and in altering the attitudes of both the intellectuals and the masses toward it.[30]

Vladimir Kosovsky (1870–1941), one of the architects of the national program of the Bund, pointed out that the theory of "neutralism" was actually in blatant contradiction to the actual operations and practical work of the Bund.

> The Bund helped develop the Yiddish language, Yiddish literature, the Yiddish school, all the elements of modern Yiddish culture. It proclaimed and strove on behalf of explicit political demands. In short, all of its work was such as to maintain and develop the Jewish nation as a community of culture. At the same time that the Bund insisted that it was neutral with regard to the outcome of the "objective process of development" of Jews as a nation, it energetically intervened in the "objective process" and in practice steered it in a particular direction, working actively against assimilation.[31]

There was a good deal of truth in the following statement published in an official organ of the Bund in 1904 :

> It is said that Jews are not a nation because they do not possess a language of their own. . . . The statistics of 1897 showed that 80 to 90 per cent of the Jewish population uses the Jargon as its mother tongue. Then is it not their folk language? It is true that the language is still underdeveloped but it has made great progress. It has a sizable literature and writers like Peretz and Abramovitsh would also be a credit to the great European literatures. . . . The movement of the Jewish proletariat, during its brief existence, has brought much vitality into the life of the Jewish people, created many new concepts and ideas, and so enriched the Yiddish language with new words and expressions that the Jargon has become almost completely transfigured and has become the cultured language of a cultured people.[32]

The Galician counterpart of the Bund, the Jewish Social

30. Cf. Baal Makhshoves, *Geklibene Verk* (New York, 1953), pp. 47–51; M. Zilberfarb, *Gezamlte Shriftn* (Paris, 1935), pp. 361f.
31. Quoted in A. Menes, p. 123.
32. Quoted in *Di Geshikhte fun Bund,* 2:23f.

Democratic Party in Galicia organized in 1905, also engaged in intensive Yiddish cultural work. Its principal organs were the Yiddish weekly, *Der Sotsyal-Demokrat* of Cracow, and *Yidishe Folks-Shtime* of Lemberg. As we shall see, in 1910 Galician Bundists led the struggle for the inclusion of Yiddish as the national language of the Jews in the Austrian census.[33]

The national consciousness of the Bund was heightened and its national program crystallized in response to the hostile criticism it met in the Russian, Polish, and Austrian Socialist movements. It was only by affirming the national individuality of East European Jewry as expressed in the Yiddish language and its culture that the Bund was able to justify its "separatist" position vis-à-vis other socialist parties.[34] An equally potent factor contributing to the growth of national consciousness and to the prestige of Yiddish in the Bund was the rise of Zionism and of the Zionist socialist parties, in particular, in Eastern Europe.

From the very beginning the Bund viewed Zionism as a reactionary, utopian, petit-bourgeois phenomenon that could only bring harm to the Jewish masses. The Bundists took issue with what seemed to them to be the conciliatory attitude of the Zionists toward the Czarist regime. They disputed the notion that the problems of Jewry could be solved by diplomatic negotiation rather than by direct action on the part of the Jews themselves. They denied the Zionist contention that world Jewry constituted a single nation and that class differences within the Jewish people were of minor importance because of the ubiquitous specter of anti-Semitism. Where Zionists denied the future of the Diaspora, considered attempts to alleviate the plight of Jews in Russia as futile, and saw statehood as the only solution to the Jewish problem, the Bundists placed their hopes in the success of the Russian revolutionary movement and in the attainment of national rights for Jews in Russia. Zionists, on the other hand, even favored Jewish immigration from Russia and

33. *Di Geshikhte fun Bund,* 3 : 413–14.
34. Cf. J. S. Hertz, "The Bund's Nationality Program and Its Critics in the Russian, Polish and Austrian Socialist Movements," *Yivo Annual of Jewish Social Science* (New York, 1969), 14 : 53–67.

viewed participation by Jews in the revolutionary movement as harming chances of enlisting Czarist support for Zionism.

Still another point of disagreement between Bundists and Zionists revolved around the language question and the nature of Jewish culture generally.[35] Linked as it was ideologically and emotionally to the East European socialist movements, the Bund's horizons were limited to the Jews of the Pale. Lacking in both geographical and historical perspective, the Bundists were gradually veering toward the definition of Yiddish as the national language, and the culture of the Jewish proletariat created in that language as the national culture, of Jewry. Russian Zionists, on the other hand, viewed Hebrew as the national language, but were divided between freethinking and orthodox elements on the definition of Jewish culture and the role of Zionism in Jewish education. The Bundist-Zionist controversy contributed a volatile political dimension to the language question.

In 1895, a group of Russian Jewish student émigrés in Berlin, many of whom were associated with nationalist groups such as Leo Motzkin's Russian Jewish Academic Association and Ahad Haam's B'nai Moshe, organized their own "Jargon Association" for the purpose of spreading enlightenment among Russian Jews in Yiddish. The association, which adopted the name "Bildung" (Education) in 1897, was nonpolitical and accepted non-Zionists as well as Zionists into its ranks.[36]

The first Zionist Congress was held in Basle, Switzerland, in 1897, the year in which the Bund was organized. At the time, Zionists and other Jewish nationalists in Galicia were already campaigning to have the Jews there recognized as a national group. One of the Galician delegates to the Congress, Dr. Shlomo Rosenhek, moved that the Austrian government be urged to officially recognize the Hebrew alphabet and the Yiddish language, which was spoken by some 750,000 Galician Jews.

35. Cf. *Di Geshikhte fun Bund*, 1:339–54; 2:163–66.
36. Y. Klausner, *Opozitsya Le-Herzl* (Jerusalem, 5720), pp. 18–21.

This would have made it possible for Jews to avoid using other languages in the Austrian courts.[37]

It is interesting to note that, from an entry in the diary of Theodor Herzl (1860–1904), the founder of the Zionist movement, dated January 9, 1895, it would appear that at first he expected Yiddish, the language most widespread among Jews of his day and the language of his potential immigrants, to be the spoken language of the projected Jewish state.

> The language will present no obstacle. Switzerland too is a federal state of various nationalities.
> We recognize ourselves as a nation by our faith.
> Actually, German is, *par la force des choses* [of necessity], likely to become the official language. *Judendeutsch* [the German spoken by Jews]! As the yellow badge is to become our blue ribbon.[38]

Nevertheless, in his major work, *Der Judenstaat* (1896), Herzl speaks of giving up

> those miserable stunted jargons, those Ghetto languages which we now employ. These were the stealthy tongues of prisoners. Our educators will give due attention to this matter. The language which proves itself to be of greatest utility for general intercourse will without compulsion establish itself as the national tongue.[39]

Three months after the publication of *Der Judenstaat*, Herzl asked Michael Berkowicz, the Hebrew translator of his book, to inform Hebrew readers that he had once again changed his mind on this issue. The language of his proposed Jewish state, he now felt, could be only Hebrew.[40]

37. S. Rozenhek, "Hebreyish-Yidish," *Di Goldene Keyt*, no. 66 (Tel Aviv, 1969), p. 159.
38. *The Complete Diaries of Theodor Herzl*, ed. R. Patai, trans. H. Zohn (New York, 1960), 1:56.
39. L. Lewisohn, ed., *Theodor Herzl: A Portrait for This Age*, (New York, 1955), p. 295.
40. Cf. I. Cohen, *Theodor Herzl: Founder of Political Zionism* (New York, 1959), p. 95, and A. Bein, *Theodore Herzl* (Philadelphia, 1941), p. 169.

Herzl's principal rival for leadership among East European Zionists was the Hebrew essayist and thinker Ahad Haam (1856–1927), the father of "cultural Zionism." In Hebrew, Ahad Haam always referred to Yiddish as "the Jargon." He offered the excuse that not all of his readers could be expected to understand the Hebrew term "Yehudit" to mean Yiddish, especially since that term had a different significance in the biblical Book of Kings. However, there was probably a psychological reason for his use of the term of opprobrium.[41] At one point, he compared the antagonism between Yiddishists and Hebraists to "the war at the time of the first Christians when the ignorant masses rebelled against the Judaism of the scholars."[42]

Yiddish was Ahad Haam's native tongue and he spoke it fluently throughout his life. He did not believe in the practicality of spoken Hebrew in the Diaspora and took issue with the extreme Hebraists in the Zionist movement who would have banned Yiddish in party publications. He realized the practical advantages of Zionist propaganda in the language but revolted against anything that smacked of Yiddishism. He became enraged at the thought that Yiddish might either usurp the place of Hebrew or come to be considered a second Jewish national language together with Hebrew.[43]

At the national conference of Russian Zionists held in Minsk in August 1902, Ahad Haam delivered an address on the problems of Jewish culture that provided a theoretical basis for Zionist cultural activities. In that address he defined what he meant by national language and national literature, erecting a theoretical wall between Hebrew and Yiddish and consigning the latter and its literature to oblivion.

Our national literature . . . is that alone which is written in our national language; it does not include what Jews write in

41. L. Simon, *Ahad Haam: Asher Ginzberg, A Biography* (Philadelphia, 1960), p. 238.

42. Quoted in L. Simon and J. Heller, *Ahad Haam: Haish, Poalo Vetorato* (Jerusalem, 1955), p. 222.

43. Simon, p. 237.

other languages. . . . A nation has no national language except that which was its own when it stood on the threshold of its history, before its national self-consciousness was fully developed—that language which has accompanied it through every period of its career, and is inextricably bound up with all its memories. . . . There is . . . no doubt that before long Yiddish will cease to be a living and spoken language. The process of its decay is an inevitable outcome of the conditions of life. . . . The Jargon, like all the other languages which Jews have employed at different times, never has been and never will be regarded by the nation as anything but an external and temporary medium of intercourse; nor can its literature live any longer than the language itself. So soon as the Jargon ceases to be spoken, it will be forgotten, and its literature with it. . . . Hebrew has been, is, and will always be, our national language . . . our national literature throughout all time, is the literature writen in Hebrew.[44]

Following Ahad Haam's address, Nahum Sokolow (1860–1936) spoke of the practical steps to be taken in order to make Hebrew the official language of the Zionist movement, foster its study and usage, and support all projects to revive it. To the delegates, Sokolow's fluent, masterful Hebrew was itself a demonstration of the possibilities inherent in the language as a vernacular. He received a thunderous ovation and his suggestions were adopted as resolutions of the conference.[45] On the practical level, Zionists had to shift to Yiddish in their propaganda in order to become an effective social force among East European Jews. But this "hard line" Zionist position on Hebrew could not fail to provoke an opposite reaction on the part of the Bund.

The Zionist socialist parties presented even more of a challenge, because they competed more directly with the Bund for the loyalty of the Jewish worker. A group of intellectuals discussed the possibility of a synthesis of Zionism and socialism as

44. Ahad Haam, *Selected Essays*, trans. L. Simon (Philadelphia, 1912), pp. 278–84, *passim*.
45. A. Raphaeli, "Veidot Artsiyot shel Tsiyoney Rusya," *Katzir* (Tel Aviv, 1964), pp. 64f., 68, 74.

early as the first Zionist Congress in Basle in 1897.[46] The following year, at the Second Congress, a group of socialist Zionists suggested that the Zionist idea be linked with the progressive objectives of mankind as a whole and Palestine rebuilt as a socialist society.[47] The idea that the inner-directed Zionist approach to Jewish questions and the outer-directed Bundist approach were not incompatible gradually found acceptance among both working-class Zionists and Zionist-oriented members of the Bund. While the former were disenchanted with the bourgeois nature of the Zionist movement, with its disregard of the problems of the Jewish worker, and with its refusal to countenance the Russian revolutionary movement, the latter could not help feeling that if the Jewish separatist policies of the Bund could be justified, so too could a Zionism of the Jewish proletariat. In 1898, Nachman Syrkin (1867–1924) began to publish a series of essays in which he attempted to provide a theoretical basis for the new movement. According to Syrkin, political socialist activity in the Diaspora could be promoted together with Zionist objectives in Palestine. Despite Syrkin's popularity, this "double area" theory was found wanting by many Zionists because it failed to establish a logical connection between socialism and Zionism.[48]

For most of his life, Syrkin saw the only solution to the problems of the Jewish people in the establishment of a Jewish socialist state in Palestine in which "the language of Isaiah" would prevail. With the publication of his *Call to Jewish Youth* (Berlin, 1901), he became a consistent "negator of the Diaspora" and of Diaspora culture. He repudiated both autonomism and the positive attitude toward Yiddish that eventually came to be associated with it. Syrkin appreciated the achieve-

46. A Duker, "Introduction," B. Borochov, *Nationalism and the Class Struggle* (New York, 1937), p. 26.
47. Z. Abramovits, "Tenuat Poaley-Tsiyon Be-Rusya," *Katsir*, p. 106.
48. Cf. Duker, p. 27, and K. Patkin, *The Origins of the Russian Jewish Labour Movement* (Melbourne, 1947), p. 218.

ments of Yiddish literature, but in essays like "The Jargon," which he wrote for *Der Yid* in 1900, he vehemently denied that Yiddish was, or ever could be, "a national language of the Jewish people."[49] Ironically, the latter formula was proposed at the Czernowitz Conference by a socialist-Zionist delegate, Lazar Khazanovitsh. Syrkin, a leading Yiddish writer and orator, used Yiddish throughout his life with the express purpose of freeing his people from it.

> Because of its Hebrew words, Yiddish became a language of the Jews, and because of the ease with which other foreign languages penetrated it, it became a "jargon," a common tongue without the durability or sanctity of the national language. . . . The Jewish people lacks a national language as it lacks a national land. Its national language is Hebrew, the language of its past, preserved in religion and literature. These guarded the sanctity of the national tongue. These provided the jargon with their national component which was used to express the deepest aspects of human thought and feeling.[50]

By 1901, some 4,000 workers were members of "Socialist Zionist" or "Zionist Workers" clubs throughout the Pale. At the conference of Russian Zionists in Minsk in 1902, H. D. Hurvitz (1865–1933) expounded the theory of "nonproletarianization," which stated that the Jewish working class would be able to develop normally only in a territory of its own. The alleviation of the basic problems of the Jewish worker was therefore dependent on the success of Zionism.[51]

Plans to unify these diverse and scattered groups at the Sixth Zionist Congress in 1903 were overwhelmed by the Uganda affair, which split Zionists and socialist Zionists alike into a variety of Palestine-centered and territorialist factions. The three subsequently established proletarian Zionist parties

49. N. Syrkin, "Der Zhargon," *Der Yid*, nos. 37–40 (Cracow 1900).
50. Quoted in S. Rozenhek, "Beyn Haketsavot," *Karmelit*, nos. 6–7, (Haifa, 1960), p. 251. See also M. Syrkin, *Nachman Syrkin: Socialist-Zionist* (New York, 1961), pp. 157–59.
51. Cf. Raphaeli, pp. 69f.; Abramovits, p. 107; Duker, p. 29.

differed on whether a Jewish national territory should be sought
in Palestine or elsewhere, on whether attempts at alleviating the
situation of the Jewish worker in the Diaspora were worthwhile,
and on the merits of Jewish participation in the revolutionary
movement.

The Zionist Socialist Labor Party (S.S.) was primarily interested in Jewish colonization in a territory other than Palestine.
The Jewish Socialist Labor Party (Seyimists) opposed any
immediate territorial solution to the Jewish problem and sought
to alleviate the problems of Russian Jews by means of Jewish
national cultural autonomy. The Jewish Social Democratic
Labor Party (Poaley Zion) strove for national autonomy in
Palestine through colonization as well as for national autonomy
in Russia.[52] All of the proletarian Zionist parties had Yiddish organs and all developed positive attitudes toward the
language.[53]

The Zionist Socialist Labor Party, despite its negative attitude
toward Jewish national autonomy in Russia, included "the
complete equality of rights of the Jewish nation and of the
Jewish language" in its program. Its position was that "the
Jewish proletariat in the countries of the Diaspora can satisfy
only those of its national needs which relate to education in its
own language." It therefore stressed the demand for instruction
in Yiddish in Jewish schools.

The Jewish Socialist Labor Party included prominent Yiddishists such as M. Zilberfarb, A. Rosen (Ben Adir), N. Shtif and,
for a time, Chaim Zhitlovsky in its ranks. Since it postponed
the solution of the territorial question to the indefinite future
and devoted itself completely to securing national autonomy in
Russia, it became the most outspokenly Yiddishist of the three
parties.[54]

52. Cf. Abramovits, pp. 107–10 and O. Janowsky, *The Jews and Minority
Rights* (New York, 1933), pp. 126–36.
53. J. Shatzky, "Geshikhte fun der Yidisher Prese," *Algemeyne Entsiklopedye*, D (New York, 1948), pp. 234f.
54. Cf. Janowsky, pp. 135f and Gregor Aronson, "Ideological Trends
Among Russian Jews," *Russian Jewry: 1860–1917*, ed. J. Frumkin, G. Aronson, A. Goldenweiser, *et al.* (New York, 1966), p. 164.

Despite differences between Hebraist and Yiddishist factions, in 1906 the Poaley Zion party adopted a program for the attainment of national political autonomy in the Diaspora. The program included freedom of national education, national-cultural autonomy, and the equality of rights of languages. Ber Borochov (1881–1917), the leading theoretician of the Poaley Zion, who learned Yiddish in connection with his political activities, eventually also achieved renown as a Yiddish philologist and literary historian.[55] In 1910, the Galician Poaley Zion participated actively in the campaign for the recognition of Yiddish as the national langage of Jewry in the Austrian census.[56] In that same year, the North American branches of the movement established the earliest Yiddish secularist schools in the United States and Canada.[57] The Poaley Zion contribution to the growth of Yiddish culture eventually became so significant that in 1913 Borochov could write that

> though the Bundists constantly propagandize on behalf of the Yiddish language, literature, and schools, they have done very little for Jewish culture, science, and education in comparison with the youthful Poaley Zion party.[58]

Socialist Zionism, in its various configurations, was therefore another major factor in the evolution and growing prestige of Yiddish in modern Jewish life and consequently in the emergence of Yiddishism.

The period of the Russian Revolution (1904–1907) was the heyday of the development of Jewish national consciousness and of the struggle for Jewish national rights in Russia. It was the period in which the various Jewish proletarian parties reached their zenith in terms of numbers and participation and truly became mass movements. The Bund's membership, for

55. See B. Borochov, *Poaley-Tsiyon Shriftn,* (New York, 1948), 2:15, and his *Shprakh-Forshung un Literatur Geshkhte* (Tel Aviv, 1966), pp. 42f.
56. O. Janowsky, pp. 141f.
57. S. Niger, *In Kamf far a Nayer Dertsiung* (New York, 1940), p. 39.
58. B. Borochov, *Nationalism and the Class Struggle* (New York, 1937), p. 117.

example, rose to 80,000 and that of the Poaley Zion to 25,000. It was also during this period that the Yiddish press in Russia and Poland first attained a mass circulation and became a powerful influence in Jewish life. One of the most important newspapers was the Bund's *Folkstsaytung* (later *Di Hofnung*), which was legally published in Vilna between 1905 and 1907.

The failure of the first Russian Revolution in 1905, the period of general reaction and political suppression which followed it, as well as the onslaught of new discrimination, disabilities, and pogroms for Russian Jewry, had enormous significance for both the Bund and Zionism. With revolutionary activities outlawed, the socialist intelligentsia turned to cultural organizations and dramatic and literary societies as outlets for its energy and zeal. Yiddish cultural activities became the major preoccupation of the Bundists. The Zionists experienced a crisis in their movement as a result of the failure of diplomatic efforts to obtain a charter for Palestine, of Herzl's death in 1904, and of the general upheaval caused by the Revolution, and they were turning more and more to cultural work in the Diaspora in addition to the colonization of Palestine.

Although both groups utilized Yiddish for their purposes, as Zionists continued to emphasize the theoretical significance of Hebrew, and Bundists that of Yiddish, the rift between them widened. Each group had its own organizations, publications, and educational facilities. A bitter battle began to be waged between them for the loyalty of the Jewish masses. Zionist publicists such as Joseph Klausner, Menahem Ussishkin, and Zalman Epstein were especially hostile to the flowering of Yiddish culture at the time.[59]

In 1906, a national conference of Russian Zionists meeting

59. See for example, Z. Epstein, "Hasakana Hazhargonit Umahuta," *Hashiloah* 6 (1910); A. Levinson, *Leom Banekhar* (Tel Aviv, n.d.), pp. 118–45; and S. Kling, *Joseph Klausner* (New York, 1970), p. 67. See also S. Niger Charney, "Joseph Klausner's 'History of Modern Hebrew Literature' and His Attitude to Yiddish," *Yivo Annual of Jewish Social Science*, 10 (New York, 1955): 197–211 and S. Bickel, *Shrayber fun Mayn Dor*, 3 (Tel Aviv, 1970): 412f. On Ussishkin see S. Kling, *The Mighty Warrior* (New York, 1965), p. 50.

in Helsingfors (Helsinki) adopted a program of *Gegenwartsarbeit* ("work in the present") in the Diaspora. The program included striving for the recognition of Hebrew and Yiddish as the national and the vernacular languages of Jewry, respectively, in the schools, courts, and other public institutions. The conference followed the lead of the Austrian Zionists who had a similar conference in Cracow that same year. At the Eighth Zionist Congress in The Hague in 1907, Chaim Weizmann presented the program of "Synthetic Zionism," which combined political goals with practical work in both Palestine and the Diaspora.

Concurrent with the emergence of Yiddishism toward the end of the nineteenth century, interest in the revival of Hebrew as a spoken language began to spread. It was especially fostered by the *Hovevey Zion* (Lovers of Zion) societies that developed following the pogroms in the eighties. As a result of the growth of the Hebrew press and literature in Russia, and of the successful attempt of Eliezer Ben Yehuda (1858–1922) and others to revive Hebrew as a spoken language in Palestine, societies for the propagation of Hebrew were rapidly multiplying throughout the world at the turn of the century. In 1907, they united in the *Agudat Hovevey Sefat Ever* (Association of Lovers of Hebrew). At the same time, the modern Hebrew school movement (*heder metukan*) was developed by Jewish educators to help spread knowledge of the language. They also devised the "natural method" of teaching it without the aid of another language (*Ivrit Beivrit*).

Hebraists felt the need to call an international Hebrew language conference immediately following the Conference of Russian Zionists in Minsk in 1902. Ahad Haam's address at that conference had actually sparked the idea of a Hebrew movement in the Diaspora, outside of the official Zionist framework. The Hebraists delayed, however, because of the hesitations of Ahad Haam, Bialik, and others concerning the possibility of actually implementing spoken Hebrew outside of Palestine. It would seem that very few of the prominent Hebrew writers were actually able to converse in the language. A conference of *Ivriah,* the first international organization for the dissemination of Hebrew, met in The Hague in 1907 and the first Congress for Hebrew Language and Culture convened in Berlin in 1909.[60]

The political struggle for the recognition of Yiddish as a Jewish national language was handicapped in Russia, where national agitation was considered illegal by the regime. It reached its zenith in the Austro-Hungarian empire, particularly in Galicia and Bukovina, in the period following the Czernowitz Conference.

In lands of immigration, too, Jews fought for the recognition of their mother tongue. One campaign of a group of Jewish intellectuals for the recognition of Yiddish as a European language was crowned with success in 1906. In that year, the South African parliament, the first government to grant official recognition to Yiddish, voted to recognize it as a European language, a cultural language, and the language of the Jewish people. In practical terms, this meant that Jewish immigrants would be able to fulfill with Yiddish the literacy requirements for entrance into the country.[61] This was but one example of how the theoretical discussions by the literati and the political realities throughout the world were converging to make the language controversy an issue of profound consequence for Jewish life at the beginning of the century.

In 1908, under the impact of this growing struggle for the recognition of Yiddish as the language of Jewry throughout the world and in the Austro-Hungarian empire in particular, and in response to the mushrooming of the Hebrew-culture movement, the Yiddishists mustered their forces at the First Yiddish Language Conference in Czernowitz. The Conference marked the conscious recognition and public proclamation of the Yiddish

60. Cf. A. Levinson, *Hatenuah Haivrit Bagolah* (Warsaw, 1935), pp. 9–21; S. Federbush, *Halashon Haivrit Beyisrael Uvaamim* (Jersulem, 1967), pp. 307–63; Y. Klausner, "Halutsey Hadibur Haivri Beartsot Hagola," *Leshoneynu Laam* 15, nos. 1–2 (Jersualem, 5724): 3–47; and Y. Klausner, *Behitorer Am* (Jerusalem, 1962), pp. 539–42.
61. Cf. Z. Reisen, *Yidishe Shprakh un Yidishe Literatur* (Buenos Aires, 1965), p. 38.

language as a factor of national significance in the life of the Jewish people. In declaring Yiddish to be a national language of Jewry, the Conference symbolized the culmination of a thousand years of Jewish linguistic and cultural creativity. It signified the consummation of several centuries of efforts to raise the status of the language. It discredited and to some extent erased the pejorative designation "Jargon," which, although accepted even by many outstanding Yiddish writers at the time, had hounded the language for more than a hundred years. It helped to officially reinstate the older and more dignified name, "Yiddish."

As an expression of modern nationalistic tendencies within Jewry at the beginning of the twentieth century, the Conference brought together adherents of a variety of trends, philosophies, doctrines, parties, and alignments in Jewish life. It highlighted important developments within each of these, underscoring areas of agreement and possible cooperation between them and pointing up disagreements and antagonisms. The Conference signaled the emergence of modern Yiddish literature and of the Yiddish press and theater as potent factors in modern Jewish life. It heralded new developments in Jewish scholarship and education such as the modern Yiddish translation of the Bible by Yehoash (Solomon Bloomgarden; 1872–1927),[62] the founding of the Yiddish Scientific Institute (Yivo) in Vilna in 1925, and the development of the Yiddish secularist school system in Eastern Europe and America in the second decade of the twentieth century. It gave added impetus to the emerging doctrines of Yiddishism that were finding expression in publications such as *Literarishe Monatshriftn*, edited by S. Gorelick, A. Vayter, and S. Niger in Vilna in 1908. It also stimulated the Hebrew-Yiddish language controversy that raged in Jewish life and letters up until the Second World War.

62. See H. M. Orlinsky, "Yehoash's Yiddish Translation of the Bible," *Essays in Biblical Culture and Bible Translation* (New York, 1974), pp. 418–22.

Nathan Birnbaum.

4

NATHAN BIRNBAUM

NATHAN BIRNBAUM, EARLY IDEOLOGUE OF YIDDISHISM AND initiator and architect of the First Yiddish Language Conference in Czernowitz in 1908, was one of the most fascinating Jewish figures at the turn of the century. A seminal thinker whom Simon Dubnow once characterized as the "noble prince of East European Jewry," Birnbaum was an early Zionist, a champion of Diaspora nationalism, and an interpreter of East European Jewish culture to the Jewish intellectuals of Western Europe.[1] Because of his manifold activities and the breadth of his achievements, he was regarded as a pivotal figure in the history of modern Jewish nationalism and culture as well as in religion.

Birnbaum was born into a moderately Orthodox family in Vienna in 1864. His father, the son of Galician *hassidim*, had come to Vienna from Cracow, and his mother, born in Hungary, was the descendant of a well-known rabbinical family. He was

1. Simon Dubnow, quoted in S. Rozenhek, *"Beyn Haketsavot,"* Karmelit, nos. 5-6 (Haifa, 5720), p. 249. Cf. D. Sadan, *Avney Bohan* (Tel Aviv, 5711), pp. 291-303.

educated in state elementary and grammar schools and received training in Jewish subjects at home. He always felt that he had been tremendously influenced by German culture without, however, ever feeling that he was a German. In his adolescent years, he shocked his peers when he came to the conclusion that the nationality of Austrian Jews was not German but Jewish. Jewry, he told them, constituted a nation of its own that should seek to regain its own land of Palestine. He began to steep himself in Jewish studies and Hebrew journals, and to learn about the Jewish nationalist movement in Eastern Europe.[2]

The journal that most influenced Jewish youth at the time was *Hashahar,* edited by the Hebrew novelist and essayist Peretz Smolenskin (1845–1885) in Vienna from 1868 to 1885. Its motto, "war against the darkness of the middle ages and war against the indifference of today!" expressed its editor's determination to equally expose the excesses of East European rabbinism and traditionalism, on the one hand, and the hollowness of West European enlightenment and religious reform, on the other. Smolenskin's opposition to the destructive aspects of the Haskalah, his emphasis on Jewish distinctiveness and modern nationalism as the keys to the solution of the problems of Jewry, and his deep respect for the Jewish masses and for the basic elements of the Jewish religion left a deep impression on Birnbaum. Indeed, the various phases of Birnbaum's ideological odyssey, including his Diaspora nationalism, may be traced to aspects of Smolenskin's writings.[3]

Birnbaum was also influenced by the thinking of the Hebrew radical writers of the day, many of whom contributed to *Hashahar,* to Aaron Lieberman's socialist periodical *Ha-emet*

2. Cf. Nathan Birnbaum, "Iberblik ber Mayn Lebn," *Yubileum-Bukh* (Warsaw, 1925), p. 10 and *Festschrift der Kadimah* (Vienna, 1933).

3. See C. Freundlich, *Peretz Smolenskin: His Life and Thought* (New York, 1965); N. Slouschz, *The Renascence of Hebrew Literature* (Philadelphia, 1909), pp. 224–70; J. Raisin, *The Haskalah Movement in Russia* (Philadelphia, 1913), pp. 260–67; A. Shaanan, *Hasifrut Haivrit Hahadasha Lizrameha* (Tel Aviv, 1962) 2:36–65; J. Klausner, *Historiya shel Hasifrut Haivrit Hahadasha* (Tel Aviv, 1955), 5:14–231; S. Spiegel, *Hebrew Reborn* (New York, 1930), pp. 223–41; E. Silberschlag, *From Renaissance to Renaissance* (New York, 1973), pp. 145–50.

published in Vienna in 1877, and to the other Hebrew periodicals of the day. The group of Hebrew writers who espoused various degrees of socialism in their writings in the seventies included Yehuda Leyb Levin (Yahalal), Yitzhak Kaminer, Morris Winchevsky (Ben-Nets), and Moshe Leyb Lilienblum, among others.[4] Lilienblum (1843–1910), erstwhile *maskil*, religious reformer, and socialist, turned to Jewish nationalism as a result of the Russian pogroms in 1881 and 1882. He became an ardent champion of the *Hovevey Zion* movement, which was formed at the time to encourage Jewish colonization and a Jewish national revival in Palestine.[5]

In 1882, the appearance of Leon Pinsker's German pamphlet *Auto-Emancipation: A Warning of a Russian Jew to His Brethren* had a profound effect on young Jewish intellectuals in Austria and Germany as well as on Russian Jewry.[6] Pinsker (1821–1891), a semi-assimilated Jewish physician in Odessa, analyzed anti-Semitism as a constant threat to Jews everywhere, which could be averted only in a land where they would form a majority. Pinsker's advocacy of a return to both national consciousness and territorial independence fired the imagination of Jewish youth with a sense of the urgency involved in finding a solution to the problems of Jewry and with feelings of Jewish dignity and self-respect.[7]

Birnbaum entered the University of Vienna in 1883. That year, together with two fellow students, Reuben Bierer and Moritz Schnirer, and with the cooperation of Peretz Smolenskin, Birnbaum founded a Jewish nationalist student organization a decade before Herzl's appearance on the Jewish scene. The Hebrew name chosen for it, *Kadimah*, meaning both forward and eastward, seemed to express the basic Zionist philosophy

4. Klausner (Tel Aviv, 1958), 6:116–314.
5. Klausner (Tel Aviv, 1963), 4:190–300; Shaanan, pp. 19–36; Slouschz, pp. 210–23; Spiegel, pp. 199–205; Silberschlag, p. 150.
6. Cf. R. Lichtheim, *Toldot Hatsiyonut Be-Germanya* (Jerusalem, 1951), pp. 14–18.
7. Cf. L. Pinsker, *Auto-Emancipation*, trans. C. S. Blondheim (New York, 1948).

that Birnbaum was expounding at the time.[8] *Kadimah* was
dedicated to the battle against assimilation, to Jewish nationalism, and to the settlement of Eretz Yisrael as a means of
furthering Jewish independence.[9] The organization, which was
the first of its kind, heralded the development of several Jewish
student societies in Central Europe that played a significant role
in the early evolution of Zionism.[10] It sponsored the *Admath
Jeschurun* Palestine Settlement Society and in 1891 became
part of the Zion student movement, which had branches in
Galicia, Bukovina, and other parts of the Austro-Hungarian
empire.[11] Following the publication of Herzl's *Judenstaat*,
Kadimah offered Herzl its services in a document for which it
obtained several thousand names.[12]

In 1884, Birnbaum issued a pamphlet entitled *The Urge to
Assimilation (Die Assimilationssucht)*. Subtitled "A Word to
the So-called Germans, Slavs, Magyars, etc. of the Mosaic
Persuasion by an Undergraduate of Jewish Nationality," it
attacked the definition of Jewry as solely a religious community
that prevailed among assimilated Jews. In the same year he also
launched *Selbst-Emancipation,* a German-language journal
named after Pinsker's pamphlet, which was already considered
a classic. The journal, dedicated to "the national, social and
political interests of the Jewish people," was published for two
years and revived again in 1890. It was in this publication,
which he served as publisher, editor, bookkeeper, typist, and
office boy, that in 1890 Birnbaum coined the term "Zionism"
and, later, "political Zionism." During the seven years in which
the tri-weekly (later a weekly) appeared, it became the rallying
point for the Westernized Jews of Central Europe who were
interested in a Jewish national renaissance and in the resettle-

8. Cf. Raisin, p. 285.
9. G. Kresel, "Zelbstemantsipatsion," *Shivat Tsiyon* (Jerusalem, 1956),
4:58.
10. Cf. Y. Klausner, *Opozitsya Le-Herzl* (Jerusalem, 5720), pp. 7–26.
11. M. Slipoy, *Haoleh Hagadol: Dr. Natan Birnbaum, Hayav Ufoalo*
(Jerusalem, 5723), p. 24.
12. M. Raisin, *Recent History of the Jews in Both Hemispheres* (New
York, 1918), p. 405 (vol. 6 of H. Graetz, *Popular History of the Jews*).

ment of Palestine.[13] During the first years of the journal, Birnbaum published it at his own expense. At one point, his mother even sold her shop of kitchen utensils to help defray the costs.[14]

Birnbaum received his Doctor of Laws degree from the University of Vienna in 1885 and spent four years working in a law firm. He was unsuccessful primarily because of the anti-Semitic atmosphere in Vienna at the time. It was impossible for a Jewish lawyer with the physical features of Birnbaum to obtain a fair ruling in the city of rabid Jew-haters such as Karl Lueger. Clients knew this and were compelled to seek other advocates.[15]

Birnbaum now decided to devote himself completely to writing and to Zionist affairs. In the early nineties, he helped organize the Hebrew cultural society (*Safah Berurah*) in Vienna. Under the pen name of Mathias Acher, which he took in 1891 to betoken his break with religious traditionalism, he sought to effect a synthesis between European modernism, moderate socialism, and Jewish nationalism. In several articles, he developed the idea of a "cultural radicalism" that would liberate Jews from the religious tradition.[16]

In 1893, Birnbaum published an exposition and interpretation of Zionist thinking, *The National Rebirth of the Jewish People as a Nation in Its Country: An Appeal to the Good and the Noble of All Nations.* By this time he had become the most distinguished intellectual among Jewish nationalists in Austria and Germany. His reading of Herzl's *Judenstaat* in 1896 convinced him of the correctness of political Zionism. He published a review of Herzl's book in *Die Zeit*, an Austrian newspaper, that same year. In 1896, he became editor of the Zionist

13. Cf. Introduction to Nathan Birnbaum, *Confession* (New York, 1947), p. 8; A. Bein, "The Origin of the Term and Concept 'Zionism'," *Herzl Year Book* (New York, 1959), 2:6; G. Kresl, pp. 55–99.

14. J. Fraenkel, "Halifat Hamikhtavim Beyn Nathan Birnbaum Leveyn Siegmund Werner," *Shivat T'siyon* 2–3 (Jerusalem, 1953):275.

15. Cf. D. Pinski, *Oysgeklibene Shriftn* (Buenos Aires, 1969), p. 279 and I. Elbogen, *A Century of Jewish Life* (Philadelphia, 1944), pp. 170f.

16. Cf. N. M. Gelber, *Toldot Hatenuah Hatsiyonit Be-Galitsya* (Jerusalem, 1958), 2:532.

periodical *Zion,* which had been founded in Berlin by Heinrich Loewe the previous year.

In 1897, Birnbaum wrote *Jewish Modernism (Die Juedische Moderne),* considered the most important publication of his Zionist period. Here he attacked assimilation on general cultural grounds. He referred to the distinction, common in German social *Wissenschaft,* between "civilization" (economic, technical, external, and therefore universal) and "culture" (a particularistic, national phenomenon). Emancipation had brought the Jew the former by making him a European but could not provide him with the latter because it was unable to make him a true member of any particular European nation.

> When we compare the so-called assimilated Jews with the environment into which they have assimilated, we see that there is a similarity between them only in that circle of ideas and emotions which is common to all European peoples. It is completely lacking, however, with regard to national particularities of individual nations. The assimilated Jew has more or less the over-all needs, approach to social justice, political maturity, courageous scientific outlook, refined desire to enjoy life, purified artistic taste, and large-scale planning of a cultured European. But he does not have, or has only to a very small degree, those particularities which characterize every race and nation in itself.[17]

In addition to obtaining equal rights for the Jews, assimilationism held out the promise of transforming him into a cultured European. Birnbaum, however, argued that this was impossible. The Jew, he said, needed Zionism not only because emancipation had failed and anti-Semitism had made him insecure; he needed Zionism because only through his own people could he become a cultured person.

Birnbaum was invited by Theodor Herzl to deliver an address on the situation of Jewish culture, "Zionism as a Cultural Movement," at the first Zionist Congress in Basle in 1897.

17. Quoted in S. Niger, "Dr. Nathan Birnbaum," *Di Yidishe Velt* 1, no. 2 (Vilna, 1914): 252.

Chaim Zhitlovsky, who also attended the Congress, later wrote that

> the most important introductory addresses, which set the tone for the deliberations, dealt enchantingly and beautifully with the question of the Jews, with anti-Semitism and the needs of the Jews, with the emptiness, harm and barrenness of assimilationist ideals. None gave expression to Ahad Haam's credo that the purpose of the Jewish renaissance was to provide a solution for the "problem of Judaism" rather than the "problem of Jewry." Only in Dr. N. Birnbaum's address did the spiritual side of the Jewish problem emerge : the return not only to our ancient land but also to our ancient spiritual world, to the social and ethical world-view of our great prophets. This point of view, which evoked the enthusiasm of the younger delegates, was developed not in opposition to pure territorialism, the ideal of a home for the Jewish people the world over, but as a supplement to it.[18]

Birnbaum was elected secretary-general of the Zionist Organization. His position as a Zionist leader and distinguished man of letters was assured. But gradually differences developed between him and Herzl. Like several other Zionist leaders at the time, including Yitshak Rilf and Carl Lipe, Birnbaum saw Herzl as a power-hungry tyrant, as a usurper and as a stranger to Jewish life who coveted the "crown of Zion." He felt betrayed when the members of *Kadimah* and other Zionist groups in Vienna pledged unqualified support to Herzl.[19] He was unwilling to play the role of a lieutenant instead of a general in the Zionist camp.

At first, not unlike Ahad Haam, Birnbaum seemed to reject only Herzl's political approach. He sought to give precedence to the work of colonization rather than diplomacy. In 1898, however, following the Second Zionist Congress, when Herzl opposed his reelection as secretary-general, Birnbaum left the movement.

> I did not remain satisfied. I gradually grew to realize that "lo zu ka-derekh" ["This is not the way"—the title of Ahad Ha-am's first essay], that the former, quieter way had been better. And

18. C. Zhitlovsky, *Mayne Ani Mamins* (New York, 1953), p. 337.
19. Cf. J. Fraenkel, pp. 276–79.

generally speaking, my Zionism became shaky. In the end I left the Zionist Organisation.[20]

Israel geht vor Zion (Israel comes before Zion), meaning that the needs of the Jewish people must take precedence over the Palestine idea, became his motto. He took issue with the Zionist "negation of the Diaspora" and even with Ahad Haam's notion that all Zionist efforts must ultimately be directed toward Palestine.

It is arbitrary to regard all cultural beginnings in the *Golus* simply as valuable cultural manure for just one potential culture on a soil which is not yet ours. Territorial concentration is not to be understood in too narrow a sense, it must not be confused with the establishment of a single territorial center.[21]

Birnbaum attributed his rejection of Zionist ideology and his departure from the Zionist movement to his close acquaintance with East European Jewry, with which he became completely obsessed.[22] In the course of an address at the First Zionist Congress he had stated that

the East European Jews, principally those who speak the Jewish "jargon," comprising three-fourths of the Jewish population, have a national individuality expressed in costumes and language, literature and art, customs and traditions, and in religious, social and legal life which proves that they possess a unique culture.[23]

At the time, however, Birnbaum had been pessimistic about the future of East European Jewish culture. It had seemed to him to be serving merely as a stepping-stone toward assimilation.

By the time of his departure from the Zionist movement, however, Birnbaum had changed his mind. It was unnecessary,

20. *Yubileum Bukh,* pp. 12, 13. Cf. Slipoy, pp. 25f.
21. Quoted in S. A. Birnbaum, "Nathan Birnbaum," *Men of the Spirit,* ed. L. Jung (New York, 1964), p. 527.
22. Cf. O. Janowsky, *The Jews and Minority Rights* (New York, 1933), p. 63.
23. N. Birnbaum, *Ausgewahlte Schriften zur Judischen Frage* (Czernowitz, 1910), 1 : 40.

he discovered, to re-create a normal Jewish people as Zionism maintained, because one already existed.

> When I found them to be a people with all the signs of a live, separate nation, it became more and more clear to me that a nation that already exists does not have to be created again *de novo*, and that what is of principal importance is preserving its life. Thus I developed my Golus-Nationalism. In Western Europe I stood up for Eastern European Jews, pointing out their lively folk existence and I requested of the latter that they guard what they possess and especially that they do not destroy it for the sake of dreams of the future.[24]

It was at this point that Birnbaum developed his ideology of Diaspora or *Golus* Nationalism. Between 1902 and 1905, under the influence of Karl Renner's *Der Kampf der osterreichischen Nationen um den Staat* and Simon Dubnow's *Letters on Old and New Judaism,* Birnbaum worked out a theory of non-Zionist nationalism that he called *Alljudentum* (Pan-Judaism). It sought to further Jewish national and cultural life in the large centers of Jewish population throughout the world and simultaneously secure the recognition of Jewry as a nationality by the world powers. Essentially an optimist who refused to take a long view of manifestations of anti-Semitism in his day, Birnbaum believed that Jew hatred was diminishing in the modern world and that it would continue to do so.

Birnbaum also refused to acknowledge the assimilation of Jewry as inevitable. He placed his hopes in the East European Jews. His analysis of their situation led him to conclude that, unlike their West European brethren whose Jewish identity had disintegrated under the impact of emancipation, social, economic, political, cultural, and demographic factors favored the survival of the East Europeans as a recognizably distinct community. Concentrated in large masses, with nationally conscious middle and lower classes determined to preserve their national rights, heirs of a rich folk tradition that they had not abandoned, Birnbaum saw every hope for their securing emancipation as a

24. *Yubileum Bukh,* p. 13.

national group rather than as individuals, as had been the case in Western Europe. He also believed that the preservation of Jewish corporate status was being furthered by the struggles of other minorities for their own rights. This too, he felt, would help guarantee the survival of East European Jewry as a national entity.[25] Unlike the Zionists, who believed in the ultimate liquidation of the Diaspora, Birnbaum believed that Diaspora Jewry was actually undergoing a renaissance in his own day.

In consonance with his new ideals, Birnbaum involved himself in Austrian politics. In 1906, a struggle for electoral reform was being waged throughout the country. In an attempt to wean Jewish support away from the Poles in Galicia, the Ukranian leader Romanchuk proposed to the Austrian Reichsrat that Jews be recognized as a nationality, with parliamentary representation of their own. The growth of the struggle for Jewish national rights in Russia at this time also had a strong effect on Jews in Galicia and Bukovina. They sought national recognition, and many groups demanded Jewish national autonomy as well.

Austrian Zionists joined hands with the only nationally inclined Jewish representative in the Reichsrat, Benno Straucher, in forming the Jewish National Party, which sought autonomy for Jews and other nationalities. In essence, this group adopted the Helsingfors program (1906) of the Russian Zionists which, as we have seen, integrated political negotiation, practical activity in Palestine, and *Gegenwartsarbeit* ("work in the present") in the Diaspora.

Birnbaum and other non-Zionist nationalists formed the *Juedischer Volksverein* (Jewish People's Association), which agitated for national rights without adopting the Helsingfors program. Together with Isidore Shalit, a leading Zionist, he headed the Association to Secure the National Rights of the Jewish Nationality which functioned in Vienna.[26]

25. *Ausgewahlte Schriften* 1:186, 237; 2:15f. Cf. 0. Janowsky, pp. 62–64.
26. S. Niger, pp. 388–89.

Birnbaum also participated in a multinational movement seeking cultural autonomy for the various ethnic groups in the Hapsburg empire. He advocated the reconstitution of the monarchy on the basis of the autonomy of nationalities rather than countries. In order to further his own political ideas and objectives, he issued the weekly *Neue Zeitung* (1906–7). He was unsuccessful, however, in his attempt to become a member of the *Reichsrat* as a representative from Eastern Galicia, where he was supported by Jews and Ukranians allied against Poles.[27] Many Jews declined to vote for him because they were afraid that if he were elected, his Jewish physiognomy would set off a new wave of anti-Semitic ridicule and slander.[28]

Birnbaum soon came to recognize that one of the most significant aspects of the life of East European Jewry was its language.

> From Golus-Nationalism, I followed a direct path to the Golus language, to Yiddish, and I began to wage a long war in order to raise its esteem among those who spoke it, among other Jews and even among other nations. I stressed its natural liveliness compared to the artificiality of the new Hebrew.[29]

He began to propagandize on behalf of Yiddish language, literature, and drama. He coined the terms "Yiddishism" and "Yiddishist." He organized "Yiddish evenings" in Vienna, translated the works of Sholom Aleichem, Y. L. Peretz, Sholem Asch, and other Yiddish writers into German, and in 1905 established *Yidishe Kultur,* the first student organization for the furtherance of Yiddish culture.[30] He lectured extensively on Yiddish and Yiddish writers throughout the Jewish world.

> One may say without exaggeration that the Yiddish language places East European Jewry and with it the entire Jewish poeple before a turning point in its national destiny. Only in the light

27. Janowsky, pp. 136–40.
28. D. Pinski, p. 279.
29. S. Birnbaum, pp. 528f.
30. *Leksikon fun der Nayer Yidisher Literatur* (New York, 1956), 1 : 307.

of this despised Golus dialect can the people's full independence ripen and Jews win their second, higher national emancipation.[31]

Birnbaum's Yiddishism was not only theoretical. He began to work assiduously to master the language himself. It took him many years and his lack of facility with it was both personally frustrating and a hindrance to his leadership of the Yiddishist camp.[32] Eventually, however, he mastered Yiddish and became a fluent orator and effective writer in the language.[33]

In 1908, with the help of fellow Galicians in America, Birnbaum made his first trip to the United States on a lecture tour. He hoped that American Jews would help him in his financial difficulties. The subject of his lectures was Golus Nationalism and the importance of the Yiddish language for the existence of the Jewish people. Both the masses and the intellectuals, he felt, had to be apprised of the significance of Yiddish. The Hebraists had to stop treating it as a "handmaiden" of Hebrew. If Hebrew was to be identified with Palestine and Zionism, Yiddish had to be identified with the Diaspora and Golus Nationalism. Yiddish had to be associated with Jewish consciousness the world over.[34]

Birnbaum also addressed several private conferences on the need to reconstruct Zionist ideology on the basis of the Yiddish language.[35] At a meeting of the commitee formed to honor him, he attacked the dominant Zionist philosophy. He accused Zionists of forgetting the Jewish people and making an idol out of Palestine. He contended that were Palestine to disappear by means of a volcanic catastrophe, Zionists would lose all contact with Jewish life and Jewish strivings. With or without Palestine, Jews had to wage their struggle for national existence everywhere.[36]

31. Quoted by N. Mayzel, *Noente un Eygene* (New York, 1957), p. 57.
32. See Lazar Kahn, "Di Tshernovitser Konferents: August, 1908" (manuscript), Yivo Archives, pp. 9f.
33. Cf. Abraham Reisen, "Nathan Birnbaum," *Forverts*, New York, May 5, 1937, p. 6.
34. D. Pinski, pp. 280f.
35. *Di Ershte Yidishe Shprakh-Konferents* (Vilna, 1931), pp. ix.
36. *Ibid.*, p. xii.

On the whole, Birnbaum found American Jews unprepared and unreceptive to his *Golus* Nationalism and Yiddishism. The masses who came to New York's Webster Hall to welcome him could not understand him. He was attacked in the Yiddish press and especially by the humor journals for delivering his pro-Yiddish lectures in German. But he was determined to do something of importance on behalf of Yiddish that would put forth its rights as a language.

At a meeting that took place in the spring of 1908 at the home of the noted Yiddish writer David Pinski, and at which Zhitlovsky and the Yiddish publisher A. M. Evalenko were present, Birnbaum presented his idea of an international conference on behalf of Yiddish. The others were taken with the idea and an animated discussion of the agenda of the conference ensued. All agreed that it was too early to proclaim Yiddish a national language of the Jewish people to the world. What was needed was a discussion of the recognition of Yiddish by Jews themselves as well as a program for the standardization of Yiddish grammar and orthography.

Zhitlovsky was chosen to draw up a proclamation, which the others signed and to which the name of the Yiddish dramatist Jacob Gordin was added at his own request.[37] Evalenko offered the use of his office and staff for the mailing of the proclamation and invitations. As the site of the conference they chose the city of Czernowitz in Bukovina, one of the countries of the Austrian empire in which Birnbaum's doctrines of Jewish national and cultural autonomy were receiving wide support at the time.[38]

Birnbaum left America without the financial support he had hoped for. But he had succeeded in arranging for a conference that would advance his plans for the Yiddish language.

In the course of his lectures and writings on behalf of Yiddish in the period preceding and immediately following the Czernowitz Conference, Birnbaum developed a complete theory

37. *Ibid.*, pp. ix, 1.
38. Cf. I. Elbogen, *A Century of Jewish Life* (Philadelphia, 1944), p. 368.

of Yiddishism that did much to advance the idea that Yiddish language and culture were integral and indispensable aspects of Jewish life in the modern age.

Birnbaum began his apology for Yiddish by pointing out that the designation "jargon" was inappropriate in describing the languages that the Jews created as a result of encounters with non-Jewish languages. That term, he said, was suitable only for the alterations that a specific class within a nation makes in its own language. There were, for example, sailor, student, and bandit jargons. The language of an ethnic group, on the other hand, whether a nation or part of a nation, could not be called a "jargon" regardless of how hybrid it might be. The term was never applied to French or English, both hybrid languages, nor to any of the Jewish hybrid languages. That Yiddish was called a "jargon" was due not to the Jewish people or to other peoples, but to those Jewish intellectuals, deeply estranged from Jewish life, who sought to spiritually dominate it according to the dry, artificial principles of the German *maskilim*.

Birnbaum pointed out that as early as 1783 Moses Mendelssohn had attacked Yiddish as though it were the work of Satan, helping to lead Jewry astray. Later Heinrich Graetz referred to Yiddish as a "semi-animal tongue" ("eine halb tierische Sprache"). Birnbaum conceded that Mendelssohn and Graetz could not have had a proper view of the entire matter in their day, but that was not true of modern East European Jewish intellectuals of the assimilationist or nationalist camps. The nationalists simply lacked an understanding of Jewish history, while the assimilationists were only too eager to insult the Jewish people.

Birnbaum recalled that in Palestine during the Second Commonwealth, Jews had stopped speaking Hebrew and had begun to create the first Jewish hybrid language. In it they wrote works of eternal value. Palestinian Aramaic was followed by many 'other Diaspora languages. "Today nine of the twelve million Jews in the world speak Yiddish, several hundred thousand speak Ladino, and an equal number speak other Jewish hybrid languages." To refuse to admit those tongues into the category of languages, said Birnbaum, was to relegate the Jewish people itself to the lowest possible status.[39]

Birnbaum dismissed the contention that hybrid languages were forced on Jewry by the conditions of exile. If that were true, Jews would have assimilated and completely accepted the languages of their captors as did other conquered peoples. Instead, they labored long and hard to confer Jewish character on their acquired tongues. Those languages were therefore not the products of exile but of the "life-strength" of Jewry.

Like Ahad Haam, Birnbaum repudiated the commonly held notion that Jews have a natural tendency to assimilate. On the contrary, their stubborn "will-to-live" was so powerful that they sometimes regretted it and wished to be free of it. As a "spiritual people" committed to "absolute ideals" (all of these terms were popularized by Ahad Haam), Jewry often forgot the relative and secular bases of its life and treated them apathetically. But it could neither renounce itself nor lose the elements that a nation needs for its existence. Its "will-to-live" would inevitably overcome its weaknesses and misfortunes. When it lost a language, it created a new one in its own spirit out of old and new elements.

> There is therefore no need for us to be ashamed of our hybrid languages. They bear witness to our power which overcomes the misfortunes which befall us and the temptations which touch us. They point to the illusoriness of our assimilation and to the facticity of our non-assimilation. They are the most salient and clearest proof of the eternal attribute of rejuvenation, of the grandiose folk loyalty of Jewry. And that is their pedigree, their primary pedigree. (p. 5)

Jews should be proud of all of the hybrid languages they created in the past, consider them precious, and treat them respectfully. But not all were of equal value and importance for the nation. Birnbaum noted that both the old assimilationist and

39. N. Birnbaum, *Der Yikhus fun Yidish* (Berlin, 1913), p. 4.

new nationalist *maskilim* refused to draw distinctions between these tongues. They knew that none of the hybrid Jewish languages could be compared to Yiddish aside from ancient Aramaic. But since this conflicted with their theories, they continued to speak of "jargons" and "*Golus* tongues," grouping them all together like the "ten plagues" of the Bible. According to Birnbaum, Yiddish speakers constituted the overwhelming majority of the Jewish people in qualitative as well as quantitative terms and the evolution of Yiddish was a factor of great national significance for the entire Jewish people.

Birnbaum saw a contradiction in the lives of the Jewish nationalists who renounced Yiddish at the very same time that they were engaged in nationalist activities and in the making of plans for the Jewish people. He believed fallacious their contention that Yiddish was not actually the language of the Jews but an alien tongue unworthy of their efforts. It was not true, he said, that a particular language or linguistic group need hold sway over a nation forever. In addition, foreign words can become naturalized if a people's spirit enters them and creates a new linguistic configuration out of them. A language did not have to offer proof of ancestry. Its pedigree was evidenced by the fact of its existence and by the fact that many people spoke it (p. 8).

The intellectuals continued to spurn Yiddish as a tongue of the masses. They referred to it as a base tongue without beauty or refinement and without ancestry. Birnbaum saw those accusations as evidence of the intellectuals' total estrangement from Jewish life. Some of them abandoned Jewry entirely. Even those who managed to return to their people via Zionism did not follow a straight path but leaped over abysses.

> They have not discovered, as have the intellectuals of other nations, that in order to link oneself to the soul of a people, one must not renounce the living language of the people but be devoted to it with love and loyalty. (p. 9)

Birnbaum contrasted these intellectuals with those of former generations. The rabbinical leaders of the past had not renounced Yiddish, though it was even less prestigious in their day. Unlike most of the intelligentsia of that time, they spoke the language of the people and taught in it. They found it suitable for the highest spiritual purposes. Birnbaum also attacked the assimilationists, who abandoned Yiddish and all it represented in order to further their own careers.

Birnbaum wrote poetically of the beauty of Yiddish as evident in the prayers of Jewish mothers at the close of the Sabbath, in the pure and hearty voices of Jewish children, in the caressing words of the itinerant preachers, in the writings of Mendele, Peretz, and Bialik, and in Yiddish folksongs, in which "a world of beauty and sacredness opens up."

Jewish nationalist opponents of Yiddish were wont to view themselves as the sole friends of Hebrew and to view devotees of Yiddish as enemies of Hebrew. Birnbaum took issue with this attitude and saw the basic distinction between the two camps in the way each viewed the ancient tongue. To the anti-Yiddish group, the significance of Hebrew lay in its hold on Jewry and its Semitic origins. To the pro-Yiddish group, on the other hand, the significance of Hebrew was found in its uniqueness as the language of the Bible.

Birnbaum believed that the eternalness and exaltedness of Hebrew did not nullify the power, intimacy, elasticity, freshness, and adaptability of Yiddish. Yiddish bore witness to the labor and genius of Jewry. It in no way detracted from the high estate, eternalness, brilliance, spiritual power, and continuous dominance of Hebrew.

It was precisely because of his own love for Hebrew, said Birnbaum, that he felt impelled to take issue with its modern devotees. Even if conditions in Palestine were to make the revival of Hebrew feasible there, no such revival was possible in the Diaspora. Why then persecute Yiddish? Why oppose a language that was the vehicle of Jewishness for nine million of the most loyal Jews, and that served as a guardian of Judaism, Jewish life, and even of the Hebrew language?

According to Birnbaum, who, as we shall see, began slowly to make his way back to religious tradition toward the end of the decade, both Yiddishists and Hebraists were guilty of succumbing to the disease of rationalism. They contented themselves with too little and avoided what was central to Jewish thought. But the Yiddishists had at least chosen the path of the folk. It was therefore difficult for them to remain aloof from the national soul and from the depths of Jewish history. They would gradually come to see the Jewish people not as the product of chance but as a nation with an inner, historical meaning. Together with the people as a whole they would develop the practical means out of which would develop "the new works, new wonders, new world-victories of the ancient, central Jewish idea" (p. 13).

Those Zionists who were hostile or apathetic to Yiddish and whose motto was "Hebrew or Russian" lacked a clear understanding of the central Jewish idea and could not even approach it. Their ideas did not stem from the national soul and therefore had no way of entering the bloodstream of the people and producing new, concrete works. They had themselves blocked the way, segregated themselves from the people, and segregated their present from the past and future.

There was a group among the Hebraists with which Birnbaum felt an internal relationship. There were those

> who feel not only that Judaism is a summary of Jewish ways and means, but that there is also a specific content, a specific objective ideal, who are in fact beginning to understand once again what this content and ideal consist of. I mean those who recognize Jews as a nation but at the same time also sense the true wealth of this nation, who together yearn for a reconsecration of our nation, for a reawakening of its religious genius. (p. 14)

The members of this group should have appreciated how important Yiddish could be in suffusing the individual and the nation with sanctity in all aspects of life. But, unfortunately, they, too, proved themselves no more than literati. Jewry had "no luck" with its Zionist saviors or its ordinary intellectuals. It stood abandoned by both. Perhaps, concluded Birnbaum, new saviors and intellectuals would arise who would understand the true pedigree of both the Jewish people and Yiddish. There were several signs, he hinted, that this was already the case (p. 14).

Birnbaum had occasion to take exception to various complaints lodged against Yiddish by its detractors. To the allegation that Jews spoke it without loving it, he responded that love manifests itself not in declarations but in unconscious feelings. Such an emotion was the feeling of relief one experienced on being able to speak a native tongue after having been unable to do so for a time. There was the pleasure one derived from the proverbs of the language, the warm feelings one could find and create only in one's own language, and the feeling of being "at home" in it.

Birnbaum saw nothing wrong in referring to Yiddish as a "Diaspora tongue" as long as that designation was intended to recall a historical fact. If, on the other hand, the term was intended to characterize Yiddish as a "language of slaves," as both Herzl and Ahad Haam used it in their writings, it was unjustified. When a people becomes free, contended Birnbaum, its language loses the "tone of slavery" and partakes of liberation.

There were many who argued that since Yiddish was not spoken by all Jews, it could not be considered a national language. The non-Yiddish-speaking groups constituted only one-fourth of Jewry, replied Birnbaum. Moreover, they were the weakest section of Jewry, from a nationalist point of view.

To the contention that Yiddish was a kind of German and not truly a Jewish tongue, Birnbaum responded that Yiddish possessed a character of its own, that it was a new creation of Jewry, and that it was no more German than was English. In spirit, it was even further removed from German than English.

Yiddish, it was claimed at the time, was not suitable for scientific purposes. The longer a language is employed for a variety of purposes, the greater its capacity to serve those purposes, answered Birnbaum. In any case, a language should be judged not on the basis of its scientific literature, but on the basis of its poetry, in which its cultural individuality is best expressed.

Had not the movement for Yiddish diminished interest in Hebrew among Jews? On the contrary! replied Birnbaum. Intellectuals who formerly took no interest in Jewish affairs had been brought back to Judaism by the movement for Yiddish and were now becoming more and more interested in Hebrew as well. The same would eventually be true of the Jewish workers.

To the claim that Yiddish works would not become part of Jewish national literature unless they were translated into Hebrew, Birnbaum replied that this was contested by the important role Aramaic continued to play in Jewish religious life. If Yiddish disappeared, the works created in the language would not fare much better.

Was there anything in contemporary Yiddish literature that might be compared to ancient Hebrew literature? The two literatures could not be compared, wrote Birnbaum, because one consisted of belles-lettres while the other was Scripture. There was no literature in the world, including modern Hebrew literature, that could be compared to the Bible. It was equally unfair to compare religious works, such as the writings of the Gaon of Vilna, with modern Yiddish writing.

To those who predicted a bleak future and the impending demise of Yiddish, Birnbaum pointed out that national minorities were becoming more and more zealous on behalf of their native tongues as they perceived the significance of these languages for national existence. Birnbaum placed great stress on such emerging factors as the movements for minority rights, cultural nationalism, and national autonomy.

Some argued that the number of Yiddish speakers totaled five or six million rather than nine million, as Birnbaum maintained. If that were true, he replied, the Yiddish speakers would still constitute a relative majority, since the remaining Jews spoke a number of other tongues. But the claim was false, he argued, and he proceeded to show that in Russia alone there were some five and one-half million Yiddish-speaking Jews. Yiddish speakers the world over, he insisted, totaled nine million of the world's twelve million Jews (pp. 15–21).

Yitzkhok Leybush Peretz.

5

YITZKHOK LEYBUSH PERETZ

ALTHOUGH NATHAN BIRNBAUM FIRST CONCEIVED THE IDEA OF THE
Czernowitz Conference and Chaim Zhitlovsky subsequently
became the outstanding theoretician of radical Yiddishism, it
was the personality of the Yiddish writer Y. L. Peretz that
dominated the Conference proceedings. Peretz emerged as the
hero of the movement that gradually and haphazardly took
shape following its deliberations. He became the leading figure
of the Yiddish cultural movement throughout the world and the
primary symbol of the coming-of-age of Yiddish. The role
became even more significant following his death. During the
period between the two World Wars, he came to be considered
the father of the Jewish secularist schools in Europe and
America.[1]

1. See Y. Turkov-Grudberg, *Y. L. Peretz: Der Veker* (Tel Aviv, 1965),
p. 18.

Peretz was not really an outspokenly militant Yiddishist until the period of the Czernowitz Conference. Even then, his attitude toward the role of the language lacked the single-mindedness and consistency of an ideologue.[2] His program for it was essentially the same as his program for Yiddish literature. He sought to make Yiddish more uniform and more modern. He wanted to enrich it and revive it, because with its help he hoped to enrich and revive its literature.[3]

Peretz was born in Zamosc, Poland, on May 18, 1852. He received a traditional Jewish education and was introduced to modern Hebrew, German, and Russian at an early age. An autodidact, he advanced rapidly from the private study of Jewish medieval philosophy to Jewish mysticism, the forbidden Hebrew literature of enlightenment and, eventually, to fiction and science in Polish.

Peretz began to write when he was fourteen. Until 1878 he did most of his writing in Polish. His first published Hebrew poem appeared in *Hashahar* in 1875. In 1876 he passed an examination that permitted him to practice law and for a decade he was a successful lawyer in Zamosc. All the while he wrote poetry in Hebrew, and topical verse in Yiddish, and rendered chapters of the Bible into Yiddish. As his Yiddish poems were set to popular tunes and achieved popularity in the vicinity of Zamosc, his reputation grew as a person concerned with social issues and as one who had an affinity for the poverty-stricken Jewish masses. He organized evening courses in writing and arithmetic and Sabbath afternoon sessions on Jewish subjects for workers. He rationalized his activities in words typical of many young *maskilim* influenced by the Russian and Polish Populists of the day :

> We can accomplish nothing with the old Talmudists and bourgeoisie. We can hope for nothing from them. Only the common people, the working masses, provide a field in which to work. They are an unhappy people but capable. They possess much idealism but need to be educated. That is why I write

2. Cf. S. Niger, *Y. L. Peretz* (Buenos Aires, 1952), p. 489.
3. *Ibid.*, p. 394.

Yiddish. I want to create a Yiddish literature, to speak and write to the people in its own language.[4]

Following the pogroms at the beginning of the eighties, the Jewish intelligentsia of Russia and Poland became increasingly "folkist" or pro-nationalist in mood. A number of outstanding Hebrew and Russian Jewish writers (Shimon Frug, Ben Ami, David Frishman, and Yitzhak Kaminer, among others) turned to Yiddish as an expression of solidarity with their brethren and in an attempt to help create a united Jewish front. In Poland, even former assimilationists expressed their recognition of Yiddish as an educational instrument for the masses.[5] This new mood also influenced Peretz to think of Yiddish more seriously than he had before.

In 1886, during a visit to Warsaw, Peretz renewed the literary contacts he had made there eleven years earlier through his friendship with the Hebrew writer Reuben Asher Broydes. His interest in literary activity was also revived during that visit.

Peretz displayed what was for its time an unusual sensitivity to the Yiddish language and a startling awareness of its deeper historical and psychological significance. In a Hebrew poem that he published shortly after his visit to Warsaw, "Manginot Hazeman," we have both the adumbration of an attitude that became more and more prominent with Peretz following the Czernowitz Conference and a foreshadowing of future apologia and paeans by devotees of the language.

> Fellow writers, be not angry with me
> For liking the language of Berl and Shmerl
> And not calling it "Jargon" with contempt.
> In their throats I hear the language of my people,
> Not the sacred tongue or tongue of the prophets
> But the exiles' tongue, the tongue of the Jews,
> The language that will ever bear witness

4. *Lekiskon fun der Nayer Yidisher Literatur* (New York, 1968), 7 : 237.
5. Cf. J. Shatzky, "Der Umbakanter Peretz," *Di Tsukunft* (July 1945), p. 445.

To the blood that was shed, to horrible slaughter,
To the devastation and evil loosed upon us
And our fellow exiles in every land.
Within it the cry of our ancestors, the wailing of generations,
The poison of our chronicles and bitterness of our history.
Its precious jewels are
Jewish tears that did not dry but were frozen.[6]

Paradoxically, however, in his first published Yiddish poem, "Monish" (1888), Peretz railed against the aesthetic limitations of the Yiddish language and voiced the wish that he might be a poet in another tongue. "Monish," despite its historic and artistic importance as the first major modern narrative poem in Yiddish, betrays Peretz's early impatience with the language and his lack of confidence in its possibilities. Even its historic role as the language of Jewish martyrdom could be construed as a liability rather than an asset.

> Differently my song would ring
> If for gentiles I would sing,
> Not in Yiddish, in "Jargon,"
> That has no proper sound or tone,
> It has no words for sex-appeal,
> And for such things as lovers feel.
>
> Yiddish has but quips and flashes,
> Words that fall on us like lashes,
> Words that stab like poisoned spears,
> And laughter that is full of fears,
> And there is a touch of gall,
> Of bitterness about it all.
>
> It is drenched with tears and blood,
> That come pouring like a flood
> From the wounds that never cease,
> Of our Jewish agonies.
> In Yiddish I have never heard
> A single warm and glowing word.[7]

6. Quoted in N. Mayzel, *Y. L. Peretz: Zayn Lebn un Shafn* (New York, 1945), p. 65.
7. Trans. J. Leftwich, *The Golden Peacock* (New York, 1961), pp. 72f.

"Monish" was published in the first issue of Sholom Aleichem's literary annual, *Di Yidishe Folks-Bibliotek* (1888), which marks the birth of collective self-awareness on the part of the modern Yiddish literati. Peretz had not even heard of Sholom Aleichem until he received the latter's invitation to participate in the new literary venture. Even Mendele was known to Peretz only in Polish translation and at first he believed that Mendele and Sholom Aleichem were one and the same person. The *Yidishe Folks-Bibliotek* brought Peretz to the attention of Yiddish readers everywhere and a number of reviews of "Monish" appeared in the press. With this poem and the short stories he wrote for Sholom Aleichem's publication, Peretz became an important figure on the Yiddish literary scene. In 1890, the first volume of his stories, *Bakante Bilder (Familiar Scenes)*, was published with an introduction by his devoted colleague and friend Jacob Dinezon.

In the course of his correspondence with Sholom Aleichem in 1889, Peretz wrote that he had consciously striven for linguistic and stylistic innovation in "Monish." He did so both because he wanted to broaden the horizons of his readers and out of his respect for Yiddish which, he felt, needed enrichment and refinement. Only if Yiddish were consciously cultivated would it achieve the status of a language.

> I do not regard the "Jargon" as a secondary medium or as a passing phenomenon. I want it to become a language and therefore we have to broaden it, increase its assets and continuously contribute new expressions so that the writer need not complain that he feels constricted.[8]

These thoughts were reiterated by Peretz almost a decade later at the Czernowitz Conference, where he argued that, despite the significance of Yiddish, because of its limitations it had not yet become a "national" language of Jewry.

From the very beginning Peretz's interest in Yiddish was practical and utilitarian. He approached the language with

8. Y. L. Peretz, *Briv un Redes*, ed. N. Mayzel (Vilna, 1929), p. 41.

almost the same feelings that Mendele and Sholom Aleichem expressed at the beginning of their careers as Yiddish writers. Yiddish was the language in which the goals of the enlightenment could most effectively be realized among the Jews of Eastern Europe. It was the duty of the true enlightener to speak to the wretched masses in their own tongue as long as they knew no Russian and Polish. Since Hebrew was the medium of the intellectuals and not of the masses, it too was wanting as a practical vehicle of Haskalah. Its centrality as the language of Jewish tradition, culture, and religion and as the language of the Jewish literature of the past could not be gainsaid, and Mendele, Sholom Aleichem, and Peretz were all accomplished writers in Hebrew as well as in Yiddish. But in their role as *maskilim* they found Hebrew singularly ineffective and impractical. Yiddish was the tongue the people spoke and the one in which they could be spoken to.

In 1889, Peretz was forbidden to practice law in Zamosc, probably because his activities on behalf of the Jewish workers made him suspect as a revolutionary. He moved to Warsaw where, in 1890, he joined a team of researchers who were investigating the economic conditions of Polish Jewry with a view to proving that Jews merited equal rights. The tour of the towns of the Pale furnished Peretz with material for *Bilder fun a Provints Rayze (Scenes from a Trip to the Provinces)* and probably for many of his short stories as well. In 1891, largely through the efforts of his friend, the Hebrew author and editor Nahum Sokolow, Peretz became secretary of the Cemetery Section of the Warsaw *Kehillah* (Jewish Communal Organization). In addition to providing him with a livelihood, this position, which he held for the remainder of his life, afforded him an unusual opportunity to become intimately acquainted with all levels of the population and with every facet of Jewish life. Peretz launched his own literary anthology, *Di Yidishe Bibliotek* (not to be confused with Sholom Aleichem's *Folks-Bibliotek*), in Warsaw in 1891. Two issues appeared that year and the third and final issue in 1895.

Populism and Enlightenment were the dominant motifs of the introductory article, "Education," which Peretz wrote for the first issue of the anthology. His essay was an expression of the new "protonationalist" emphasis of the Haskalah movement. The "education" of which Peretz spoke was no longer the facile cosmopolitan and individualistic enlightenment of the East European *maskilim* of the 1860s. It was a broader concept, including the history, cultural heritage, and folk traditions of one's people. He urged the Jewish intellectuals of his day to shun shallow cosmopolitanism and work on behalf of the betterment of their own people.

Don't assume, Jewish intellectuals, that you are doing your duty, by working for a greater entity, for so-called humanity-at-large . . . Humanity-at-large does not yet exist. Cultural groups, distinct peoples, differing civilizations are now the actors on the stage of the world. . . . Come back to your own people; be for it a pillar of cloud by day and a pillow of flame by night; lead it and guide it but do not run ahead and do not abandon it in the desert. . . . You are lighting a fire beneath the open sky, while your own family in your own house is freezing or is suffocating with smoke. . . . Help the people to recognize the sun's rays as early as possible.[9]

This was Peretz's first attempt at writing a serious essay in Yiddish and it established his reputation as an essayist of importance with a style of his own. Peretz's direct, terse sentences went a long way in altering the verbosity and homiletical tortuousness of the Yiddish and Hebrew essayists of the period. In addition, the ideas expressed in "Education" eventually became a kind of Yiddishist credo. Peretz's words voiced the particular blend of particularism and universalism, Jewish traditionalism and social radicalism that came to be associated with Peretz and with those who saw in him the symbol of the modern Jewish humanist with deep roots in his own culture and tradition.

In "Education" Peretz dealt with the question of the

9. Trans. in S. Liptzin, *Peretz* (New York, 1947), pp. 335–38.

languages of the Jewish people in a forceful, direct manner. Knowledge of Hebrew, he felt, was indispensable. Hebrew made the Bible in its original tongue accessible to the Jew and united him with his people of the past and present. The modern Jew also had to know the language of the country in which he dwelt. The existence of Yiddish and its function as a "third language" of Jewry was also indispensable and had to be reckoned with. The Jewish intellectual who wished to serve his people had to familiarize himself with Yiddish as well. "It would be better," wrote Peretz, "if we could get along with a single language, or with two; but we are forced to know all three. . . ."[10]

In the period following the Czernowitz Conference, when the Hebrew culture movement rallied to the threat posed by the Yiddishists, Peretz's early pronouncement on the two languages seemed to favor Hebrew over Yiddish. Hebraists could claim that the later Peretz had been deflected from the right path by Czernowitz. Had he not been a Hebrew writer, maintaining close contact with the circle of Hebrew writers in Warsaw for several years after his arrival there? Had he not been a member of the Hebrew culture club in Warsaw (*Safah Berurah*), before which he had frequently delivered lectures in Hebrew? His true feelings and those which, in fact, expressed the true spirit of Jewish history were for the Hebraists those Peretz had expressed two decades earlier in "Education":

> We want every Jew to know Hebrew, so that he does not forget the Bible. . . . The Hebrew language, which Jews in all lands understand, is the belt which holds together all the ringlets and prevents their falling apart. It is the cement which binds together our scattered units. . . . The Hebrew language also holds together the ringlets in the chain of time. It links us with Moses and the Prophets of old, with the creators of the Talmud and with all the great luminaries that once shone in our firmament. The Hebrew language knits us with the pyramid-builders, with the warriors who shed their blood in defense of Jerusalem's walls, with the martyrs whose last words at the stake were *Shma*

10. *Ibid.*, p. 334.

Yisroel. . . . To forget the Hebrew language means to forget the Books of Moses, the Prophets, our history. It means to tear ourselves away, a solitary branch, from the trunk of Judaism, to rot a while, and to disappear.[11]

By contrast, Peretz's reply to the question "Why was Yiddish needed as a third language along with Hebrew and the state-language?" appeared sparse and halting.

This question is answered by the reality about us. The third language exists. Three million people speak it. If we want to educate these three million Jews, we cannot wait until they acquire a thorough knowledge of other tongues. . . . Whosoever wants to understand the Jewish people, whosoever wants to teach them, must be able to read and write Yiddish. . . . No language is holy *per se;* no language is good or bad in itself. Language is a means whereby human beings communicate with each other and whereby the educated influence the uneducated.[12]

It has been suggested that the views on the language question expressed in "Education" are representative of the assimilationist backers of the *Yidishe Bibliotek* rather than of Peretz himself. This notion has been convincingly refuted, however, by an analysis of the social, political, and economic views expressed in the essay. These could not possibly have been held by Polish-Jewish assimilationists at the time. There is therefore no sufficient reason to suggest that with regard to the language question alone Peretz expressed views other than his own. Perhaps even more significant is the fact that Peretz did not alter the text of the essay when he prepared his collected works for publication in later years.[13]

The key to Peretz's view of the language question in this essay and throughout his career was his conviction that, as he put it, "language is a means" and that "no language is holy *per se.*" He drew a sharp distinction between content and form,

11. Ibid., pp. 332–34.
12. *Ibid.*, p. 334. Cf. *Tsuzamen,* ed. S. L. Schneiderman (Tel Aviv, 1974), pp. 479–84.
13. Cf. S. Niger, pp. 212f.

concept and expression, idea and language. Yiddish was a means toward enlightenment and education and, in addition, toward the development of a modern Jewish literature and culture. It was not a final goal in itself. Nor was it destined to replace Hebrew or the "language of the land." Two years before the Czernowitz Conference, Peretz reiterated this view in a letter to Bialik. He had translated several of Bialik's poems into Yiddish and urged Bialik to turn directly to the people in Yiddish himself. "It is not language," he wrote, "which is the main thing but the living person who speaks the language."[14]

Peretz's preference for Yiddish is best explained in terms of his affinity for the common people, whose inner life he sought to depict in his stories. The swift, direct, impressionistic writing so characteristic of Peretz seemed unattainable to him in the aristocratic and pedantic Hebrew of his day.[15]

In 1894 Peretz joined two other Yiddish writers, David Pinski and Mordecai Spektor, in the publication of the literary anthology *Literatur un Lebn (Literature and Life)*. In the introductory article Peretz felt the need once again to explain the motivation for his literary activity in Yiddish. The ideas expressed were virtually the same as those in "Education."

> He who wishes to reach rich, intellectual or middle class homes may use other languages; he who would reach the hearts and minds of the ordinary common people, those whom the higher classes disparagingly call "the masses" must write "Jargon."[16]

Unable to obtain permission from the Russian government to publish either a daily newspaper or a monthly magazine in Yiddish, Peretz joined hands with Pinski and Mordecai Spektor in the publication of *Yontev Bletlekh (Holiday Leaves)*, a periodical that appeared in the form of individually titled anthologies for Jewish holidays. Under several pseudonyms,

---

14. Quoted in N. Mayzel, *Yitzkhok Leybush Peretz un Zayn Dor Shrayber* (New York, 1951), p. 357.
15. Cf. N. Sokolow, "Peretz" in *The Way We Think*, trans. and ed. J. Leftwich, vol. 2 (New York, 1969), pp. 558, 563.
16. Quoted in S. Niger, p. 224.

Peretz authored most of the fictional and nonfictional material and won the acclaim of his readers especially for his satirical writings, which explored the social inequities in the Jewish community of the time. The entire venture was tremendously successful and the seventeen anthologies issued between 1894 and 1896 mark the beginning of the Jewish socialist press in Russia and the emergence of the radical socialist trend in modern Yiddish writing. They represent the development of a new level of sophistication in Yiddish poetry and prose, the growth of a new linguistic and stylistic awareness more in tune with European literature than anything that had appeared previously in the language. The enterprise won the admiration of Russian-Jewish student émigrés in Berlin interested in Zionism and Hebrew culture.[17] But it also evoked the opposition of the renowned Hebrew critic David Frishman, who attempted to ridicule the publication out of existence. The conflict, however, only served to strengthen the popularity of the *Yontev Bletlekh* and Peretz was invited by a Hebrew publisher to issue a similar publication in Hebrew. In a memoir, Pinski recorded how delighted Peretz was with the opportunity to do similar work in both tongues, since "both languages were one with him." *Hahetz (The Arrow),* the Hebrew counterpart of the *Yontev Bletlekh,* was not so successful however and only one issue appeared. *Ha-ugav (The Organ),* a volume of Hebrew love poems by Peretz issued at this time (1894), was better received and even acclaimed by some critics as a major breakthrough in modern Hebrew literature. Peretz wrote love poetry in Yiddish at this time as well, disproving his own contention in "Monish" that Yiddish had no words for the expression of erotic love.[18]

Through Pinski, Peretz became personally acquainted with the leaders of the Jewish workers, both those who belonged to the Polish Socialist party and those who in 1897 helped create

17. Cf. Y. Klausner, *Opozitsya Le-Herzl* (Jerusalem, 5720), p. 18.
18. Cf. David Pinski, "Dray Yor mit Y. L. Peretz," *Di Goldene Keyt,* no. 10 (Tel Aviv, 1951), p. 18.

the Jewish Labor Bund. More and more, his writings reflected the socialism, anti-Zionism and anti-Hebraism of the readers of *Yontev Bletlekh*. Peretz was sympathetic to the revolutionary ideals of the workers and, although he did not participate directly in political activities, both he and Spektor were imprisoned for two months in 1899. In the rising Jewish proletariat Peretz found readers who understood and identified with his writings and who were sympathetic to his vision of an all-embracing modern Yiddish literature. The influence of the socialists on Peretz is evidenced in the polemical articles that he wrote at this time against the "bourgeois" *Hovevey-Zion*, Ahad Haam's theory of a "spiritual center," and contemporary trends in modern Hebrew writing.

Peretz's radical socialist period represents only a transitional phase in his evolution from didactic *maskil* to romantic nationalist, a process paralleled in the experience of many Hebrew and Yiddish writers during the last decade of the nineteenth century. Peretz was not a socialist in any doctrinal sense. When the Yiddish Zionist weekly *Der Yid* was established in 1899, Mendele, Sholom Aleichem, and Peretz all became contributors. Here Peretz published many of his Hassidic and folk tales, works that eventually secured his position as a member of the classical triumvirate of Yiddish literature. Peretz was never actually an opponent of Zionism. His criticism was always reserved for what he considered to be the "utopian" and "petit-bourgeois" aspects of the movement.[19]

Peretz's fascination with Jewish folklore in general, and Jewish folksong in particular during this period was an expression of his own deep interest in the folk. It was also symptomatic of the times. An interest in Jewish folklore developed among Jewish intellectuals toward the end of the eighties. In Poland emancipated young Jews were among the accomplished folklorists and some of them had begun to evince interest in Jewish folklore studies.[20] Peretz collected and published Yiddish folksongs and

19. Cf. N. Sokolow, pp. 556, 565.
20. Cf. M. Schweid, *Dos Lebn fun Y. L. Peretz* (New York, 1955), p. 222.

encouraged his protégés to do likewise. At the Saturday afternoon gatherings of intellectuals and writers in his home, these songs were sung regularly.[21]

Peretz became the guiding spirit of Yiddish literature in the 1890s, assuming the role of major literary figure as well as mentor of the younger authors that Sholom Aleichem had played a decade earlier. Peretz's reputation for hospitality and magnanimity spread throughout Poland and young writers, artists, and actors from all over the country came to see him. No Hebrew or Yiddish writer in modern times has possessed the personal magnetism, charm, and charisma of Peretz.

The young intellectuals and would-be authors were attracted to Peretz's vision of the role of the Yiddish language in Jewish life and of the mission of modern Yiddish literature as much as to his aestheticism, romanticism, and intellectualism. His house became the center of Jewish culture in Warsaw. To the Polish Jewish youth from all sectors of the population who flocked to his modest home, Peretz was a kind of secular Hassidic rabbi who preached the importance of aesthetic values and modernism in Jewish life and on whom they could confer the loyalty and adulation their parents and grandparents reserved for the Hassidic leaders.

From the very beginning of his career as a Yiddish writer, Peretz had believed that Yiddish literature must abandon its provincialism and become universal and modern. Its horizons could no longer be limited to belles lettres. History and scholarly research had to be brought into its ken. Peretz had himself written a number of popular scientific articles for his anthologies. In addition, Yiddish literature had to become a literature of the entire Jewish people, as Peretz saw it. It had to appeal to the intellectuals as well as the masses, to the Polish Jews as well as to their Lithuanian and Ukranian brethren.[22] Where Mendele and Sholom Aleichem had sought to capture the

21. Cf. S. Asch, "My First Meeting with Peretz" in Y. L. Peretz, *In This World and the Next*, trans. M. Spiegel (New York, 1958), p. 349.
22. Y. L. Peretz, *Briv un Redes*, pp. 15–18.

Jewish ethos of the past, employing Yiddish as the traditional folk language, Peretz seemed to be concerned with preparing the groundwork for a new, modern Jewish life in which Yiddish would become a modern Jewish language in the fullest sense. In Peretz's writings, Yiddish did indeed appear to be transformed into a language capable of expressing the nervousness of urban life and the nuances of sophisticated modern thought. Peretz's works are replete with neologisms, foreignisms, and new expressions.

To many of the young people who came to him, Peretz also seemed to provide an approach to the burning issues of the day: socialism and Bundism, nationalism and Zionism, cosmopolitanism and assimilationism, secularism and modernism, religion and personal values. In place of a national territory or religious regimen as the unifying factor of Jewish life, Peretz offered the Yiddish language. In place of formal religion, he pointed to the religious ecstasy, emotionalism, and ethical impetus of the folk tradition and Hassidism, which could be duplicated by the modern Jew without a sacrifice of intellect. The definition, rationale, and program for Jewish living that Western European Jewry sought in the modern Jewish religious movements, the Europeanized Jewish youth of Russia and Poland found in the literary works and personality of Peretz. He taught that Judaism was the unique Jewish approach to things, "seeing the world through Jewish eyes," the Jewish *Weltanschauung* that was the product of the Jewish historical experience. He stressed the individual's need for community and solidarity with his people and unmasked the dangers of cosmopolitanism and rugged individualism in Jewish life. His approach to Judaism was dynamic, evolutionary, cultural, and spiritual. It was optimistic and inspiring, rooted in the Jewish past and confident of the future.

Despite their lack of precision, these ideas placed Peretz in the center of the Jewish cultural renaissance in Eastern Europe at the turn of the century. They hinted at a new secularized Jewish way of life in the making.[23] Peretz's modern humanistic

23. Cf. Jacob Glatstein, "Peretzes Yerushe," *In Tokh Genumen* (New

interpretation of tradition eased the feelings of radical discontinuity that plagued those who had but recently come from traditional and Hassidic homes. His call for a return to the study of the Bible, a revival of the deeper values of the religion of the past, and a knowledge of both Hebrew and Yiddish resounded throughout the Jewish world as a call to self-respect. Peretz represented the synthesis of European rationalism, aestheticism, and modernism with the ethical and cultural values of Judaism. It is against this background that his central role at the Czernowitz Conference and in the Yiddishist movement must be viewed.

In 1901 Peretz's fiftieth birthday and the twenty-fifth anniversary of his literary career were celebrated by Zionists, socialists, Hebraists, and Yiddishists alike, both in Europe and in America. In Warsaw, even outspoken Jewish assimilationists partook of the three-day festivities. This was the first time that a literary anniversary was viewed as a major event in Jewish life. Members of the Bund presented Peretz with a tattered copy of his *Yidishe Bibliotek,* which imprisoned Jewish revolutionaries in Warsaw had passed from hand to hand. In connection with the celebration, a large volume of Peretz's *Collected Works* was issued. It was reprinted during the next few years in Russia, Poland, and the United States. In addition, four volumes of Peretz's writings appeared in Hebrew with a laudatory introduction by Joseph Klausner. Peretz's popularity grew and his literary career reached a peak in the first decade of the century. In addition to *Der Yid,* he was a regular contributor to *Der Fraynd,* the first Yiddish daily in Russia; to *Der Veg,* another daily; and to such Hebrew weeklies as *Hador* and *Hatzofeh.* He contributed essays and articles to virtually all of the Hebrew and Yiddish newspapers and magazines of the day. To this

York, 1947), pp. 484–514. See also A. Shaanan, *Hasifrut Haivrit Hahadasha Lizrameha* (Tel Aviv, 1962) 2:205–23; I. Howe and E. Greenberg, Introduction to I. L. Peretz, *Selected Tales* (New York, 1974), pp. 7–19; B. Zuckerman, *Eseyen un Profiln* (Tel Aviv, 1967), pp. 157–68; Y. Yanasovitsh, *Penemer un Nemen* (Buenos Aires, 1971), pp. 255–61; Y. Kahan, *Oyfn Tsesheydveg* (Tel Aviv, 1971), pp. 11–17; Y. Shpigl, *Geshtaltn un Profiln* (Tel Aviv, 1971), pp. 28–38; H. Sloves, *In un Arum* (New York, 1970), pp. 18–27.

period also belong his activities on behalf of the Yiddish theater in Poland, as dramatist, producer, and critic. Thus, at the beginning of the twentieth century, Peretz was the leading figure in the field of Yiddish culture throughout the world.[24]

Peretz's initial reaction to the invitation to participate in the Czernowitz Conference was negative. The proclamation issued in New York, which I shall discuss in chapter 8, was suspect in his eyes both because of the negative experiences he had had in dealing with American publishers and because the style of the proclamation seemed "immature" and "coarse" to him. He took exception to the opening sentence: "In the last several decades the Yiddish language has made great progress," which he considered an exaggeration. "We need a conference to demand development and progress," he and Dinezon wrote in a reply to the committee.[25] Together they drafted an alternate invitation and suggested that the Conference take up the following questions: orthography, grammar, the use of foreign words, a dictionary, Bible translation, the press, literature, drama and the theater, the significance of the language as a national or folk language and its relation to Hebrew, and "moral international literary property insurance." This last item was probably related to Peretz's own experience with his American publishers. It was not included in the official invitation issued in New York but was soon mentioned in connection with the Conference in the Yiddish press, both in Europe and the United States.[26]

In spite of his initial misgivings, Peretz decided to attend the Conference. He was destined to play a major role in its deliberations and one issue that he raised, concerning the relation of Yiddish to Hebrew, would be a major source of contention during the Conference and in the years that were to follow.

---

24. Cf. N. B. Minkov, "Peretz in Amerike," *Literarishe Vegn* (Mexico, 1955), pp. 41-62, and Chaim Zhitlovsky, *Yitzkhok Leybush Peretz* (New York, 1951), pp. 15-48.

25. *Di Ershte Yidishe Shprakh-Konferents* (Vilna, 1931), p. 4.

26. *Ibid.,* pp. 20, 50.

Matisyohu Mieses.

6

MATISYOHU MIESES

THE MAJOR PRESENTATION AT THE FIRST YIDDISH LANGUAGE
Conference in Czernowitz in 1908 was delivered by Matisyohu
Mieses, a relatively unknown young Hebrew linguist who wrote
polemical articles in defense of Yiddish and debated with
prominent Hebraists, including Nahum Sokolow and Ahad
Haam, in the Hebrew press. His address, the first scientific
essay in the area of Yiddish linguistics in modern times, as well
as his other writings, are of major importance for an understanding of the emergence of the Yiddish-language movement
and of Yiddishist ideology. Mieses provided Yiddishism with its
basic intellectual scaffolding by demonstrating the linguistic
maturity and authenticity of Yiddish and convincingly refuting
the arguments of its opponents.[1]

1. Cf. G. Kresel, "Matisyohu Mieses un di Polemik vegn Yidish,"
Di Goldene Keyt, no. 28 (Tel Aviv, 1957), p. 143.

Mieses was born in 1885 in Przemysl, Galicia, where his father was a successful merchant and well-known communal leader. The young Mieses received training in secular studies as well as traditional subjects and had had two books published by the time he reached his twentieth birthday. Beginning in 1910, he spent many years studying in the libraries of the universities of Berlin and Vienna. He apparently never took an academic degree and preferred to remain a businessman for most of his life.

In addition to Yiddish philology, Mieses published in the fields of ancient Jewish history (*The Ancient Peoples and Israel*, 1910, in Hebrew), the history of Polish Jewry (*The Poles and the Jews in History and Literature*, 1905, in Hebrew), and anti-Semitism (*Germans and Jews*, 1917; *On the Race Question*, 1919; *The Beginning of Jew-Hatred*, 1923, all in German).[2] He also published hundreds of political and scientific articles in the journals *Hamitzpeh, Haolam, Hayarden,* and *Heatid.* He contributed to the Hebrew encyclopedia *Otzar Yisroel* edited by J. D. Eisenstein, to the Polish press, and to German-Jewish and general German publications.

Although Mieses never saw Zionism as a solution to the problems of Diaspora Jewry, one of his first contributions to *Hamitzpeh,* under the *nom de plume* "Dr. Judaicus," was a call for the redemption of Jewry "from physical and spiritual exile."[3]

In June 1907, Mieses published an essay, "In Defense of the Yiddish Language," in the Hebrew journal *Haolam,* edited by Nahum Sokolow and issued by the Zionist Organization. It was here that he began his polemic on behalf of the Yiddish language. He sought to show that, because of its importance, Yiddish merited a place alongside nationalism and Zionism in the consciousness of the modern Jew. He provided a point-by-point refutation of anti-Yiddishism and an explicit, technical

2. Zalmen Reisen, *Leksikon fun der Yidisher Literatur* (Vilna, 1926), 2 : 378.
3. G. Kresel, *Leksikon Hasifrut Haivrit Badorot Haaharonim* (Mer-haviah, 1967), 2 : 344.

exposition and defense of Yiddish as an authentic Jewish tongue.

Along wth Mieses's article, the following editorial note by Sokolow appeared :

> We are publishing this article, which casts light on an important national and scientific question, especially because of the significance of its scientific enlightenment. We are in disagreement with several points in the author's nationalistic reasoning and will return to this question from our point of view in the future.[4]

Mieses began by pointing out that the idea that the folk tongue of East European Jewry was nothing but bad German with a corrupt admixture of Hebrew and Slavic, an unnatural conglomeration and a coarse patois, prevailed among all enlightened Jewish groups with the exception of a few "Jargonists." In practical terms this meant that whether Jews wanted complete emancipation and integration or a renewal of their national existence, they had to rid themselves of "this pernicious and despicable medieval residue" that hindered their attainment of spiritual perfection and prevented their inner liberation. Zionists and assimilationists, two conflicting and contradictory parties in Jewish life, concurred in this view, said Mieses.

> Jews who go to Eretz Yisrael in order to kindle a great light with all the sparks of Judaism they can gather to one center, and traitors who choose the fleshpots of Egypt and sell their souls and their people for transient pleasures, unite in deciding upon the destruction of a tongue which millions speak and in which they experience and express their joys and sorrows. It is bitter to contemplate that the pioneers of the future who seek to restore their people to a complete existence begin their work with destruction, estrangement and negation. Under normal conditions, it is continuous affirmation which expresses the national self-recognition of a rising nation. The desire to cut out a large part of the people's heritage is therefore a sign of

4. M. Mieses, "Bizehut Hasafah Hayehudit," *Haolam,* no. 22 (Cologne, June 5, 1907), p. 269.

senility and a pathological phenomenon which evokes sad
thoughts. There is no competition betwen Hebrew and Yiddish
that can account for the war which the pioneers of Zion are
waging against Yiddish.

Mieses felt that Yiddish and Hebrew readers came from
completely different social groups and had their own intellectual
orientations. The strengthening of Yiddish posed no threat to
the existence of the sacred tongue. It was inconceivable that
Hebrew would ever take the place of the Jewish vernacular
among the masses. Where Yiddish was silent, it was not Hebrew
but the national European languages that were heard.

> If Yiddish is abandoned, its true adversary, the language of
> the country, will be victorious and complete assimilation, the
> destruction of our nation, which our traitors anticipate, will
> come about. With the destruction of the most important criterion
> of our nationhood, the language which stamps us with a unique
> individuality, our nation will lose its solidity and disintegrate.
> With its language our people will lose its individual content, its
> soul, a unique world of spirit and life.[5]

According to Mieses, the invisible but true reason behind
the holy war against "Jargon" was unconscious anti-Semitism
or self-hatred on the part of Jews. "The hatred of Judaism
which formerly led to betrayal and national suicide continues
its devilish work even in the ranks of the most ardent Zionists,
albeit secretly and in disguise." There was no point in
arguing with those who on principle denied everything Jewish
and desired to erase every trace of the existence of Jewry. There
was no point in proving to them that the language of the Jews
had already attained a thorough integration, that from its disparate elements a unified synthesis had emerged, and that such
a synthesis had "the same right to exist which is accorded
without reservation to the Romance languages and to English."
People whose desire it was to completely assimilate would not
change their minds on the basis of such arguments.

5. *Ibid.*

If anything worthy of keeping alive, anything that has the ability to escape annihilation and that can grow and develop, is still to be found in Judaism, all the worse for it; it must be quickly uprooted. For the detractors, proof of the right to exist for anything Jewish leads to an even more enthusiastic ravaging.

But if people who were accustomed to show great love for their nation and were zealous on behalf of its past and future decreed an end to Yiddish and decided to rob Jewry of its living language, then there was no time to rest and gaze peacefully at the natural course of events. "For nationalistic reasons we must not permit the grim reaper who destroys nations to perform this senseless destruction which, in the end, will frighten us all."

Mieses characterized the viewpoint of the devotees of Hebrew with regard to Yiddish as follows: Yiddish, they say, is a linguistic hodge-podge, a residue of the ghetto that shames them with its barbarism. Every Jew who longs to restore the luminous Hebraism of the Golden Age and to return to the glorious period of independence, must rid himself of this indigestible and corrupting burden.

Why, asked Mieses, was the pejorative designation "Jargon" more suited to Yiddish than it was to French, Italian, Spanish, or English, which were also polyglot?

The tongues of Molière and Victor Hugo, of Cervantes and Lope de Vega, of Dante and Tasso, of Shakespeare and Byron are as much jargons as is the language of Mendele and Morris Rosenfeld. A difference in language does not betoken corruption. The Irishman does not consider his strange polyglot a "Jargon." It is time we ceased applying the pejorative term "Jargon" to our Jewish language. Only conscious or unconscious anti-Semitism can lead us to view Yiddish as a jargon, as a contemptible patois. This verdict dooms to abhorrence our people's unique development of the vocabulary which the Jew took during his exile in Ashkenaz. From a philological viewpoint, in its development our people's tongue is not below the Romance languages.

Aside from the philological reasons, the devotees of Hebrew

refused to hear about Yiddish because they considered it strange and alien.

> God of Abraham! For hundreds of years the Jew's soul breathed in his language; he watered it with streams of bloody tears; in it he gave expression to his turbulent sorrow over the Exile of the Divine Presence, of his community and of his soul. He made it a mirror of his suffering and hoping soul. He made it a reflection of his pain and anticipation, of the sufferings he bore at the hands of tyrants and of his songs of the future, of groans before the beatings of an unmerciful destiny and of morning songs of a dawn soon to break forth. The Jew exalted the group of German words until it became the best interpretation of his soul and of his inner world. He made it a truly Jewish language. How then can it be alien to him?

It was not unusual, said Mieses, for a group to make a foreign tongue its own by reworking it.

> For the same reason that the Frenchman considered the language derived from Latin spoken in his land as his own, even though as a descendant of Celts and Germans he had no national connection with the Romans, Jews could consider the German-derived language spoken by their people Jewish.[6]

According to Mieses, the fact that the vocabulary of a language was etymologically derived from another proved nothing. It was not words but the animating spirit of a language that constituted its essence.

> The material is passive; the spirit which dominates it is everything. . . . Why should we be concerned if many words, which are nothing but empty sounds, come from Germany? The soul of the language, its essence, is completely new or, better, completely old and truly Jewish.[7]

Due to hypersensitivity, some Jews complained about Yiddish and argued against it on ethical grounds. They claimed that as the inheritance of the German ghetto, Yiddish bore the signs of

6. *Ibid.*
7. *Ibid.*, p. 270.

slavery and was not fit to be spoken by a free people. Yiddish was a profane burden weighing heavily on Jewry and restraining its self-liberation. Such hypersensitivity was a sign of pettiness and narrowness, said Mieses. Did anyone really sense in Yiddish the ancient servitude that once compelled the Jews to accept it? Internally, the Yiddish language was completely free. What harm was there in the fact that the historical reason for its acceptance had been compulsion?

Were happier songs sung at the cradle of the French language? The Roman colonists, veterans of the armies of the Caesars, who settled beyond the Alps and spread the knowledge of Latin were to no less a degree merciless, devouring tyrants, oppressors of the people and tramplers upon the poor, than were the nations of Europe with regard to us. There is only one big difference between us and the Romance peoples : our fathers were only physically enslaved, theirs were also enslaved spiritually. The Jew's submission to Christianity, even in the deep darkness of the domain of the law of the fist, was outward, external. In his heart he was free, proud of his surroundings, full of suppressed sorrow and silent over the rule of wicked, nations. As a royal son exiled from his father's table among wild savages, the Jew awaited the moment when he would be restored to greatness. Internally, the Jew never debased himself and the mirror of his soul, his language, was never debased. If the Frenchman and Englishman are not ashamed of their languages which were brought to them by their conquerors, our people has even less to be ashamed of.[8]

Some were troubled by the thought that Jewry possessed two languages. Mieses pointed out that the Irish, in addition to their principal Celtic language, which they still used somewhat, also spoke English. They did not seem to be afraid of having two national languages. And for the Irish, English was "the language of the overlords who exploited their land and strangled their life-spirit for hundreds of years." The Egyptians who used the language of the Mameluks, their oppressors, had three languages : the contemporary Arabic dialect; medieval Coptic,

8. *Haolam,* no. 23 (Cologne, June 12, 1907), p. 281.

which the poor Christian farmers still spoke; and primitive Egyptian.

Mieses stressed the point that the Yiddish language had both a national and a philological right to existence. Its uniqueness was attested by the revolutionary changes it had undergone among the Jews. Not only were its grammatical rules, its phonetic forms, its spirit and soul completely altered, but even the simple meanings of many of its words had changed completely. The Jew had left his own mark on the language that he had acquired during his wanderings on the banks of the Rhine.

> The language which life brought to the dwellings of Israel, which the dispersion of the Exile compelled him to speak, was digested by Judaism and converted. The dispersion of the Exile, the atomic fission of the homeless wanderers, assisted the language in penetrating deeply into the tents of Jacob. The Jew was unable to withstand it with collective strength. Necessity was the determining factor and compelled the Jew to alter his language. The stable surrounding life won its victory but the victory was incomplete. Necessity was not the determinant everywhere. In spite of the wild, volcanic storm which mercilessly raged about him, Jacob's strength did not leave him and he did not faint from weakness. He was not so dejected as to reject as a sponge, to respond like a reed in the abyss to every single stream that was poured upon him. . . . Necessity succeeded only in the external world. Only neutral matters of the world of perceptible phenomena acquired new names whose source was Germany. These and no more. At the threshold of spiritual life the gate was closed before the foreign destroyer. He could not desecrate the inner protection, the fortress of Judah. The world of thought and the soul, all subjective phenomena continued to be Hebrew. . . . Music is the expression of the inner soul and the language of music remained Hebrew. . . . Time is related to the subjective and it too is usually referred to with Hebrew nouns.

A narrow ideology, said Mieses, would constrict Judaism and confine an entire historic community to a Procrustean bed. It would tailor the soul of a whole people to fit some artificial model. Those who dreamed of the Hebrew language of the future did not want to know about the Yiddish language of the present.

The love of that which is distant, the longing for the promised land, the pining for a national center, the authentic striving for a completely independent and full national existence wishes to pass thoughtlessly over that which is nearest, wishes to gather that which is closest to our people and declare it obsolete.[9]

A holy war was being proclaimed against the folk tongue. Mieses felt that the Jewish nationalists, to whom the future of the people was dear, had to oppose it.

Those whose goal it was to enhance the true spirit of the Jewish people had to prevent "the domination of implausible ideological axioms which are arrived at routinely without reference to true facts." Only a national language, Mieses believed, could protect Jewry in the face of growing involuntary and unconscious inner assimilation. The Yiddish language could be the armor that would protect Jewry.

The times do not favor the independent existence and unhampered development of our people. Life passes over everything Jewish with the fury of a destructive storm, removing national characteristics, uprooting future blossoms, ravaging all the treasures of our spirit. In spite of the surprising popularity of the Zionist idea among all classes of our people and the election of Zionists to the government councils, in spite of all the glittering externalities, the source of Judaism is becoming depleted, the basis of our nationhood is shriveling, especially in terms of quality. We stand without protection before the onrushing waters of the peoples of Europe which carry everything along with them. We must erect a dam against them. Only a language spoken by the entire people, bearing a Jewish stamp and containing impressions of a large part of its history, only the Yiddish language, can serve as such a dam. The primary and principal demand of the nationalists must be its recognition as the language of our schools and public life wherever Jews

9. *Ibid.*, pp. 281–82.

live. Only a Jewry which speaks its own living language will be spared gradual disintegration and will renew its life as the phoenix. The sole salvation of the Jewish nation is the Yiddish language ! [10]

In his reactions and comments, published together with the second half of Mieses's article under the title "Clarification," Nahum Sokolow, editor of *Haolam,* accused the young linguist of exaggerating the opposition of Jewish nationalists to Yiddish. It was true that they gave preference to Hebrew. "Yiddish-Daytsh" (Judeo-German), he said, "was not unlike Judeo-Spanish, Judeo-Arabic or Judeo-Persian." There was only one truly "Jewish" language and that was Hebrew. For a thousand years Jews had invested their spirit in Judeo-German, Ladino, and their other foreign vernaculars, but they had been investing it in Hebrew for four thousand years. The principal inspiration of Jewish genius in thought and learning in all times and in all lands had been Hebrew. Jewish nationalists did not scorn Judeo-German and did not belittle its value as a language with anger, abuse, and disdain, as did the assimilationists. Sokolow agreed that Mieses's arguments against assimilationists were well taken, but his strictures against the nationalists could not stand up to criticism. Zionism had no disdainful or belittling attitude to Yiddish. On the contrary, most Hebrew writers also wrote in Yiddish.

Nahum Sokolow was himself no opponent of Yiddish. Although he never considered himself a "Jargonist," he was sympathetic to the flowering of the language and its literature. He viewed Yiddish as a folk language of great national importance.[11] As editor of the Hebrew newspaper *Hatsefirah,* he devoted ample space to articles about the language, to reviews of Yiddish books, and to notices of translations from Yiddish into other languages. In his own articles and columns he missed no opportunity to mention Yiddish literature. In bibliographical notices, which he wrote for almost every issue of *Hatsefirah,* he

10. *Ibid.,* pp. 282-83.
11. Cf. A. R. Malachi, "Nahum Sokolow un di Yidishe Shprakh," *Ykuf Almanakh* (New York, 1961), p. 473.

noted every publication in Yiddish, often with critical comments and explanations.[12] He even defended Yiddish from the attacks of the Hebrew scholar Aaron Kaminka, who in a series of articles in *Hatsefirah* denied Yiddish every historical and philological right to existence.[13] Sokolow also wrote a large number of articles as well as several books in Yiddish. For several years he even edited a Yiddish newspaper, *Der Telegraf* of Warsaw.[14]

According to Sokolow, a just defense of Yiddish did not require the "exaggerated notion" that because it contained many Hebrew words it could take the place of Hebrew. Sokolow suggested that if Mieses read the new Yiddish publications of England, of America, and of the socialists in Russia, he would find very few Hebrew words in them. Individual words did not, in any case, constitute a language. As to the future of Yiddish, Mieses was deluding himself. It was gradually withering, being absorbed by the general culture, and becoming more and more of a jargon. It would eventually be absorbed by the native tongues of the lands in which it was spoken. The sphere of Hebrew, he said, was limited, but it was as strong "as tradition, as Judaism, as our people." Yiddish had a large sphere but lacked deep historical roots and could be uprooted by any wind.

For Sokolow the Hebrew language alone was the "tree of life" of the entire Hebrew nation. It was the thread that linked the past to the future as well as all sections of the nation in the present. Its life was eternal. "Its current deplorable state," he wrote, "is our own fault. We must write it, speak it, teach it and propagandize in its behalf." Hebrew had been improved and its scope had been broadened during the past generation. Sokolow felt that the confusion in the ranks of Russian Jewry was bound to pass. The sources of Jewish national feeling had not dried up and the development that had been arrested would

12. *Ibid.*, p. 471.
13. *Ibid.*, pp. 472–73.
14. Cf. S. Kling, *Nahum Sokolow: Servant of His People* (New York, 1960), p. 47. See also F. Sokolow, *Mayn Foter Nahum Sokolow* (Tel Aviv, 1972).

begin anew. In the land of Israel, Hebrew truly blossomed and the emergence of any other general language there was inconceivable.

> Let us be clear and concise on this matter. We will not allow Hebrew to be pushed aside by Yiddish. On the contrary, whereever we can replace Yiddish with Hebrew we will do so zealously and thereby sustain the source of our national spirit and restore the crown to its rightful owner. Where the choice is Hebrew or Judeo-German, without hesitation we will decide for Hebrew. But where outsiders would limit the rights of "Jargon" and refer to it with scorn and contempt, we will protect it in every possible way. Our opposition to Judeo-German because of our preference for our national language is in no way akin to the opposition which stems from assimilation, defection and contempt for the Jewish masses.[15]

In a second article, "A Few More Words About the Yiddish Language," published in *Haolam* only a few weeks later, Mieses countered Sokolow's objections and developed his own thoughts further. He took up the question of the primacy of Yiddish among the folk languages of the Jewish people. It was true, he said, that small groups of Jews used languages other than Yiddish. But that was not at all unusual. Similar situations existed among other nations. Always, however, the national minority was disregarded and, out of a sense of patriotism, it surrendered to the majority. Out of eleven million Jews in the world, eight million spoke Yiddish, two million were assimilated and had no knowledge of Hebrew or Yiddish, and the remaining million spoke the other Jewish languages. How could the latter group be compared to the bloc of eight million Yiddish speakers? What was more important, almost all lacked literatures in those languages. The only exception was the Sephardic group, which possessed a literature, was unified and stood out among the non-Yiddish-speaking groups. Their language was customarily viewed as a competitor of Yiddish. But could the languages really be compared? Ladino contained far fewer Hebrew words

15. *Haolam,* p. 283.

than did Yiddish, and therefore lacked national permanence and direct contact with the past. Moreover, Ladino had not been absorbed by Jewry. It had not been shaped into a new linguistic unit by the creative genius of the Jewish people.

The essential difference between books in Yiddish and books in Ladino is that in the latter case, were the old Spanish words removed, the language would differ slightly, if at all, from normal literary Spanish. For this reason, Ladino books are sometimes published in Latin characters.[16]

It was obvious, wrote Mieses, that the constructive power of a community of eight million was something that the Sephardic community of half a million or the smaller communities could not achieve.

Who can expect impoverished and depressed communities, sunk in lethargic sleep for hundreds of years, without excellence, without any cultural or literary achievement, without real signs of life, to gather enough strength to breathe a new spirit into their languages and give them an inner richness? Who can expect them to fill languages that they were forced to accept passively with the fullness of independent life? Those who speak other dialects are for us petrified, half-dead, lifeless limbs which cling to Judaism out of inertia. Not one of them participates in our revival. There is not even one Hebrew writer who has come from outside the Yiddish Pale. In this respect, the Sephardim, the cream of those who speak other dialects are no different from their wretched brothers in the East. Should we, the majority of Jewry, comport ourselves according to the dry and withered parts of our people? If they wish to return to a national life, to band together under our flag of revival, let them acquiesce to us and to the language in which the literature of the majority of our people is written. There is another possibility and it is that both Yiddish and Ladino be recognized as national languages. The national unity of the Belgian people, for example, does not suffer because of two languages. (pp. 318f.)

16. *Ibid.*, p. 318. Mieses quotes this statement from *Zur Semitischen Sagenkunde* by M. Gruenbaum.

For Mieses, the Yiddish language was the language of the majority of the Jewish people, the language of the entire living nation. It was a language that had achieved integration and it possessed a Jewish character that was expressed in its unique grammar and in its psychological adjustment to Judaism. In all its characteristics Yiddish could be distinguished from the other jargons, which Mieses characterized as no more than insubstantial dialects.

The Yiddish language had been thoroughly Judaized and had become a true folk tongue. It alone could guard Jewry from encroaching assimilation. Yiddish had great power because it had a national tradition, and because it linked Jewry with Hebrew. If words alone constituted a language, Yiddish would indeed be only a German dialect since, according to Mieses, over 80 percent of its words stemmed from German.

> It is not words which constitute a language, but the spirit which animates it. I stressed this repeatedly in my article. The spirit which animates the Yiddish language is truly Hebraic. Its rich folklore, its emotions and its wit, its Hebraic grammatical forms, etc., testify to this. But most of all I tried to show that the Jewish spirit which animates it is so strong that its most import-ant idioms remain Hebraic. I agree that words by themselves prove nothing but the method proves much. It reflects the power of the spirit which creates it.

Mieses wrote that if there were a choice between Hebrew and Yiddish, he would not hesitate for a moment and choose Hebrew. But there was no such choice. Whoever ceased to speak Yiddish, spoke the language of the country—Russian, Polish, German, Ruthenian, English, and so on. Hebrew did not inherit the abandoned place of Yiddish.

> The editor is correct when he says that Yiddish deteriorates under the influence of the general culture. That is why I advocate an end to scorning it and an attempt at strengthening it and preventing its deterioration. The general culture or, better, the national cultures of the various lands deny the foreign minorities, pulverize them until they are no longer

recognizable and devour them completely. The national cultures put an end to our independence and drag us into their midst. They do not intend to wait until we rid ourselves of Yiddish and put Hebrew in its place.

The advocates of Hebrew expected to replace Yiddish with Hebrew. To Mieses it was inconceivable that the overwhelming majority of the people could learn Hebrew so well that they would not need another language. He estimated that in the entire Diaspora, there were at most 100,000 Jews who could read Hebrew well. They formed a strong nucleus, but one that was steadily diminishing and that propaganda and education could not bolster.

A knowledge of Hebrew as a modern language which would enable one to use it for every purpose and in every situation is probably beyond the ability of the average person. The life of a nation must rest on a broad foundation. Only Yiddish can provide such a foundation.

As Yiddish attained strength through usage and growth, its power of resistance would increase and the influence of the dominant languages on Yiddish would cease. Yiddish had enormous potential as a barrier against assimilation. "Jargonization" and assimilation by an environment were possible only for a community that did not intend to preserve its identity and that assimilated because of internal weakness.

One day our people will shake off the slag which engulfs its essence and remove the obstacles and submissiveness which prevent its inner liberation and autonomous development, and will return to its historic path. A negative horoscope based on a temporary situation is a false prophecy. One can neither add to nor detract from Yiddish on the basis of the publications of the Bund or the American Yiddish press. The decrease in Hebraisms in literature of that kind will pass; it is the artificial work of tendentious reporters. The folk continues to speak Yiddish with its Hebrew materials.

In America, said Mieses, conditions were unusual. There a

new nation was being created that organically integrated the various national characteristics and contrasts that could not be integrated in Europe. Mieses predicted that in America Jews would cease to exist in a national sense. In this they would follow the larger immigrant groups of Germans, Irish, and Poles, whose numbers in some cases exceeded the world Jewish population. In ancient times, when the eastern coast of the Mediterranean united to form one Hellenistic community, Jews had been part of it. In America, this phenomenon was destined to be repeated.

> Here in Eastern Europe, however, where Jewish communities are strong and contiguous, and where the synthetic power of America is absent, we can gather our forces and protect our language from destruction and degeneration.

The only protective wall that could restrain the alien streams from inundating the Jewish camp was the Yiddish tongue.

> We are told that Hebrew is blossoming in Eretz Yisrael and that it will eventually replace Yiddish and revive Judaism. Would that this were so! How our hearts will rejoice at the sight of the national flowering of our literary language, at the sight of letters abandoning the pages of withered books and embarking upon a free and flourishing life, a vital and stable development! But why should we delude ourselves? What strength does a community of five thousand farmers have? No one will count the sixty or seventy thousand *halukkah* beggars in the ranks of our revival. (p. 319)

The new institutions being developed in Palestine were still too young to be relied upon, said Mieses. The time had come to stop being excited at the sight of children babbling in a few hundred Hebrew words in a Palestinian village.

> The sin of self-deception is very grave for all sins may be corrected in the course of development except the sin of self-deception and self-delusion. We will gaze at the light ascending from the villages of Judea, while sections of our people disintegrate and are lost. Who will then be able to bring Israel up

out of the ocean of peoples and clothe the lost and dispersed with an identity foolishly abandoned? (p. 320)

Sokolow continued the discussion by stating that space had been given to Mieses in *Haolam* because he had presented everything that could be said on behalf of Yiddish with greater precision and depth than had theretofore been accorded the subject by others. Sokolow then went on to clarify his own position :

(a) The crusade against Yiddish on the part of "liberal" gentiles in countries like Poland and Galicia resulted from enmity, opposition to Jewish separateness, and the desire to assimilate Jewry.

(b) Some assimilationist Jews had joined the ranks of the liberal gentiles in order to show their patriotism.

Sokolow opposed the campaign against Yiddish for the following reasons :

(1) If any existent language had a right to exist, Yiddish, a language spoken by millions, had such a right. The philological, historical, and aesthetic arguments against Yiddish were groundless.

(2) The truly liberal meaning of equality and liberty for the Jews was equality for them as they were, without any restrictions or conditions. If they wished to use the language to which they were accustomed not only for conversation but for legal purposes, for education and for literature, no one had a right to prevent them from doing so.

(3) In addition to not placing legal or technical obstacles before them, it was forbidden to exert moral coercion by berating their language, and by having other "cultural" languages treat it insolently as "barbaric," "despised," etc.

On these points, said Sokolow, he agreed with Mieses, as he had stated in his first response. But with regard to the question of Hebrew versus Yiddish, his views differed. The language, he said, should not be called Yiddish (meaning "Jewish") but Judeo-German, since there were other "Jewish" languages. Even if Mieses's statistics were correct, that kind of designation could not be awarded on the basis of statistics alone. The rights of minorities had to be protected and the half-million Ladino speakers were not to be discriminated against because their language was less Jewish than Judeo-German. For them, Ladino was as Jewish as Judeo-German was for Ashkenazim.

In addition, Mieses's statistics were not impeccable, said Sokolow. Yiddish speakers in various parts of the world did not form one bloc. America could not be dismissed so lightly. It had become the center of the Diaspora and there Yiddish was becoming anglicized. The same was true of England. The "synthesizing" power that Mieses attributed to America was equally true of Europe generally and of Hungary, where Yiddish was spoken only by the extremely orthodox of the small towns, in particular. Mieses had also dismissed the "new Jargon" of the socialist publications too lightly. It was significant and there were profound reasons for it.

All of this, said Sokolow, pointed to the fact that Yiddish was disintegrating. The Hebrew components of Yiddish had resulted from an all-embracing religious life that was now becoming secularized. Yiddish literature was, in fact, no more widespread than Hebrew literature. Acquiring Hebrew was not so difficult as Mieses suggested, and there was much that was more easily conveyed in Hebrew than in Yiddish.

For Sokolow, there was no such thing as Yiddish—the Jewish language, but "an ever-changing Judeo-German which continues to exist by force of habit, is geographically determined and open to every influence in the world" (p. 320). Hebrew, while not much understood at present, was *sui generis*; it united the "best of the nation," contained the creativity of various periods, and encompassed "the continuity of past, present and future."

Which has a better chance of surviving and to which shall we dedicate our efforts? To this question, we respond unequivocally : to Hebrew. What Mieses wants for Yiddish, we want for Hebrew. The revival of Hebrew is no more impossible than the revival of other languages to which Mieses refers in his article. Mieses finds the achievements in Palestine minimal. So do we! But this is not because achieving more is impossible but because more effort is required. Can the strengthening of Yiddish, its defense and the improvement of its literature be achieved without effort? (p. 321)

Sokolow took courage from the revival of Flemish in Belgium. Could Jews do less for their historic language? If Yiddish had the advantage of being widespread, it also had the disadvantage of being spread extensively rather than intensively. It was spoken in a variety of accents, carelessly and without respect.

When assimilation leads Jews or gentiles to attack Yiddish we will defend it. But to propagandize on its behalf is absurd. The majority of Yiddish speakers are extremely orthodox and their attitude toward the language is well known. With them, it is merely a matter of habit; a secular language with some translations "for women." The Bundists show an extreme fondness for it but cannot be relied upon. Their fondness is not intrinsic but opportunistic; they view the language as a means of more easily spreading their ideas. It stems either from the idea that languages should have equal rights or from the idea that as long as Jews have not learned another language or not learned it well enough to use, Yiddish may be employed. Some of them use Yiddish more because of hatred for Hebrew than because of love for Yiddish. "The holy tongue," "tradition," "bourgeoisie," "Eretz-Israel," "Beth Hamidrash"—all of these have become antiquated and degenerate for them. This ferment, rooted in a crisis of narrowness, servitude, and frivolousness, is but one of a thousand Galut psychoses. They shout: Let us protect the things that are ours! What things are ours if not the Hebrew language, the Torah, Hebrew literature, the Land of Israel, the tradition, the Synagogue, the hope for our future? What is left to us if we insist that we have no more than the Torah of Rabbi Marx, or that temporarily we must use the Jargon and transpose all the scientific terms into Hebrew script? Afterwards, when mandatory studies are offered in the general schools, why will we need special schools? What special things will they offer that will make them necessary? Saying *der kind* (as do the Lithuanians) and not *dos kind*? Will people be willing to sacrifice for that?

Mieses claimed that "modern life" helped Yiddish and hindered Hebrew. But the modern Jew knew other languages and used them. According to Sokolow they were more practical than Yiddish. The modern Jew sent his children to general schools where they studied every language but Yiddish. To change that situation national enthusiasm and sacrifice were necessary. It was therefore not the revival of Hebrew but the establishment of Yiddish as a national language that was fantastic. Hebrew had deep roots on which to rely, which Yiddish lacked. "As much as we like Yiddish, see the need for it, and protest when it is maliciously attacked, we have but one national language—Hebrew!" (p. 322).

The battle was joined. The antagonists appeared to be evenly matched. But Mieses had not yet shown all his cards. He was saving his powers for the Czernowitz Conference and for the polemic with the principal foe of Yiddish in the Zionist camp, Ahad Haam, which followed it. Sokolow had responded forcefully to Mieses's arguments without vanquishing them. Yiddishists took heart, for never before had the case for Yiddish received such incisive and thorough formulation. They invited Mieses to address the Czernowitz Conference on "The Recognition of Yiddish."

Chaim Zhitlovsky.

7

CHAIM ZHITLOVSKY

CHAIM ZHITLOVSKY WAS THE OUTSTANDING THINKER OF THE
Jewish cultural renaissance in the Yiddish language in the
twentieth century. He was a leading theoretician of Jewish
socialism, nationalism, and radical secularism, and the principal
exponent of Yiddishism in Eastern Europe and the United
States. An influential philosopher, orator, educator, literary
critic, and journalist, he was active in a variety of political and
cultural organizations and publications that helped shape the
contours of modern Jewish life.[1]

Zhitlovsky was born in a small *shtetl* near Vitebsk in 1865

1. See I. Knox, "Zhitlovsky's Philosophy of Jewish Life,"*Contemporary
Jewish Record* (April 1945); Y. Mark, Introduction to Zhitlovsky's *Gekli-
bene Verk* (New York, 1945); R. Mahler, *Historiker un Vegvayzer* (Tel
Aviv, 1967); M. Epstein, *Profiles of Eleven* (Detroit, 1965); S. Goodman,
"Chaim Zhitlovsky—His Contemporary Relevance," *The Reconstructionist*
(June 25, 1965); B. Zuckerman, *Eseyen un Profiln* (Tel Aviv, 1967);
Y. Kahan, "Dr. Chaim Zhitlovsky," *Di Tsukunft* (December 1965); A. Almi,
Kheshbn un Sakhakl (Buenos Aires, 1959); Y. Rapoport, *Zoymen in Vint*
(Buenos Aires, 1961); S. Bickel, *Shrayber fun Mayn Dor* (New York, 1958).

and was raised in Vitebsk. His father, who had studied for the rabbinate in the famed *yeshiva* of Volozhin, combined within himself rabbinical erudition, an attachment to Hassidism, a knowledge of the literature of the Haskalah, and business acumen. As a successful merchant, he was able to provide the young Chaim with Hebrew and Russian tutors as well as training in the traditional subjects. In adolescence Zhitlovsky was influenced greatly by his friend S. Z. Rapoport (S. Ansky; 1863–1920), who subsequently became famous as the author of the Jewish Labor Bund hymn *Di Shvue* and the Yiddish play the *Dybbuk,* and as a founder and leader of the Russian Social Revolutionary party. At the age of fourteen Zhitlovsky entered the third class of the gymnasium where from his fellow-students he learned for the first time of Marx and Lassalle and of the *Narodnaya Volya* ("People's Will") movement, which sought to propagate socialist ideals among the Russian peasants.

Convinced of the truth of the populist doctrines of the Russian writers Peter Lavrov and Nicholas Mikhailovsky, Zhitlovsky left the gymnasium, assumed the Russian name Yefim, and spent a year and one-half in the city of Tula, where he hoped to propagate socialism among the peasants. He devoted most of his time, however, to the reading of revolutionary literature. During an extended visit to an uncle in his home *shtetl,* he also read Hebrew periodicals and became impressed with the writings of Moshe Leyb Lilienblum and other early Zionist thinkers.

A number of personal experiences during this period influenced Zhitlovsky's decision to work among Jews and interest himself in their plight. When he tried to explain socialist ideas to his grandfather, the latter told him about the Essenes who had lived in the communes in Palestine during the Second Temple period and reminded him of the social protests of the prophets and the prayers for "one world" in the High Holy Day Prayer Book. On reading Goethe's *Faust,* he saw in its heroine, Gretchen, a symbol of the fate of the Jewish people, which in refusing to choose freedom for itself was abandoned by its intellectuals. One day, upon hearing a young woman beside a grave bewail her deceased husband with the words, "To whom have you abandoned me?" he made an oath never to desert the Jewish people. He pledged himself "always to remain true to my two-fold duty as a Jewish intellectual, to serve the ideals of general progress in the light of my responsibility for their destiny among my own people."[2]

Another important experience in the life of the young Zhitlovsky was his reading of a story by the celebrated anti-Czarist writer Mikhail Saltykov, who wrote under the pen name of Schedrin. In 1884 Saltykov published three tales in the style of Aesop's fables. One of these, "The Old Wolf," Zhitlovsky interpreted as an allegory of the life of the Jewish people. Zhitlovsky resolved, after reading the tale, which ends with the death of the wolf, that he would not permit his people to die through either natural causes or assimilation. The Jewish people was not like a wolf and death was not the solution to its problems. "Jewish diaspora-nationalism was born within me at that time," writes Zhitlovsky in his memoirs. "Jewish national rebirth on the basis of socialist elements in Russia—was the first clear formulation of its goal."[3]

Although sympathetic to the proto-Zionist stirrings within Jewry, Zhitlovsky was unable to identify himself with them. He agreed with the view of many of the *Hovevey-Zion* that the social and economic basis of Jewish life was degenerate. He approved of the emphasis on agrarianism as a solution to Jewish problems. He was impressed with the Russian-Jewish students who formed the *Bilu* group and went to Palestine as agricultural pioneers in 1882. He dissented, however, from the negative attitude of the *Hovevey-Zion* toward international socialism. He disagreed with their Hebraism and with what he viewed as their reactionary alliance with the rabbinate and the religious forces.[4] Zhitlovsky was convinced of the truth of

2. *Geklibene Verk*, p. 345.
3. *Ibid.*, p. 341.
4. Cf. Mahler, p. 114.

socialism, while these "Lovers of Zion" despaired of it as a
panacea for the problems of Jewry. They had abandoned the
notion that socialist progress would spell freedom for their own
people. They did not share Zhitlovsky's populist inclination
toward Yiddish rather than Hebrew and, unlike him, were not
rabidly anti-clerical.

Zhitlovsky therefore decided to organize a Jewish branch of
the *Narodnaya Volya* movement that would publish its own
journal and be called *Teshuas Yisroel (Salvation of Israel)*. In
1886, the leadership of the larger movement, which consisted
primarily of assimilated Jewish students, refused to authorize
the establishment of such a branch. Zhitlovsky was shocked by
this manifestation of assimilationism. He plunged himself into
the study of Jewish history with the hope of achieving some
historical perspective on what had occurred.

The result was his first published work, *Thoughts on the
Historical Destiny of Jewry* (1887), a book of 125 pages in
Russian. The survival of the Jewish nation, wrote Zhitlovsky,
could not be explained on the basis of persecutions and excep-
tional laws as it usually was by assimilation theory. Jewish
survival was the product of a national will-to-live and struggle
for existence. The Jewish nation had a right to survive because
it was the bearer of the concept of social justice first expressed
by the Israelite prophets and the Essenes.

In 1892, under the name H. Khasin, Zhitlovsky published
his analysis of the condition of Russian Jewry, *A Jew to Jews.*
It was issued in London by the Fund for the Free Russian Press
to which many exiled intellectuals belonged. It contained original
ideas on the synthesis of socialism and Jewish nationalism in
Russia.[5]

The basic ideas of the brochure, consisting of an interesting
amalgam of Jewish nationalist and socialist ideas with Russian
non-Marxist populism and revolutionary romanticism, were as
follows :

5. Cf. Y. Maor, *Sheelat Hayehudim Batenuah Haliberalit Vehamahapk-
hanit Berusyah* (Jerusalem, 5724), p. 122.

1. The proclamation of the independence of the Jewish people. ("We are not 4% of anyone else but 100% of ourselves.")
2. Socialism and nationalism are not opposites.
3. The interests of the workers and peasants are in accord. A socialist party must defend both.
4. The proclamation of the existence of a Jewish working class in Russia, and therefore of a Jewish worker's problem, a Jewish worker's movement and a Jewish socialism.
5. The difference between West European and East European Jewry and the criticism of the former.
6. The connection between Russian revolution and Jewish liberation; the need to participate in the Russian revolutionary struggle as a Jewish nation and in the socialist movement as a Jewish working class.
7. The socialist criticism of Jewish economic life and its parasitic character. The need for a Jewish agrarian socialism.
8. The need to establish Jewish life on the basis of work and science.
9. The Jewish intelligentsia must belong to the Jewish people. . . .
10. We should fight for national equality not only for civic equality.[6]

In 1887 Zhitlovsky had settled in Zurich, Switzerland, where he took an active part in the organization of Russian socialist émigrés. With Charles Rapoport he developed an ideology that eventually served as the basis of the Social Revolutionary party in Russia. He also helped organize the overseas branch of the party in Zurich and wrote a number of essays and brochures on its behalf. He published articles on the history and philosophy of socialism in German. In 1892 he was awarded a Doctor of Philosophy degree by the University of Bern. His thesis dealt with medieval Jewish philosophy.

Although inconsistencies and even glaring contradictions may be discovered in Zhitlovsky's writings of various periods, there was one area in which he remained consistent and single-minded throughout his life : his attitude to Yiddish. Zhitlovsky's Yiddishism may be traced to his populism and his opposition to bourgeois Zionism, as well as to an early fondness for the

6. Chaim Zhitlovsky, *Gezamlte Shriftn* (New York, 1917), 6:8–9.

language. Toward the end of the eighties he was writing Yiddish poetry. In his views on the Yiddish language, literature, and culture, he was always a consistent and uncompromising fighter.[7]

In 1896 Zhitlovsky organized a group of Jewish socialists in Switzerland for the purpose of preparing socialist literature in Yiddish to be published by the Jewish Labor Bund of Russia and Poland. Zhitlovsky wrote an introduction to the first book of the series but the Bund, which could not accept Zhitlovsky's views, published the work without the introduction. Three years later it appeared as an essay, "Why Specifically Yiddish?" in the Yiddish socialist newspaper *Forverts* in New York.

Zhitlovsky began his article by noting with approval the changes that had taken place since the publication of *A Jew to Jews* five years earlier. Young Jewish socialists were now vigorously engaged in bringing the ideas of socialism to the Jewish people in the Yiddish language. Socialist literature in Yiddish was appearing in London, America, Galicia, and Russia. In addition to this "illegal" literature, men like Peretz and Sholom Aleichem were creating a "legal" Yiddish literature, which sought to awaken the man in the harried Jew and arouse his desire for education and knowledge.

There was nothing unusual in creating a new literature in a language formerly considered fit only for insignificant purposes. The Flemish in Belgium had done it. So had the Ruthenians in Galicia, the Latvians in Russia, and others. But none of these had behind them a literature comparable to that of the Jewish people. Yiddish literature was only the latest link in a literary tradition going back to the prophets. Was Yiddish literature, as some predicted, merely the last gasp of a dying people? Other nations had but one language and one literature and their writers could be reasonably assured that their works would be read and have an impact on the life of their people. On the other hand, Jewish literature in three languages, Russian,

7. N. Mayzel. *Dr. Chaim Zhitlovsky: Tsu Zayn Hundertstn Geboyrnyor* (New York, 1965), p. 29.

Hebrew and Yiddish, had been singularly ineffective in enlightening the Jewish masses and improving their thoughts and feelings. Jews in the larger cities may have accepted the outer trappings of modernity and education, but until recently they had remained deaf to the higher aspirations of the *maskilim*.

Zhitlovsky expressed the hope that with the appearance of socialist literature in Yiddish a new page in the history of the Jewish people would begin.

> The Socialists do not speak to the people in a language that it had long forgotten. They also do not go to their neighbors to borrow a language. They speak the mother-tongue and convey thoughts which every mother might well learn by heart and teach to her children every day—thoughts which teach us how the poor, oppressed and exploited section of our society may free itself from its unfortunate condition.[8]

Zhitlovsky noted that although a socialist literature for Jews already existed, it had been created in Hebrew for the Jewish middle class and for the *yeshiva* students who marveled at the fine language in which socialism was clad but could not appreciate the validity of its ideas. The new Jewish socialists, he said, addressed themselves to the Jewish worker, for whom socialism was not a fad but a matter of economic necessity. The old Jewish socialists knew how to write hymns of praise to socialism. As workers, the younger socialists came to the people not only with talk about the socialist future but with plans to improve life now. There was every reason to hope for the success of this new undertaking in the life of Jewry.

In 1897 Zhitlovsky attended the first Zionist Congress in Basle, Switzerland. Although he was registered as a journalist and not as a delegate, he participated in a conference of the Russian delegates that took place before the opening of the Congress. Zhitlovsky offered a resolution to the effect that the Zionist movement be constituted as a league that members of all parties and movements in Jewish life might join if they

8. *Geklibene Verk,* pp. 109–10.

agreed with the purpose of Zionism. He hoped to prevent the Zionists from forming a political party of their own because that would mean the denial of political and revolutionary work on behalf of Jewry in the Diaspora. The defeat of the resolution led him to conclude that "for West European Jewry Zionism may be a progressive phenomenon but utterly and completely bourgeois; for East European Jewry it is absolutely reactionary and harmful."[9]

On the day following the Congress, a meeting was held to acquaint the delegates with the program of the new *Tsayt-gayst* publishing house, which had been established in Berlin a year previously by a group of radical Jewish students headed by the Yiddish writer David Pinski. At that meeting Zhitlovsky delivered an address that held the quintessence of his future Yiddishist program.

Zhitlovsky equated the recognition of Yiddish with the affirmation of Jewish life. Whoever was opposed to Yiddish was, *ipso facto,* a proponent of assimilation. If Jews possessed a land of their own, it might serve to rescue them from assimilation. Without it, language became its substitute. "If we hold on to our language, it becomes a raft which can save us from drowning," he said. "We can swim further without fear of the waves about us." The language of Jewry was Yiddish, which the people loved and recognized. At the time of the Haskalah, Yiddish was opposed by the *maskilim,* and now the growing intelligentsia was estranged from it. That was the cardinal sin of the Jewish intellectuals. They had divorced themselves from Yiddish and in so doing estranged themselves from their people. The Jewish masses had no leaders and had consequently lost their senses. "Return to Yiddish," urged Zhitlovsky. "Reunite yourselves with the masses. Unify the separated limbs of our people. Return it to its senses!"[10]

These thoughts were even more forcefully expressed in

9. Cf. Chaim Zhitlovsky, *Mayne Ani Mamins* (New York, 1953), p. 336 and *Zhitlovsky Zamlbukh* (Warsaw, 1929), p. 222.
10. *Zhitlovsky Zamlbukh,* p. 222.

another essay, "Zionism or Socialism," which appeared in the sixth issue of *Der Yidisher Arbeter* (March 1899), a publication of the Bund. The significance of this essay lay in the fact that socialism and nationalism were not viewed as opposites but as complementary. Zhitlovsky's main point was the notion that Zionism, a movement of the Jewish borgeoisie, was completely utopian in its aims, distracting the Jewish worker from improving his own plight and from contributing to the growth of socialism, a movement of the Jewish proletariat, in the here and now. A reconciliation of the two movements was impossible and the Jewish worker had no choice but to espouse socialism and reject Zionism. (In footnotes penned in 1908, Zhitlovsky conceded that Zionism and socialism could indeed be merged as they had been in the Poaley Zion party and that he had been wrong in identifying Zionism only with the interests of the Jewish middle class. His attitude toward Zionism had reflected the views of Jewish socialists at the time. But he was still opposed to the anti-Diaspora tendencies of the Zionists.)

Zhitlovsky conceded that at first the socialists were set upon aiding the Jewish worker as an individual, as a worker, and not as a Jew. But as they began to understand socialism more profoundly, it became clear to them that socialism did not intend to abolish all peoples. Socialism wished every people to develop its own qualities and talents as long as all peoples lived in peace and assisted one another in the struggle for existence, so that no people would lord it over another. For socialism no peoples had special advantages; none were "chosen." All were equal and all possessed attributes and failings. The meaning of the word "internationalism" as Zhitlovsky understood it was that all peoples were equal brothers and as such had to live as brothers among themselves.

Zhitlovsky countered the Zionist accusation that the socialists were bereft of Jewish feelings. The contrary was true. The Jewish feelings of the Zionists were reactions to anti-Semitism. The Jewish feelings of the socialists, on the other hand, were "natural" and "healthy," like those of the ordinary Jewish worker. The worker's national sentiments were normal. He felt closer to other Jewish workers and to his impoverished folk generally than he did to non-Jews. At the same time he had a healthy social sense and therefore felt closer to workers of other peoples than to his own Jewish middle class. The Jewish socialists, like the workers, had no need to display their Jewishness because of its normalcy while the Zionists constantly spoke about theirs because it was unhealthy.

The Jewish socialists hoped for an end to capitalist exploitation and the end of class differences. In the future all men would be workers and the Jewish people, too, would be free of its "bloodsuckers." But as Jews, the Jewish socialists had additional hopes. They looked forward to the flowering of Yiddish literature, to the day when it would equal the most beautiful European literatures. They looked forward to the enrichment in works and expressions of the Yiddish language, which was as precious to them as Jews as other languages are to other peoples. Yiddish was still impoverished because the educated Jews did not write in it. That situation would be remedied in the future. As Jews, the Jewish socialists also looked forward to the establishment of an international organization of Jewish workers that would protect the interests of Jewry and help the nations among which Jews lived to attain socialism and freedom. In the free socialist community of the future, the Jewish people would conduct its life as it saw fit. It would establish its own educational system that would extend from the elementary school through the university.

> If three million Swiss can maintain ten universities, the seven to ten million Jews who speak Yiddish will most certainly be able to maintain twenty-five. Thus, the Jewish people will become one of the most educated of peoples.[11]

Zhitlovsky applied the views of the Austrian socialists Karl Renner and Otto Bauer to the situation of the Jewish people. In the past, he said, nationhood and statehood were viewed as

11. Chaim Zhitlovsky, *Gezamlte Verk* (New York, 1917), 5:50.

identical. In the present, however, nationhood was equated with culture and education. It was therefore possible for the Jewish people to retain its identity while remaining dispersed among the nations. The development of Jewish culture and education would make Jews proud of their people and evoke admiration for it from other peoples. If the world eventually became one nation, the Jewish people would cease to retain its individuality, but until then it would continue to exist as an equal among all the other nations. The Jewish socialist approach was both idealistic and a response to the reality of Jewish life, while Zionism endangered that reality with its negative attitude toward the Jewish worker and to Jewish life in the Diaspora.

The editors of *Der Yidisher Arbeter,* in which this essay appeared, added their own comments to Zhitlovsky's article. They were strongly in favor of efforts on behalf of equal political, economic, and national rights for Jews. (This was a departure from previous statements, which mentioned civic but not national rights.) But they expressed misgivings about whether the "Jargon" would be able to develop sufficiently to become a language of culture, and whether a specific Jewish literature and science, that is, a specific Jewish culture, could be developed in it. Whether Jewish schools and universities would be feasible and whether it was necessary to unite Jewish workers of various lands living under different circumstances were also moot or "difficult to answer at the present time."[12] A short time later, the Bund published this essay as a separate brochure without the concluding section dealing with Yiddish culture and Jewish particularistic needs.

In 1903, as a result of the Kishinev pogrom and the deteriorating situation of Russian Jewry, Zhitlovsky added the principles of Territorialism to Autonomism and *Golus* Nationalism in his Jewish program. He saw the need for the establishment of an autonomous agriculture-based settlement of Jews that would help alleviate the sore plight of his brethren in Russia.

In 1904, Zhitlovsky published an essay "The Jewish People

12. S. Lew, *Prokim Yidishe Geshikhte* (New York, 1941), p. 71.

and the Yiddish Language," which had a tremendous impact. In this essay, strongly reminiscent of the Austrian socialist thinkers and the Russian Slavophiles, Zhitlovsky drew a parallel between the fate of the Jewish people and that of Yiddish. The former was denied the status of nationhood because it lacked a land of its own while the latter was denied the status of a language because it lacked a grammar.

> As important as its own land may be for the life of a nation, it is no more than a condition, a qualification, an aid to life, but not a part of its being in the world. A nation does not consist of water, earth, hills, valleys, forests and fields. The forests and fields cannot be even the smallest part of the nation which consists rather of living people, with a unique body and soul, with different levels of attainment, with attributes and defects; in whom with the best microscope there cannot be found even one grain of sand and soil, even one atom of land.[13]

To say that Jews did not constitute a nation when they were recognizably distinct from all the other nations of the earth was absurd, said Zhitlovsky. It was even more foolish to claim that Yiddish was not a language. Yiddish always possessed a grammar because there is no such thing as people using a vocabulary without a grammar. Like all other languages, Yiddish has a syntax of its own, which may not be violated. Yiddish philology was still in its infancy and the rules of Yiddish grammar had not been adequately researched, but that Yiddish was a real language could not be doubted any more than that Jewry was a nation.

The Jewish nation and the Yiddish language were also alike in that both were terribly impoverished. The reasons for the poverty of Jewry had been explained by political economics, but the poverty of the Yiddish language remained a great riddle. It could not be attributed to a lack of ideas, because Jewry possessed an abundance of ideas.

At this point, Zhitlovsky attacked the notion that Hebrew, a language that he conceded was rich in means of expression,

13. *Geklibene Verk,* p. 114.

was the language of Jewry rather than Yiddish. Hebrew was only the written language of a small section of the Jewish intelligentsia, which cultivated Hebrew and neglected Yiddish because it did not wish to know the folk. This accounted, in part, for the poverty of Yiddish. The nation on the whole, however, did not share the view of the Hebrew intelligentsia.

> Just as the ancient Hebrews with weapons in their hands conquered the land of the Canaanites and Philistines, irrigated the *alien* land with their blood and sweat, invested Jewish labor in it and gave it the name "Eretz Yisrael," the Land of Israel, so did the Jews in the Germanic lands accept an *alien* tongue, one of the German languages, recast it in a new form, fill it with Jewish intelligence, wit and feeling, and give it the name "Yiddish." And just as the alien land of the Amorite, Girgashite, Hivite and Jebusite became the Jewish people's own land, its fatherland, so did the alien tongue of the Germanic peoples which the Jews appropriated become their own tongue, their mother tongue.[14]

Jewry never viewed Yiddish as an alien tongue. It distinguished between the precursors of Yiddish, "Taytsh" and "Ivri-Taytsh," which it viewed as gentile and alien, and Yiddish, which it considered Jewish. Most alien of all to the masses was Hebrew, which depended for its status upon the survival of the world of religious superstition! The true Jewish language was not Hebrew but Yiddish.

> He who ridicules Yiddish ridicules the Jewish people. He who does not know a word of Yiddish is in fact half a gentile.[15]

Zhitlovsky attributed the poverty of Yiddish to the fact that Jews did not view language as an end in itself, but solely as a means of communication. Lacking an interest in aesthetics, they were not concerned with the condition of their language.

The Jewish nation and the Yiddish language were also alike in that neither was tolerated by the Jewish intelligentsia. But

14. *Ibid.*, p. 123.
15. *Ibid.*, p. 124.

even members of the intelligentsia who loved the Jewish nation
had no regard for Yiddish.

> If they truly love the Jewish nation . . . how can they despise
> the Yiddish language in which the Jew's soul lives and in which
> all the attributes and defects of the Jewish nation are reflected?
> Thousands and millions of Jews believe that there is no more
> beautiful language in all the world than Yiddish. And I am
> confident that thousands and millions of Jews will agree with
> me when I say : More beautiful to me than all images is my
> mother's face; more precious to me than all languages is my
> mother-tongue ! [16]

In 1904 Zhitlovsky visited the United States with Catherine
Breshko-Breshkovskaya, the "grandmother of the Russian revolution," in order to gain American support for the Russian Social
Revolutionary party. This party rallied the surviving elements
of the Russian populist movement and sought to preserve the
maximalist traditions of the revolutionary intelligentsia.[17] Breshkovskaya had been one of the active members of the *Narodnaya
Volya* movement in the 1870s. In Brno in 1893, she had formed
the Union of Social Revolutionaries Abroad with the Jewish
revolutionary Gregory Gershuni. Zhitlovsky had been one of the
seven founders of this organization, out of which the Social
Revolutionary party developed in 1901. The assassination of
the Russian prime minister, Wenzel Von Plehve, by a member
of the party in 1904 brought it tremendous prestige among
socialists outside Russia. The delegation of Breshkovskaya and
Zhitlovsky was sent to the United States to capitalize on those
sentiments. Since the party leadership considered New York
"Jewish territory," it was deemed advisable to have a Jew who
was a good lecturer accompany Breshkovskaya. Zhitlovsky was
chosen because he was especially close to two other leaders of
the party, Victor Chernow and S. Ansky.[18] The party agreed

16. *Ibid.,* p. 128.
17. Cf. H. Kohn, *The Mind of Modern Russia* (New York, 1955), p. 254.
18. Cf. D. Shub, *Fun di Amolike Yorn* (New York, 1970), 1 : 80–81
and V. Chernov, *Yidishe Tuer in der Partey Sotsyalistn Revolutsyonern*
(New York, 1948), pp. 52–90, 280–312.

to permit Zhitlovsky to advocate his own Jewish nationalist program among American Jews during his stay. Thus, in addition to his lectures on socialism he also spoke on Jewish questions.

Zhitlovsky discovered that the East European Jewish immigrants in the United States were under the influence of an intelligentsia dominated by assimilationist and cosmopolitan ideas. They viewed Yiddish literature and culture as a passing phenomenon and were unable to combine radicalism and nationalism in their thinking. Zhitlovsky set out to combat these notions both in print and from the lecture platform. A highlight of his trip was a public debate on "Nationalism and Internationalism" with the successful Yiddish dramatist Jacob Gordin, an avowed cosmopolitan and internationalist. Gordin was also a popular essayist and journalist who wrote frequently on philosophical as well as literary themes. He had no knowledge of the literature on the nationalist question that had been published in Austria-Hungary and Russia in recent years and was therefore at a disadvantage in debating this question with Zhitlovsky.[19]

Gordin accused Zhitlovsky of not being a true Jew when he spoke of Jewish nationalism. His Jewishness was manifest only when he addressed himself to the larger international questions and to universal philosophical issues. There were only two nations in the world, according to Gordin, the nation of productive mankind and the nation of man's inhuman oppressors and exploiters.

The war which is being waged between these two nations will lead sooner or later to the establishment of one nation, one people, one kingdom, one culture, one civilization, one great union which will be called by the great and sacred name : mankind.[20]

Gordin also dissented from Zhitlovsky's views on Yiddish.

19. Shub, p. 88.
20. Quoted in Y. Marmor, *Yankev Gordin* (New York, 1963), pp. 162f.

He did not feel that a specific Jewish national culture had been created or would be created in the language. Nor did he agree that the Jewish people would be united on the basis of the language. For him Yiddish was only a means by which the Jewish masses could be familiarized with world culture. Yiddish was a temporary phenomenon and Hebraists and advocates of the languages of the lands in which Jews lived could not be ruled out of the Jewish people as Zhitlovsky contended. Gordin felt that in his own field of the drama the attempt to write Jewish national plays resulted in caricatures. Yiddish dramatists would write best if they imitated the forms of world drama. Gordin's own most successful plays were adaptations of classics from world literature. If Jews possessed any unique cultural forms, Gordin felt that they were to be found in the Bible and the Talmud and not in Yiddish literature.[21]

Zhitlovsky set about contesting these views with all the force and vigor at his command. From the lecture platform and from the pages of every American Yiddish newspaper and magazine that would publish his writings, he called for a synthesis of international socialism and national culture, of political radicalism and Yiddish culturism. He favored local autonomy for Jews wherever they lived, as well as the establishment of national territories where Jews would constitute the majority population and be free to devote themselves to agricultural pursuits and the development of their cultural heritage. Zhitlovsky's influence was tremendous. He altered the thinking of a section of the immigrant intelligentsia and working class, which was assimilationist, cosmopolitan, far from Jewish thought and culture, and opposed to Zionism.[22]

Among Zhitlovsky's most significant achievements were the lectures he delivered in the United States between 1904 and 1906 on "Jewishness and Humanity" and "The Future of the Peoples in America." The former, one of his classic essays, contains his most important statements on the nature of modern Jewish culture.

21. *Ibid.*, p. 163. See also M. Epstein, pp. 135–58.
22. Cf. Meyer Brown, *Mit Yidishe Oygn* (New York, 1958), p. 252.

Zhitlovsky analyzed the Haskalah slogan "Be a man on the street and a Jew at home," which posits a conflict between humanity and Jewish identity. The Jewish radicals had carried that slogan to its logical conclusion and dissociated themselves from Jewish life. Zhitlovsky admitted that in his youth he had been one of their number, but was now a "repentant sinner." The more human one was, the radicals had felt, the less Jewish. While this may sometimes be true, said Zhitlovsky, frequently Jewishness and humanity were not in conflict. There were even occasions where the more Jewish one was, the more human.

Zhitlovsky defined the concepts "humanity" and "Jewishness." Humanity consisted of the love of reason, science, one's fellow men, justice, beauty, and human dignity. "The more one is suffused with these characteristics and with love for them, the more human one is." "Jewishness" in the modern world was defined by birth, religion, or nationality. Zhitlovsky associated himself with the third definition and explained the necessity of national cultures despite the chauvinism they frequently engendered among extremists. Cosmopolitans were correct in attacking the extremes of national egoism and the anti-progressive elements of national cultures. But there were cultural phenomena that could not be measured in terms of "progress" and "humanity." There were national differentia that had to be viewed as different ways of expressing a common humanity.[23]

In the case of language, said Zhitlovsky, the formula "the more human, the less Jewish" was absurd. A language could not be objectively evaluated as being more human than another, because every nation preferred its own. The more human one was, the more one developed a love for one's own native tongue.

> I have dealt at much length with language and the love of language because it is one of the most important rocks against which the waves of cosmopolitanism break. If the question of language is significant to someone, if his love of language grows with the development of his humanity, and if human reason cannot decide which language is the most human, there is not the slightest chance of realizing the cosmopolitan ideal of the

23. *Geklibene Verk*, pp. 31f.

disappearance of national cultures into one culture and one language. (pp. 54f.)

Cosmopolitanism has missed the fact that there are many branches of culture which each people expresses in a different national way but which are nevertheless all equally human, all of equal value and can all possess the same degree of truth, justice, beauty and human dignity. For that reason there is no sense in demanding of any people that it cease to be a people and become human. In all mankind there is no form in which an aspect of culture expresses itself that has more of a right to a people's love than its own national form. (p. 56)

Abandoning one's own nationality was not cosmopolitanism but surrender to the chauvinism of a foreign nationality. Humanity was manifest in a person's interest in the "higher branches" of culture. The more interested in culture one became, the more natural it was to feel bound to the national forms of one's own people. The more human a Jew became, the more Jewish he became. His love for his own culture was an expression of his humanity.

A person's love for his people also encompassed the historical past, which provided him with inspiring heroes, tales, and events. A member of another nationality might appreciate the higher achievements of a foreign culture, but only to the native were the minor figures and events in its history of importance. Zhitlovsky had been among those who saw nothing of value in the Jewish past until he began his study of Jewish history in 1885. He then became aware of much in that past from which modern Jews might draw pride and self-respect. He emphasized the significance of seeing the past in historical perspective, of not "berating Moses for having failed to read Darwin."

In a masterful survey of the Jewish cultural heritage, Zhitlovsky demonstrated the historical and contemporary significance of the Bible, the Talmud, Gaonic literature, medieval Jewish philosophy, Hebrew poetry, mysticism, Hassidism, Jewish historical research in the nineteenth century, Haskalah literature, and modern Hebrew and Yiddish writing. Lack of familiarity with all of this was not proof of a Jew's humanity, said Zhitlovsky, but of his ignorance.

The concept of humanity also implied the freedom of a people to develop itself in all those areas of culture where universal human reason could not dictate a common rate of progress for mankind. It was therefore necessary for each people to determine its own fate and be autonomous in the cultural sphere and, at times, in the political sphere as well. This was not segregation from the rest of mankind but "the realization of universal human progress which has no executors other than the individual peoples" (p. 83).

Cultural domination of one people by another was an affront to that sense of justice that was essential to humanity. Every people had the duty to fight for its own freedom, independence, and cultural progress. This was doubly true of the Jewish people, which was undergoing a cultural catastrophe because of the estrangement of its intellectuals. Jewry was also experiencing a moral degeneration, due to its illegal economic and juridical situation in Eastern Europe and its cultural destruction everywhere. The Jewish people was without respect in the eyes of other nations, who refused to accord it the status of a nation. For the Jewish people to become more human, it would have to become more Jewish, assert itself, and fight for its own dignity.

Addressing himself to the religious Jew, Zhitlovsky argued that in the religious sphere it was equally true that the more human the Jew was, the more Jewish he would be. The Jewish religion provided amply for the needs of the religious personality.

To the Jew by birth, Zhitlovsky pointed out that national characteristics were inescapable.

The higher the cultural level of a people, the stronger the creative powers of its members. The more their soul has absorbed the rich culture of generations, the clearer the national creative form is crystallized in them. So that the more human a Jew is, the stronger his human creative powers, the more salient must be his national powers and the more Jewish he must be. (p. 97)

In 1908, Zhitlovsky settled in the United States, where he became one of the founders of *Dos Naye Lebn (The New Life)*, a monthly magazine devoted to "science, literature and socialism." Zhitlovsky edited the magazine from 1908 to 1913 and contributed many important philosophical, sociological, and literary articles that helped alter the approach of the radical Jewish intellectuals to general as well as Jewish questions. The articles influenced the Jewish labor movement in the United States significantly and helped provide a theoretical basis for Yiddishism throughout the world.

When Nathan Birnbaum visited the United States in 1907, Zhitlovsky was delighted to find a person whom he considered to be a distinguished German Jew who shared his own view of the centrality of Yiddish in modern Jewish life. He was taken with Birnbaum's idea of convoking an international conference and establishing an organization on behalf of the language.[24] Zhitlovsky played a crucial role at the deliberations in Pinski's home and it was he who drafted the invitation to the Conference.

At a public meeting held in New York on March 11, 1908, to win support for the idea of the Conference, Zhitlovsky said that

> if the cultural level of our people is not high it is due to the lack of a language. Philosophy is the mind, poetry—the heart, and language may be likened to the blood. If the body lacks blood it becomes anemic. . . . It is not popular works that we need to publish in Yiddish but the creation in the language of an entire literature so that our intellectuals may obtain their entire education from their own source. . . . Let even assimilationist theories and profound thoughts, not propaganda brochures, be written in Yiddish.[25]

24. D. Pinski, *Oysgeklibene Shriftn* (Buenos Aires, 1961), p. 282.
25. *Di Ershte Yidishe Shprakh-Konferents* (Vilna, 1931), p. 2.

Zhitlovsky was not only one of the signers of the invitation. He was the only member of the group of American initiators to attend it. Pinski, Evalenko, Gordin, and Harkavy, the Yiddish philologist who also addressed the public meeting, were all unable to attend for personal reasons or because of other commitments. Zhitlovsky's arrival was looked forward to with great anticipation in Czernowitz because of his great influence among both American and Russian Jewry.[26]

26. *Ibid.,* p. 13.

Delegates to the Czernowitz Conference together with members of the student society "Yidishe Kultur" (*second row:* first from left—Nathan Birnbaum; first from right—Y. L. Peretz; *third row:* first from left—Sholem Asch; fourth, fifth, and eighth from left—Abraham Reisen, H. D. Nomberg, Chaim Zhitlovsky).

8

THE CZERNOWITZ
CONFERENCE

which was prepared by Zhitlovsky and distributed by Evalenko,
read as follows:

Honored Sir!

In the past several decades the Yiddish language has made
great progress. Its literature has achieved a level of which no
one had imagined it capable. Yiddish newspapers are distributed
in hundreds of thousands of copies daily and weekly. Yiddish
poets write songs which are sung by the people, stories which
are read by the people, plays which the people eagerly flock
to see. Every day the language itself becomes more refined and
richer.

But it continues to lack one thing which older tongues
possess. The latter are not permitted to roam about freely and
wildly in the linguistic world to attract all sorts of diseases,
defects and perhaps even death. They are guarded as a precious
child is guarded. No one, however, pays heed to the Yiddish
language. Thousands of Yiddish words are replaced by German,
Russian and English words which are completely unnecessary.
The live rules of the language which are born and develop with

183

it in the mouths of the people go unrecorded and it appears not to possess any such rules. Each person writes it in another way with his own spelling because no standard authoritative Yiddish orthography has thus far been established.

True, the disgrace attached to Yiddish in the past has diminished. People are less and less ashamed of the contemporary language of our people. It is gradually coming to be reckoned with and respected. It is coming to be understood that in Yiddish the Jewish spirit is reflected and its value for the survival of our nation is beginning to be comprehended. But it is still an object of ridicule and contempt. People are still ashamed of it. And is this not because of the faults noted above?

If this be true, a stop must be put to these things. A fence needs be established, some sort of protection for our precious mother-tongue so that it not wander about aimlessly as until now, so that it not become chaotic, tattered and divided. All who are involved with the language, writers, poets, linguists, and those who simply love it—must confer and find the appropriate means and methods of establishing an authority to which all will have to and want to defer.

Honored Sir! If you share the views herein expressed, you are invited to attend the Conference which we are calling on behalf of the Yiddish language.

The Conference will be held on ....
in Czernowitz (Bukovina, Austria) and will deal with the following items :

(1) Yiddish orthography, (2) Yiddish grammar, (3) foreign and new words, (4) a Yiddish dictionary, (5) Jewish youth and the Yiddish language, (6) the Yiddish press and the Yiddish language, (7) the Yiddish stage and Yiddish actors, (8) the economic situation of the Yiddish writer, (9) the economic situation of Yiddish actors, (10) the recognition of the Yiddish language.

If you wish to attend the Conference, please send your name and address to the main office of the Conference (...................)
immediately, so that we may send you the additional announcements which we will distribute. If you have any practical suggestions for the Conference and especially for the Yiddish language, we ask you to please write to us as soon as possible and thank you in advance.

Nisan 5668—April, 1908.[1]

1. *Di Ershte Yidishe Shprakh-Konferents* (Vilna, 1931), pp. 2, 3.

Attached to the invitation was a letter signed by Birnbaum, Gordin, Evalenko, Pinski, and Zhitlovsky, urging the addressees to permit their names to be signed to the invitation. When the invitation appeared in the press it included the name of Mendele Mokher Seforim, which naturally drew the attention of many readers. The date of the Conference was eventually set for August 30 and it was to last five days. The press releases announced that all individuals in agreement with the purposes of the Conference could attend as delegates, whereas others would be welcomed as guests. The delegates did not officially represent any parties or movements in Jewish life, although together they did constitute a gathering representative of the major groups interested in Yiddish at the time.

Czernowitz, capital of Bukovina, one of the constituent countries of Austria, was chosen as the site of the Conference because of Birnbaum's great influence there and because of its proximity to two countries where Yiddish flourished, Russia and Rumania. It would have been impossible to hold the Conference in Russia at the time because of governmental restrictions. Czernowitz was also an ideal location for the Conference because it symbolized the multinational character of the Austrian empire. The city was populated by Germans, Ruthenians (Ukranians), Rumanians, Jews, and other groups, all engaged in the struggle for national minority rights, which included the recognition of their respective languages. Jews and Rumanians got along well together in Bukovina, which for a time was called the "Eldorado of the Jews." The Jews of Bukovina actually had *de facto* recognition as a nationality group. Czernowitz had had a Jewish mayor several times, and its representative in the Reichsrat at the time of the Conference was a Jew who consciously followed a Jewish policy, Benno Straucher.[2]

The technical aspects of the Conference were handled by an arrangements committee headed by Birnbaum, who moved to

2. Cf. I. Elbogen, *A Century of Jewish Life* (Philadelphia, 1934), p. 368 and *Di Geshikhte fun Bund* (New York, 1966) 3 : 421.

Czernowitz at this time. It included the twelve members of the student society "Yidishe Kultur," which Birnbaum had founded in Vienna, all of whom attended the Conference, the local Jewish student organizations "Hasmonai" and "Emunah," and the local "Poaley Zion" organization. On the whole, the Conference was very poorly arranged and no adequate records were kept. The proceedings were reconstructed some twenty years later on the basis of newspaper reports and memoirs.

Although about seventy persons were registered at the Conference, only forty were voting delegates. The others were the members of "Yidishe Kultur," local dignitaries, and representatives of the Yiddish and general press. There were fourteen Russian delegates, mainly from Poland, fourteen or fifteen delegates from Galicia, six or seven from Czernowitz (Bukovina), and one each from the United States, Rumania, and Switzerland. Sholom Aleichem, who was ill at the time, sent a telegram, as did Mendele, who had planned to attend but was unable to do so. Seven or eight of the delegates were members of the Poaley Zion party, three or four members of the Bund, and two or three were general Zionists. The list of delegates included Samuel Eisenstadt (Bern), Sholem Asch (Koszmer), Gershom Bader (Lemberg), Nathan Birnbaum (Czernowitz), Moyshe-Leyb Halpern (Zlochev), Abraham Heisler (Kosov, Galicia), Michael Vaykhert (Galicia), Vaynreb (Buczaz, Galicia), Chaim Zhitlovsky (New York), Leybl Toybish (Czernowitz), Lazar ("Kasriel") Khazanovitsh (Lemberg), Matisyohu Mieses (Przemysl), H. D. Nomberg (Warsaw), N. Sotek (Braila, Rumania), Noah Prilutzky (Warsaw), Y. L. Peretz (Warsaw), Esther Frumkin (Vilna), Lazar Kahn (Lodz), Joseph Kisman (Czernowitz), Anselm (Moshe) Klaynman (Lemberg), Yonah Krepl (Cracow), and Abraham Reisen (Cracow).[3]

Birnbaum's energy, political tact, reputation, and visibility in the Jewish world were indispensable in calling the Conference together and getting Yiddish writers and other important Jewish

3. Cf. *Di Ershte* . . . , p. 61.

public figures to participate. In a newspaper interview held nine days before the Conference, Birnbaum stated :

> Our objective is purely cultural. We wish to raise our vernacular to the level of a cultural language. As with every cultural activity, this must be achieved by means of painstaking work among the masses. Our decisions will, of course, not obligate anyone. . . . From the point of view of cultural activity, it seems to me that no one can be opposed to our work. Some Zionists are hostile to our program because for them the question of language is tied to their political program and world-view and we understand them very well. But they are the only opponents among the conscious portion of Jewry.[4]

Birnbaum delivered the opening address at the first session of the Conference on Sunday morning, August 30, 1908. He opened his remarks by pointing out that people who choose new paths are frequently ridiculed. They should nevertheless hold to their ideals until they gain wider acceptance. The movement for Yiddish was an example of this. Decades before, a few people had recognized the inconsistency of regarding the tongues that various peoples created out of other languages as independent creations while ridiculing and labeling as "jargon" the language that Jews formed from German, Hebrew, and Slavic elements. When the Jewish intelligentsia became nationalistic, it viewed Yiddish only as something to be tolerated. It did not grasp the significance of the language of the folk and considered using Yiddish beneath its dignity.

The new period of Jewish history, however, required Yiddish for the purpose of educating the masses, and the Jewish people needed it in order to bestir itself out of its long slumber. A new intelligentsia had arisen that saw Yiddish as the unique product of Jewish experience and sought to remove from it the cloak of shame placed upon it in the past. Indeed, this cloak hampered the Jew's attainment of true self-respect. "If we remove the ban of excommunication from our language, a new

4. *Ibid.,* p. 13. Cf. p. xii.

Jewish loveliness will emerge from us to illumine our lives" (p. 72).

Along with this newer national awareness came the development of Yiddish literature, the contribution that its writers had made to the growth and standardization of Yiddish, and the demand that it be recognized as a separate language. The ridicule of the past, concluded Birnbaum, had been unable to destroy Yiddish and the coming together at the Conference of those who loved it or were at least interested in it should make the participants in the Conference fearless in their efforts on behalf of the language (pp. 71–74).

Birnbaum was applauded frequently in the course of his remarks, but the impression he made on the press was unfavorable. The correspondents of newspapers opposed to the Conference ridiculed his German pronunciation, his use of German in the debates, and the fact that he read his address. "Everyone understood," he was later to write, "that the power and the rights of Yiddish do not depend on the fact that a Jew who was born and educated in Western Europe learned the language late in life and could not yet speak it at the time of the Conference" (p. x).

Birnbaum was elected president of the Conference and Zhitlovsky vice-president. Birnbaum's participation in the deliberations was inhibited by his limited knowledge of Yiddish and the barring of other languages from the Conference sessions. Had he mastered the language before the Conference, he would probably have been able to make use of his acclaimed oratorical skills and play a dominant role in the Conference. According to Zhitlovsky, however, Birnbaum's interest in the Conference simply waned after it was convened. He was too deeply engrossed in his future plans, in which he saw the Conference as only a first step. Once chosen, he left the Conference to its own resources. In effect, it was Zhitlovsky rather than Birnbaum who chaired the Conference (p. xii).

The newspapers attacked Birnbaum and labeled him a radical for the position he took during the debate on the status of

Yiddish, which eventually became the major issue at the Conference.

> I cannot recall another instance in which so many lies were written and published as there were concerning the Czernowitz conference and my role in it. . . .[5] Throughout the conference, I was the one who least insisted on strong words and who most opposed radicalism and demanded practical accomplishments.[6]

Birnbaum drafted a resolution to the effect that the Conference was of the opinion "that the recognition of the Yiddish language in cultural, national and social respects is absolutely necessary."[7]

Birnbaum defended his resolution at an all-night closed session of the Conference in which he was permitted to speak German and at which he apparently had a tremendous effect upon the other delegates.[8] But his resolution was nevertheless defeated and in its place another, to the effect that Yiddish is "a national language of the Jewish people," was adopted over the formulation "*the* national language" suggested by the Bundist delegate, Esther Frumkin. The newspapers reported that the extremist position had been adopted and that Birnbaum was its chief advocate. Actually, Birnbaum opposed Esther Frumkin's position throughout the Conference.[9] He was an advocate of moderation, steering the Conference between the Bundist "left" and Zionist "right."

When dissension over the resolution on the status of Yiddish threatened to wreck the Conference, Birnbaum did all in his power to encourage the delegates to go on with their work. He emphasized that although they were not official representatives empowered to act on behalf of the groups to which they belonged, the entire gamut of Jewish life had indeed found expression in their deliberations. It was incumbent upon the

5. N. Birnbaum. *Der Yikhus fun Yidish* (Berlin, 1913), p. 21.
6. *Di Ershte Yidishe* . . . , p. x.
7. S. A. Birnbaum, "Nathan Birnbaum," *Men of the Spirit*, ed. L. Jung (New York, 1964), p. 530f.
8. L. Kahn, "Di Tshernovitser Konferents: August, 1908" (manuscript), Yivo Archives, p. 18.
9. *Di Ershte Yidishe* . . . , p. x.

delegates to fulfill the desires of the Jewish people and create
a unified body to advance Jewish literary and cultural interests.
He urged them not to disperse without laying the cornerstone
of an organization that would unite all Jews interested in the
furtherance of Yiddish. He warned them not to do anything
that might estrange either Zionists or Bundists. Disagreements,
he felt, were theoretical and the delegates were actually united
on objectives.[10]

At the final session, Birnbaum was unanimously elected
president of the organization established to implement the
resolutions of the Conference. In his closing remarks he reiterated
his view that the Conference had represented all viewpoints and
trends in Jewish life. He felt that the airing of attitudes toward
Hebrew had been of special importance. Never before had the
matter been so openly discussed. It would now be possible for
the delegates to orient themselves on this important question.[11]

In assessing its accomplishments, Birnbaum wrote :

> The Czernowitz Conference was called for practical cultural
> purposes, and if afterwards it dealt with the theoretical language
> question, this was, first of all, because enemies of Yiddish
> sneaked into it and, secondly, because the mood of the friends
> of Yiddish was a more radical one at the time.[12]

On the whole, his evaluation of the Conference was positive.
"The Conference stirred the little Jewish world . . . it
strengthened the energies of all those for whom Yiddish was
and is precious." [13]

The relationship of Yiddish to Hebrew had not been included
in the original invitation as an item to be discussed at the
Conference. At the planning session held immediately prior to
the Conference, when the issue was raised by the Yiddish writer,

10. *Ibid.*, p. 111.
11. *Ibid.*, p. 122.
12. *Der Yikhus fun Yidish,* p. 21.
13. *Di Ershte Yidishe* . . . , pp. ix, x.

H. D. Nomberg, Peretz changed his mind and opposed its inclusion on the agenda. This may have been due to the controversy between Hebraists and Yiddishists, which the announcement of the Conference had already stirred in the press. Peretz probably also wanted to avoid a clash between Bundists and Zionists at the Conference.

Nomberg felt that the Conference would not be doing its duty unless it clearly expressed a sympathetic attitude toward Hebrew.

> The people want from us a clear perspective on all our modern national and cultural values and we must not avoid the question of our attitude towards the Hebrew language which is tied to Jewish history and all of Jewish culture. With regard to this matter we must adopt a clear resolution which, according to my deepest conviction, will state : We express our true sympathy with the Hebrew language.[14]

Peretz believed that the Conference could not be accused of shirking any obligation if it failed to adopt a resolution on this issue.

> Not adopting a resolution does not mean silencing the question and avoiding an answer. That is not our intent. We have gathered together here for practical work on behalf of the Yiddish language and only positive activity interests us. The question concerning Hebrew is a theoretical one and the discussion will not be fruitful. Everyone will hold to his own opinion. No one will accuse us of hating Hebrew for this. That is incorrect. My own attitude to Hebrew is well known to all. Were a conference now called to deal with questions of Hebrew literature, I would gladly participate.[15]

In the ensuing discussion, S. Eisenstadt pointed out that Peretz was the only Hebrew-Yiddish writer at the Conference. The others, he said, had declined to participate because they suspected the Conference of anti-Hebraism. Abraham Reisen

14. *Ibid.*, pp. 64f.
15. *Ibid.*, p. 65.

even accused Peretz of divorcing himself from the mainstream of the Conference in refusing to discuss the relationship of Yiddish to Hebrew. At this point Peretz felt the need to clarify his stand. He expressed his concept of Hebrew as the Jewish national language and Yiddish as the "folk language." His definition of "national language" was strikingly similar to that of Ahad Haam, as we shall see in the following chapter.

By national language I mean the language which was born with the given nation and can disappear only if it degenerates. That is Hebrew. By folk language I mean the language which in a certain period is the spoken language of a certain portion of the people; the language which was not born together with Jewry and whose destiny is not as organically bound to the destiny of the people. Our meeting has the purpose of dealing with several important questions related to the Yiddish language. There will be no talk of Hebrew at this time. Of course, each of us has the right (and as for myself, I consider it a moral obligation) to express his attitude to Hebrew as a matter of course. Others may agree with him but we do not require unity on this question because this is not in our practical platform now.[16]

Nomberg's concern that failure to deal with this question would lessen the popularity of the Conference and weaken its authority was not taken seriously at this time. It was felt that somehow it would be possible to discuss the recognition by Jews and gentiles of Yiddish as a Jewish language without dealing with the Hebrew-Yiddish question. In the course of the Conference, as we shall see, this proved impossible. The issue could not be overlooked and the delegates were compelled to take a collective stand.

Peretz's address at the opening of the Conference, a kind of Declaration of the Cultural Independence of Yiddish, was enthusiastically received by the delegates. He began by analyzing the factors that had created the movement on behalf of the language. Hassidism, which expressed the will of the Jew of the masses

16. *Ibid.*, p. 66.

"to live his own poor life alone," without dependence on the wisdom of the scholar or the charity of the magnate, was the first factor.

Yiddish does not begin with Isaac Meyer Dik. The Hassidic folk tale is its genesis. "In Praise of the Baal Shem Tov" and other legendary tales are folk creations. The first folk poet is Rabbi Nakhman of Bratzlav with his "Seven Beggars."

The second factor in the emergence of the movement was the women's literature in Yiddish and the recognition of the language as the tongue of the ordinary masses and, especially, of the Jewish woman. *Ivri-Taytsh,* the language of the Women's Pentateuch, had become a "mother-tongue."

The rise of the Jewish working class with its proletarian culture in Yiddish was the third factor. With the worker's need to live his life in Yiddish, modern Yiddish literature was born. The fourth factor, according to Peretz, was the emerging recognition of nationality rather than statehood as the primary force in modern civilization. National minorities, weak and oppressed though they were, were rising to claim their rights and fight for their cultures.

Let the state no longer falsify the cultures of peoples and no longer extinguish particularity and individuality—this is what is proclaimed and sounded throughout the camp. We already stand in the ranks beneath our own flag and in the name of our own cultural interests. . . . We proclaim to the world : we are a Jewish people and Yiddish is our language. In our language we want to live our lives, create our cultural treasures, and no longer sacrifice them to the false interests of the state which is only the protector of ruling, dominating peoples and the bloodsucker of the weak.

Peretz praised Bukovina and the city of Czernowitz, "where diverse nationalities and diverse languages live together," as the proper setting for the Conference. Here it was easy for the Conference to convey its message to Jewry and the world at large.

In the evening we stroll through the street and the sounds of various languages emerge from the windows, the music of various peoples. We want to have our own window, our own independent theme in the symphony of peoples.

The Conference was an expression of Jewish national and cultural unity and of the Jewish people's desire to no longer permit itself to be splintered and sacrificed on behalf of the various nation-states. With the Yiddish language as the bond uniting all Jews, the creativity of the Jewish people would be stimulated and enhanced and it would contribute to the cultural growth of humanity as a whole. Peretz suggested both that the Hebrew-Aramaic literary heritage be translated into Yiddish and that the best works of Yiddish literature be transcribed in Latin characters so that they be made more easily accessible to the world at large.

Jews are one people whose language is Yiddish. In this language we wish to gather our treasure, create our culture, further stimulate our spirit and unite ourselves culturally in all lands and in all times. Warsaw and Bukovina, New York and Russia must now be united in the Yiddish language. Antiquity and modern times, the past and the present must express themselves through it. The Jewish cultural treasures must become the property of the whole world and the whole world must hear and learn to understand us.[17]

In his memoirs, Matisyohu Mieses recalled the impression that Peretz's address made on his hearers.

We awaited Peretz's opening address with anticipation and spiritual hunger at that time. He did not disappoint us. We heard powerful, mighty words from him. . . . I recall the electricity that ran through my limbs and the insight I gained into the soul of Peretz the man when he said "the state is the greatest criminal. . . ." In those few words I had before me the mirror of Peretz's weltanschauung.[18]

17. N. Mayzel, ed. *Briv un Redes fun Y. L. Peretz* (New York, 1944), p. 373.
18. Quoted in N. Mayzel, *Y. L. Peretz: Zayn Lebn un Shafn* (New York, 1945), p. 215.

In the elections, with which the opening session concluded, Peretz was voted a Vice-President of the Conference, together with Leybl Toybish and Dr. Chaim Zhitlovsky. During his remarks at the mass meeting held subsequently, Peretz expressed concern over the fact that Jewish intellectuals were serving alien cultures. If the cultural treasures of Jewry were disseminated in Yiddish, he reasoned, a uniform Jewish culture would be achieved. Thus, when Sholem Asch delivered his address on the need to translate the Bible into Yiddish, Peretz responded warmly. The generation of Yiddish writers that was intimately acquainted with the Bible in Hebrew was passing and it was imperative that younger writers be enabled to discover their roots in the traditional literature.[19]

At the third session of the Conference, Peretz delivered an address on the question of organizing a Yiddish literary and cultural union. He felt that the time was ripe for the creation of such a body. He did not regard as a deterrent the fact that the participants in the Conference were not elected delegates representing specific constituencies. The large number of guests and the greetings that the Conference had received from leading Jewish figures the world over seemed to indicate that the Conference truly expressed the mood of the Jewish masses at the time. Peretz had prepared the by-laws of the proposed organization together with the other officers of the Conference.

The "Conference of the Yiddish Language" has the following objectives :

a) the recognition and attainment of equal rights for the Yiddish language.

b) the advancement and dissemination of culture and art in the Yiddish language.

c) the unification of the Jewish people and its culture in its language.

To attain the objectives the Conference will create an organization and an office which will be temporarily stationed in Czernowitz.

19. *Di Ershte Yidishe* . . . , p. 83.

Organization : The organization consists of Jews of at least eighteen years of age who are in accord with the objectives of the "Conference of the Yiddish Language" and contribute at least 1 ruble (2 ½ crowns, 2 marks, etc.) to it annually.

Agency : The executive organ of the organization is the Agency which it elects. The Agency is to be called "Central Agency of the Conference of the Yiddish Language." The Agency must collect the stipulated monetary contributions and execute the decisions of the Conference.

In addition, the Agency will

a) solicit members for the organization

b) establish societies, committees, groups and other units to work on behalf of the objectives of the Conference according to the provisions of the various national laws

c) publish and support the publication of cultural and artistic materials

d) establish libraries

e) organize lectures and public readings

f) assist in the translation into Yiddish of all the cultural and artistic treasures of the Jewish past and especially of the Bible

g) assist in the publication of model textbooks

h) establish and support model Yiddish schools

i) establish and support a circulating model theater

j) establish professional unions of writers and artists

k) arbitrate disputes between writers and artists, on the one hand, and publishers, book dealers and the public, on the other

l) create a body to serve as an authority in questions of Yiddish orthography, grammar and other language questions

m) propagandize for the recognition and attainment of equal rights by the Yiddish language, and call periodic conferences.[20]

During the discussion of Peretz's resolution, the question of Hebrew vs. Yiddish was raised again. Abraham Heisler, an elderly Galician Zionist, accused Peretz's proposal of being inimical to the Zionist organization. The abandonment of Hebrew as the national Jewish language by the Conference would turn it into an "apostasy *(shmad)*-conference" rather than a "language *(shprakh)*- conference." Esther Frumkin, the Bundist delegate, also opposed the resolution, albeit for other reasons.

20. *Ibid.,* pp. 86f.

She feared that the establishment of any international Jewish organization without regard to class divisions within the Jewish people would weaken the class consciousness of the Jewish proletariat. Other delegates, including Noah Prilutzky and Lazar Kahn, felt that Peretz had emphasized the Agency and not dealt adequately with the organization as a whole.

Peretz addressed himself to the various criticisms and objections. In reply to the Zionists, who contended that an organization such as he envisioned could be established only by a government, Peretz pointed to the fact that for the time being the best Jewish institutions were organized and funded voluntarily by Jews themselves. He admitted that his proposals for the organization were not perfect but said that they would be improved in the course of implementation. He expressed his sympathy with the Bund but pointed out that the various political organizations were too subjective in their cultural work and had merely flooded the literary market with propagandistic brochures.

Before Peretz's resolution was carried as a platform, the details of which were to be discussed subsequently, Esther Frumkin put forth her view of Yiddish as "the sole national language of Jewry." Although her counterproposal that Peretz's resolution be scrapped and that a purely educational agency be established with practical work to be carried out by the various national organizations and institutions was voted down, her theoretical formulation provided fuel for the subsequent debate on the status of Yiddish.

When the discussion on the status of Yiddish was finally begun, Peretz found himself in an uncomfortable position. He had responded enthusiastically to Matisyohu Mieses's address (see below) and had even moved that it be issued by the Conference in a special brochure as the first scientific study of the Yiddish language. Peretz's motion aroused the ire of those who took exception to Mieses's negative view of the role of Hebrew in modern Jewish life. The reaction of the "Hebraists" was so strong that Peretz felt the need to retract his motion and apologize for having offended anyone. In addition, Esther Frumkin's remarks had turned the discussion of Peretz's proposal into a discussion of the "national" status of Yiddish and its role vis-à-vis Hebrew.

Peretz defined the terms "nation," "folk," "national language" and "folk language" as he used them and stated explicitly that he was opposed to adoption by the Conference of any resolution concerning a national language. The question was a theoretical one and the respective delegates were entitled to their own opinions. Such an issue could no more be determined by majority vote than could the question of the earth's rotation.

Whether or not Peretz reiterated his view that Hebrew was the national language and Yiddish a folk language in the course of the debate is not clear. After the formulation of "a national language" was adopted by the Conference, Peretz expressed his dissatisfaction with it.

> The addresses delivered here have not convinced me. The argument that the political situation in Austria, especially in Galicia and Bukovina thoroughly necessitates declaring Yiddish a national language has not moved me. Such a declaration is definitely not within the province of the organization which this Conference is creating. A political, pragmatic purpose cannot and should not influence our convictions. All that is necessary is the recognition of Yiddish as a language. Asch tells us of the living Hebrew language of the Bokharian Jews which even he is not opposed to. If we recognize Yiddish as the national language, if we relegate Hebrew only to the past, to history, then we conceive the Hebrew language as alien. To whom, then, do we relinquish our past? To whom do we sell our Prophets? I remain convinced that :
> 1) Hebrew is not a folk language. Hebrew is no longer living.
> 2) To mechanically revive a language is to create a new jargon.
> 3) As long as our cultural treasures remain in Hebrew, Yiddish is only a folk language.
> 4) The Conference therefore has only the right to do what is needed to help the folk language raise itself to the level of a national language.
> Although I do not acquiesce to the majority, I remain a

member of the Conference. I withdraw only from the presidium, the staff and the practical duties until the next Conference which will certainly content itself with the sentence : "Our language is Yiddish."[21]

Although Peretz's viewpoint has been attributed to his desire to protect his position in the world of Hebrew letters, it is far more plausible to attribute it to the realistic situation that prevailed in Yiddish literature at the time. Peretz felt that a national language must afford access to the entire national culture of its people and enable an intelligent person to adequately live his life in it. Yiddish, at present a folk language, had to be gradually transformed into a national language by incorporating the literary treasures and values in the millennial culture of the Jewish people.[22]

It is nevertheless apparent that Peretz did not remain unaffected by the radical winds blowing at the Conference. The role he assigned to Hebrew seems to have diminished and to have approached the view of some of the other delegates that Hebrew was a "dead language." During the final session the question was raised as to whether he could be elected to the executive committee in spite of his disagreement with the resolution on the status of Yiddish. At this point Peretz explained that he was essentially in agreement with the desire of the Conference to make Yiddish a national language but that his definition of "national language" was different from that of the other delegates. Nomberg moved that Peretz be admitted in recognition of his achievements on behalf of Yiddish, because of his desire to work on behalf of the goals of the Conference and especially in light of his own statement that he was essentially in agreement with the resolution and differed only in his definition of "national." The resolution was carried and Peretz was elected to the exectuive committee of the new organization.[23]

21. Ibid., pp. 108f.
22. Cf. M. Ravitch in *Tsum Yoyvl fun der Ershter Yidisher Sprakh-Konferents* (Montreal, 1968), p. 9.
23. *Di Ershte Yidishe . . .* , pp. 121f. See also S. Eisenstadt, *Pyonerishe Geshtaltn* (Tel Aviv, 1970), pp. 143–56.

To all intents and purposes, then, Peretz came to accept the view of the Conference and to place himself firmly in the newly emerging militant Yiddishist camp. It is not surprising that in later years he was wont to refer to the Conference as the "holy Conference." In Czernowitz, Peretz experienced not only an inner conflict of ideals and realities, but also a revelation of the potential inherent in the Yiddish language as the language of the Jewish renaissance. As we shall see, however, his Yiddishism never diverted him from the larger dimensions of Jewish culture.

Following the Conference, Peretz, Asch, Reisen, and Nomberg embarked on a lecture tour of Galicia and Bukovina in order to raise funds for the new organization. Although generally successful, they met with the heckling and opposition of the Hebraists in many towns. Peretz concluded one of his addresses with the following words:

> We do indeed have our ancient Hebraic cultural language and it may conceivably have a future. It would, however, be impossible for it to become a folk language overnight. The people needs a language of its own today in order not to be drawn into the assimilationist stream. We have to be concerned with today if we want to survive until tomorrow. (p. 126)

The details of Matisyohu Mieses's participation in the Conference are vague except for the fact that at its fourth session he delivered an address full of scholarly arguments that sought to prove that Yiddish is a language equal to all others. Many of the arguments were new at the time and many participants in the Conference heard them for the first time. His remarks served as a scholarly basis for the deliberations of the Conference on the status of Yiddish.

Mieses opened his address with a description of language as the most important factor in the establishment of national identity. He cited the Irish as an example of a people which, having lost its national language, had lost its soul. The history of the Jewish people had taught it to appreciate the significance of language as a unifying and sustaining force in national life.

> The Jew always had a language of his own in which to converse. . . . Even when compelled to speak foreign languages, he utilized their vocabularies as raw material, infusing them with his own spirit and placing his own seal upon them. . . . Aramaic and Judaeo-Greek testify to the fact that the Jew always saw to it that his soul might express itself in its own way and that his world-view might have its own form of expression. . . . The Jews of Spain, on the other hand, except for the period known as the Golden Age, were handicapped in producing original works of Jewish culture and in enabling their masses to attain a creative identity by not having a language of their own. . . . The Sephardic language spoken by the Jews of the Orient is neither their own language nor an original dialect. A few Hebrew words and old Castillian expressions do not make it an original tongue. Its grammar and pronunciation do not differ from Spanish. The name by which those who speak it refer to it—Ladino—means "Latin." . . . The other Jews of the Orient are Arabic-speaking and culturally assimilated, constituting only lame limbs of our people. (pp. 144ff.)

The strongest and most powerful of all the languages acquired by the Jewish people in exile, the one most transformed into an independent tongue, was that which the Jews of Central and Eastern Europe had obtained from the Germans. Unlike the Sephardim, the majority of Ashkenazim never broke with their past. Their traditional culture represented a creative continuation of the Talmud. The Polish or Ashkenazic Jew was a new type with deep roots in his people's past. He who was free of gentile prejudices, and could appreciate something original, would divorce himself from the usual attitude that Jewish intellectuals bore toward the old Polish Jew in his caftan with his pilpulistic reasoning. "If we measure the contribution of Ashkenazic Jewry to the civilization of Western Europe since the Emancipation, we cannot but be impressed by its ability and talent" (p. 147). Mieses quoted approvingly the statement of Nietzsche, whose sole knowledge of Judaism was derived from assimilated German Jews, to the effect that Jews are born to nationhood (*natio nata*), where other nations are artificially contrived (*natio facta*).

The Ashkenazic branch of Jewry, endowed with great strength and resiliency, did with German what their ancestors had done with Aramaic and Alexandrian Greek. It tailored the alien elements to the Jewish spirit, altering the pronunciation and grammatical rules and including hundreds of new words. Estimating that some eight million Jews spoke Yiddish, Mieses concluded that they had a right to consider it a national language.

Mieses countered the claim that Yiddish was only a jargon by stating that the most significant European languages, including English, French, and Italian, were all "jargons" and were originally all held up to contempt.

> The Jew's lack of respect for his language is nothing but a capitulation to the anti-Semitic feeling of the Germans who ridicule the Jewish version of their own language. Even the loyal Zionist and ardent Hebraist is not free of such unconscious anti-Semitism. Anti-Semitism attacks everything that is considered Jewish and this is especially true in the case of a hybrid language created by the Jews themselves. (p.149)

But a hybrid language, Mieses insisted, was not necessarily something to be ashamed of. Only the languages of wild tribes were pure and free from admixture. The more cultured a nation was, the more it was subject to foreign influences. The German language too had all the signs of being an amalgam, a hybrid language and a jargon. Just as the Romance languages were a historical development of Latin, Yiddish represented a Judaized evolution of German. Mieses offered a large number of illustrations to support his view of Yiddish as a more highly developed version of the German language.

Mieses discussed a number of prejudices that plagued Yiddish. It was claimed that as "the language of the narrow ghetto, the dank cellar and the small Jewish street," Yiddish was not worthy of attention. Mieses pointed out that the external circumstances in which Yiddish evolved served to strengthen it and concentrate its energies. Nineteenth-century Polish literature, too, was a product of oppression, but nevertheless it had great artistic merit.

Did not the fact that Jews were overwhelmingly urban dwellers preclude their language from describing nature and depicting landscapes? Contemporary Yiddish literature disproved that contention. Classical literature was also deficient in nature scenes. Contrary to widespread opinion, romantic love had also found its way into modern Yiddish writing despite the Jewish tradition of prearranged marriages.

The argument that Yiddish was vile sounding was purely subjective, said Mieses. Similar views had been expressed in the past concerning English and German. Native-born Yiddish speakers, it was often claimed, found difficulty in speaking other languages, but that was equally true, according to Mieses, of those who spoke other tongues.

"Yiddish is a natural language; Yiddish is our language with a distinct stamp of our spirit" (p. 163). The fact that three-fourths of the Yiddish vocabulary could be traced etymologically to German was unimportant, said Mieses. It was not the empty sound of words but the spirit that vivified it that constituted a language.

> The national essence is not in the bare words; it expresses itself in the internal construction, in the contents breathed into the received elements, in the phonetic form and, principally, in the whole sea of feelings, images, associations, jokes, etc. which have grown into the mute, blind material. (p. 163)

For Mieses it was not raw material but "spirit" that is decisive in the formation of a language. Spirit, as he described it, was a racial or individual characteristic manifest in the poetic treatment of raw material by a group or an individual artist. Under the microscope, all languages, even the most ancient, appear to have foreign elements.

Some Jews had rejected Yiddish out of national pride. Was it fitting, they asked, that an ancient Semitic people speak a

comparatively recent Indo-Germanic language? Youth is no
sin, replied Mieses. It was time Jews stopped priding themselves
on their antiquity.

Was it not a sign of servitude for Jews to accept as their
own the language of their erstwhile oppressors? For Mieses,
sentimentalism was a sign of weakness and exhaustion. Yiddish
was Germanic only from a linguistic standpoint. Moreover, why
should Jews be ashamed to speak it simply because of what the
ancestors of the present-day Germans did to their ancestors?

> Our ancestors, who in Germany acquired the Germanic elements
> of Yiddish, did not do so out of inner servitude. The Jew's soul
> was never enslaved. The "serf of the chamber" never denied
> his own worth. He always had the feeling that his proud *poritz*
> [nobleman] was a robber [*poritz* actually means robber], a
> morally inferior individual. The Jew always felt that together
> with his ancient Torah he stood opposed to the half-savage
> Europe of those days. At most, under the worst conditions of
> Exile, the Jew's life became constricted and exhausted. But his
> soul was never bowed. He gazed at the world as a free man
> with his own culture. Only outwardly was he enslaved. (p. 168)

In contrast, the proud nations of Europe had also been inwardly
enslaved to Rome, from which they learned Latin and which
conquered them with both the sword and the crucifix. Mieses
felt that Jews ought to look upon the Middle Ages as a time
when, in spite of persecution, their people manifested strength
of soul and developed their own culture, including a language of
their own. Such a language was therefore not a sign of servitude
or shame.

In dealing with the problem of non-Yiddish-speaking Jews,
Mieses took a position which, as we shall see, was later espoused
by Zhitlovsky. He read off the two million assimilated Jews in
Europe and America. They did not belong to the Jewish nation.
Only race and, at best, religion still bound them to East European Jewry. The one million non-Ashkenazic Jews spoke a
variety of languages. The remaining eight million Jews in the
world who spoke Yiddish constituted the overwhelming majority
of the Jewish people, both quantitatively and qualitatively.

In the camp of the Ashkenazim may be found all the national strength that our people pessesses. The overwhelming majority speaks Yiddish. Those who do not, constitute a minority and are unimportant. (p. 170)

What about the contention that Yiddish was a "folk language" but not a "national language"? (This was the position that Peretz had presented earlier.) The term "folk language" was undemocratic, according to Mieses. It was what aristocrats called the language of the masses and was not fitting in modern times. Those who supported the designation "folk language" also sought to prove that Yiddish was suitable only for jokes and satires. They were obviously under the influence of anti-Semites like Wagner, who once said that it was impossible to put a Jew on the stage without laughing at him. "The truth is that all we can conclude from the Jewish joke is that the Jewish people has an abundance of spirit which Yiddish expresses well" (p. 173). The French, Mieses noted, were also embarrassed by their humorous spirit. The dramatic genre in which they were original and spontaneous was comedy. Perhaps Yiddish humor was not specifically Jewish and only a product of circumstances. Jokes depend upon contradictions and unlikely contrasts, which abound in times of transition when the old has not yet died and the new is already in evidence. At such times humorous situations that give rise to comedy and satire abound.

Another objection frequently raised against Yiddish was that a dispersed nation could not create a literature truly representative of its spirit. The language in which that literature was written could not be termed a "national language." Mieses pointed out that this was equally true of Hebrew and reminded his listeners that the major part of Hellenic culture was created in Asia Minor, where the Greeks constituted a minority group. Polish culture, too, produced its greatest writers among the Polish minority living in Lithuania. Mieses believed that the future of Jewry depended upon the production of great works in Yiddish. The designation "folk language," he believed, smacked of despondency and a lack of self-confidence.

Responding to the question, "What should be our attitude toward Hebrew?" Mieses answered that it should be viewed solely as a literary language. It was inconceivable to him that Hebrew would ever again become the spoken language of dispersed Jewry. He was also skeptical about the ability of the Jews in Palestine to revive it.

Mieses took an extremely combative position toward Hebrew. For him the sacred tongue had taken leave of life more than two thousand years ago. Hebrew was the language of the past; Yiddish the language of the present. Hebrew had to continue to play the important role of binding the Jew to his past and reminding him of his people's ancient glories. Hebrew as a living language was artificial, its words fossilized, mummified, and without psychological underpinning. It was incapable of adequately reflecting modern life in all its variations and its future as a medium of belles lettres was bleak.

> Our living language will be Yiddish and the language of Jewish research Hebrew. . . . Hebrew can still play a larger role than just the language of the synagogue and religion. . . . The two languages will live together as good neighbors in our serious literature and our educated class will read Hebrew as well as Yiddish. . . . No conflict between the languages need exist as long as the Hebraists realize that the role of Hebrew is solely that of a literary tongue. . . . The number of Jews who actually understand Hebrew is minimal and the desire of some Hebraists to relegate Yiddish literature to the status of a literary genre and plaything in a folk dialect therefore meaningless. . . . Yiddish is not a dialect but is actually an independent language of the contemporary Jewish nation. (pp. 177ff.)

Yiddish was the language of *Yidishkeyt* (Judaism). It alone could protect Jewry from assimilation and shield it from alien attacks. Where Yiddish ceased to be spoken, the unity of Jewry was endangered. The strengthening of Yiddish would not harm Hebrew. On the contrary, when Yiddish was silenced Judaism became mute and assimilation eventually triumphed.

Whether we are Yiddishists or Hebraists we must organize to preserve this language which aside from religion is the only thread uniting East European Jewry. . . . The Jewish people must rid itself of self-contempt and make itself aware of the significance and sacredness of Yiddish. (p. 182)

Mieses insisted that the Yiddishists were not creating something new or denying historical continuity but rather continuing the thread of Jewish historical development. Modern Yiddish developed slowly and was the result of a process that had gone on for hundreds of years. The large number of Yiddish words taken from Hebrew was evidence of the fact that Yiddish was a continuation of the past. It was not only the terminology of religion and custom that came from Hebrew.

The life of the soul and of society, generally, is usually expressed in Hebrew terms. . . . The Jew sensed that it would be a desecration to appropriate foreign words for such a purpose. . . . The Hebrew words in Yiddish are not the result of chance but of a pattern which flows from the Jewish national spirit. . . . The same is true of Yiddish grammar and even Yiddish phonetics bear the stamp of ancient Judaism. (pp. 184ff.)

Mieses insisted that because Yiddish was a continuation of the past and was based on ancient Judaism, it was essential that it retain the Hebrew alphabet. He presented a number of arguments against the substitution of the Latin alphabet for the Hebrew, which some Yiddishists were proposing at the time.

Mieses summed up his case for Yiddish as follows:

From a linguistic standpoint Yiddish is a language like all others; from a Jewish historical standpoint it is our national language; from the modern standpoint of the psychology of nations, this language comprises a large folklore, hundreds of tales, and thousands of emotional and conceptual associations of our people. We treasure our past but refuse to live with it alone. As Yiddish speaking Jews we are good Jews because our language is completely suffused with our spirit and because it is a continuation of our past. (pp. 191ff.)

Mieses concluded his address with the thought that a nation could not have a normal existence without its own language. It was his sincere conviction that Hebrew had no chance of becoming a living language of the Jewish people.

> He who holds the future of his people dear and who does not want Judaism to disappear must join those who seek the emancipation of Yiddish. Yiddish must have equal rights in the schools so that it may develop naturally and its literature must be accorded equal status with other literatures. The nineteenth century created the rights of man, the twentieth has the responsibility of creating the rights of languages. Affording Yiddish the right to develop is a sacred national cause and a contribution to the progress of humanity. (p. 193)

The reaction to Mieses's address was overwhelming. His attitude to Hebrew and his use of terms like "graves," "cemetery," "mummy," and "pulse-less" in connection with it, aroused the anger of several delegates and some actually broke into tears. Peretz was completely taken with Mieses's presentation despite the divergences in their views. He reprimanded the Hebraists for their conduct and suggested that the address be published in a special brochure as the first scientific essay on the Yiddish language. According to a newspaper report of the session,

> the address of Herr Mieses stirred a bit of conflict among some Conference delegates for whom Hebrew was still precious and sacred. Then, when Y. L. Peretz suggested that the address be printed in a separate brochure, a storm which threatened to become a fist-fight broke out. . . . The Hebraists began to whistle loudly and the Jargonists were ready to defend Herr Mieses' address with their fists. . . . One of the shouting Hebraists sat down in a corner, began to cry terribly and was unable to calm himself. Not far from him stood two Hebrew-speaking girls who cried along as they looked at him. (pp. 96–97)

As noted above, Mieses's single contribution to the Conference was his address. There is little record of his participation in the ensuing discussions.

It is recorded that when

Peretz took serious note of Mieses at the Conference, the latter began to withdraw. In jest Peretz remarked to his friends concerning Mieses, "He is a strange young man. He is like a sack filled with nails. Nails are useful, without them one cannot build, but it's hard to touch a sack of nails with one's hands."[24]

Following the election of officers during the first session of the Conference on Sunday, August 30, Zhitlovsky addressed the "people's rally" and told the large gathering that Yiddish had no competitors. No other language, however beautiful, could harm it. He believed that the Conference, and later the organization that the Conference would establish, "should strive to develop the Yiddish language into the Jewish national language because that was the best means to Jewish national existence."[25]

Zhitlovsky developed the thought he had expressed in his American lectures about the abyss that had been created in modern times between the concepts "Jew" and "man." Jewish students in the Russian universities felt compelled to choose between socialism and humanity, on the one hand, and Jewishness and miserable *Golus* existence, on the other. But with the development of Yiddish that abyss had vanished. Yiddish had established an organic connection with European civilization and now the advancing life of the Jewish people was tied to the language. Yiddish was still "slightly anemic," but it could and would develop.

Zhitlovsky also dealt with the relationship between Yiddish and Hebrew. He depicted a wise old grandmother who handed over the keys to the cupboards and closets in the house to her daughters and daughters-in-law. The young women treated grandmother respectfully and provided a beautiful funeral for her when her time came to depart this life. This was how Hebrew and Yiddish should have been treating each other. Instead, grandmother refused to surrender the keys and there was constant wrangling.

24. M. Ravitch, p. 11.
25. *Di Ershte Yidishe* . . . , p. 78.

That evening was devoted to literature and Zhitlovsky spoke briefly about the literatures of oppressed peoples with special reference to Yiddish writing. He opened the second session the following morning and responded favorably to Sholem Asch's lecture concerning the need to translate the Bible into Yiddish but insisted that it was equally important that the Talmud and other great works of Jewish literature also be translated.

By translating the Bible and other Jewish cultural treasures into Yiddish, we will open for the Jewish people the great sea, which the great Jewish masses have not seen until now. Whatever our approach to the Bible, we must admit that it is necessary to create the means for every Jew to understand it. (p. 84)

Zhitlovsky offered a resolution to the effect that "the Conference deems it necessary to translate into Yiddish, the ancient Jewish treasures which are written in Hebrew and, first of all, the Bible" (p. 84). Asch took issue with this resolution because he felt that translating the Bible was of far greater importance than the translation of any other work at the time. Another question that aroused discussion was whether the translation of the Bible was necessary as a contribution to the Yiddish language or to Jewish culture and the Jewish spirit generally. This was no academic discussion since there were both religionists and avowed atheists and secularists among the delegates. Both concepts were accepted and combined when the resolution was passed (pp. 84–85).

In the debates concerning the status of the Yiddish language, Zhitlovsky stressed that the differences between the delegates on the relationship between Hebrew and Yiddish reflected differences within the Jewish community. The Jewish people, he said, needed a national language. "When we fight for our national rights, when we demand Jewish schools, etc., we must be able to show that we have a national language. Our national language cannot be Hebrew but Yiddish" (pp. 105–6). For Zhitlovsky, Yiddish was the Jewish national language primarily because it was spoken by the overwhelming majority of the Jewish people. With Asch and Nomberg, Zhitlovsky drafted a resolution to the effect that "Yiddish was *the* national language of the Jewish people but each member of the Conference and the future organization is free to think of Hebrew as his personal convictions dictate" (pp. 106f.). The resolution that was finally passed, declaring Yiddish *a* national language of the Jewish people, was milder than Zhitlovsky would have liked but a victory for Yiddishism to which he always looked back approvingly.

The following year Zhitlovsky published a report on the Czernowitz Conference. An occasion that had simultaneously aroused so much enmity and hope, he wrote, could not be considered an accident in the history of a people. Whatever the verdict of the future, the Czernowitz Conference had to be viewed as an important event.

> The future will show whether the entire Yiddish language movement was only a small paragraph in the history of the Jewish people or the title page of a new chapter. In the meantime, we must concede that the Yiddish language movement has grown out of Jewish life itself, i.e., it is a part of Jewish history.[26]

Zhitlovsky felt that the recognition accorded Yiddish at the Czernowitz Conference was justified on socioeconomic, cultural, and national grounds. The experiences of multinational states proved that national legal equality and the legal equality of languages were the same. "The socioeconomic interests of the Jewish masses which demand without any concession legal equality for the Jewish people, demand at the same time legal equality for the Yiddish language."[27] The cultural elevation of the Jewish masses could not be achieved unless Yiddish was recognized and made the language of the intellectual class. Moreover, only Yiddish could serve as the cementing force in

26. Chaim Zhitlovsky, *Gezamlte Shriftn*, 4:112.
27. *Ibid.*, p. 116.

Jewry that the Jewish religion had been in the past. The modern religious Jew who clothed his religion in European form and the Jewish nationalist attached to Hebrew culture were less visibly Jewish to the outside world and less attached to the Jewish people as a whole than the assimilationist or apostate who read a Yiddish newspaper publicly.

> I personally believe that whatever the future of the Jewish people in future generations, in the present situation of the Jewish people it is simply a matter of respect for every Jew —whether he be nationalist, assimilationist, religious or secularist—not to publicly abandon his people but to demonstrate his attachment to the persecuted people. If earlier, in the assimilationist period, it was a matter of respect for intellectuals to demonstrate their attachment to European civilization at every opportunity, then in our time a new moral imperative has evolved from that : *to show with every breath and with every pulse-beat of your heart your membership in the Jewish people and your solidarity with its historic destiny!* And this is possible for all Jews, for all parties, classes and movements in one way only : in the form of attachment to the Yiddish language.[28]

Zhitlovsky conceded that the same needs that propelled the Jewish masses toward Yiddish urged the intellectuals toward Hebrew. All the polarizations in Jewish life had been reflected in the Conference : intelligentsia and masses, Zionists and Bundists, religionists and secularists, middle class and proletariat. Were all Jews living together in their own land, wrote Zhitlovsky, Hebrew, Yiddish, and Ladino would all have equal rights, as did the three official languages of Switzerland. All three were, in fact, national Jewish languages. Circumstances had necessitated the public declaration that Yiddish, a language tied to the socioeconomic, cultural, and national needs of the Jewish masses, be no longer treated as a stepchild but as a national language. This declaration and the establishment of

28. *Ibid.*, p. 118.

an organization to champion the cause of Yiddish were practical necessities of Jewish life and constituted the historical
significance of the Conference.[29]

The chances of the Czernowitz Conference for success were
limited from the very start by the wide diversity of orientations
and views represented in its ranks. There were "unpleasant
incidents" and resignations throughout the deliberations. Zhitlovsky, Mieses, and possibly Birnbaum, were alone in viewing
the primacy or centrality of Yiddish as the overriding problem
of Jewry at the time. The literati were disgruntled and divided
by Peretz's refusal to acknowledge Yiddish as a national
language and by his lack of clarity and resolve on the role
of Hebrew. For neither Bundists nor Zionists was Yiddish
really a major concern. The former were primarily concerned
with socialism and the latter with Palestine, where Hebrew
was establishing itself as the Jewish vernacular. Both found it
more advantageous to independently foster their own partisan
interests with the help of Yiddish rather than compromise on
theory and surrender a modicum of sovereignty and self-
jurisdiction in order to foster the growth of Yiddish itself.
Thus the Conference and the organization it sought to create
were robbed of the validation and participation of the two
political movements without whose cooperation they were
doomed to ultimate failure. The representatives of the various
socialist Zionist parties found themselves caught in the ideological juggernaut created by the two major movements.

The Zionist participants saw Hebrew as "the sole bond of
Jewish national existence," with Yiddish as merely "the
necessary language of the Jewish exile."[30] Vaynreb, a Galician
Zionist, typified the Zionist dilemma at the Conference. Before
the resolution on the status of Yiddish was passed, he expressed

29. *Ibid.*, pp. 120–21.
30. *Di Ershte Yidishe* . . . , p. 82.

the view that only Hebrew could be considered the national language and that Yiddish was only a means of preserving Judaism and of attracting Jews to the revival of Jewry in the Hebrew language. Nevertheless, he conceded the need to work with those who saw Yiddish as the sum total and eternal aspect of Jewish culture, provided they did not hurt the feelings of the Hebraists. He urged that the concept of "Jewish culture" be discussed instead of that of "national language" (p. 103). Once the resolution on Yiddish was passed, however, he withdrew from the Conference, explaining that he would continue to work on behalf of Yiddish in accordance with his Zionist convictions. Yiddish, he said, was not a national language but a language actually spoken by a great portion of the Jewish people. It was for that reason that he loved it and wished to help it develop (p. 107).

L. Khazanovitsh, a Poaley Zion publicist from Lemberg, whose nom de plume was "Kasriel," expressed the Poaley Zion view at the Conference. The Poaley Zion, he maintained, although both socialist and Zionist, took a position independent of both the Bund and the Zionist movement (p. 100). The resolution that he drafted during the discussion on the status of Yiddish read as follows:

> Yiddish is a national language of the Jewish people and we demand complete political and social equality for it in the lands of compact mass settlement by Jews. (p. 106)

Although he approved of Peretz's general idea of an international organization and accused the Bundists of assimilationism and of contributing to the disintegration of Jewry in opposing it, he went along with Esther Frumkin's minimalist program for the organization until the calling of another conference (pp. 89, 115). In a report that he published in an Austrian Poaley Zion organ immediately following the Conference, Khazanovitsh explained the positions of his party.

> Whoever wishes to proclaim Yiddish as the sole national language, now and always, not only takes the risk of being

judged a false prophet by history but also excludes various groups in Zionism from collaboration. Without Zionism no great cultural institution can be created. Those who remain unconvinced by the arguments of Zionism must at least reckon with its power and influence. . . . We could not agree to the notion that a cultural organization for all social classes and partisan trends is possible. No one can completely free himself of the class influences under which he was raised and one cultural organization for all would still have had to bear the character of a particular class. We could not join such an organization without a party decision and we would therefore have had no influence on its formation. All socialist groups at the Conference (Poaley Zion, Seymists, Bundists) agreed on this and because of our unified stand we succeeded in seeing to it that for the time being there be formed only a central office consisting of representatives from various countries which would be limited to organizational and informational activities and primarily to the preparation of the next conference. If our point of view had not been accepted, the Conference would have fallen apart. (pp. 208–9)

The Bundist position was basically inimical to the purposes of the Conference. The Bund clearly continued to shun all practical manifestations of Jewish national consciousness that transcended class interests because it viewed them as detrimental to the Jewish proletariat. Although local members of the Bund filled the public sessions and gave the deliberations a sense of urgency, Esther Frumkin, the Bundist newspaperwoman and educator, was the most intransigent and inflexible of the delegates. She may be credited with undermining the deliberations and wrecking all chances for the creation of a centralized and effective international Yiddishist organization. Her position was reported in the Bundist press and unofficially adopted as that of the Bund toward the Conference. In a detailed report that she published in a Bundist organ, she justified the inflexibility of the Bundist position and her unwillingness to cooperate or compromise with any kind of "general Jewish politics."

However modest the objectives which the Conference takes upon itself and however insignificant it views the language question, one thing is clear : Only those who believe in the future of Yiddish can consciously work for its development, enhancement and improvement. How can those whose activities ridicule the mother tongue; who attempt to develop themselves and train their children in a language which is alien to the Jewish masses; who wish to be leaders of the folk masses while deciding to make Hebrew their official tongue; who publish their official organ in Hebrew which is completely incomprehensible to the masses—how can they fight for the rights of the mother-tongue? If the Conference is fated to achieve anything it can only be to the detriment of the Hebraists and can only bury Hebrew.[31]

Frumkin found the resolution on the status of Yiddish, with its reference to the position of Hebrew as a matter of personal choice, completely inadequate. Verbal symbols, she believed, were important, and the resolution gave the impression that the Conference supported Zionist "utopianism." The Conference, in her opinion, truly represented neither the masses nor the intelligentsia. It consisted only of individuals who had come together to form an organization which, in her opinion, had to be limited to the dissemination of information concerning Yiddish. The Conference had no right to pass resolutions on matters of principle and should have been concerned only with calling another, more representative, conference.[32]

Frumkin opposed and eventually helped defeat Peretz's proposal for a central organization because she believed that culture could be propagated solely along class lines and that the struggle for the equality of Yiddish could be carried forth effectively only by local organizations. Since, in her opinion, any organization founded by the Conference would have to be no more than an information bureau, it could not engage in the political struggle for the equality of Yiddish or in educational activities such as the establishment of schools. Its publications would have to be limited to statistics, bibliographies, and the like, and it could,

31. Esther Frumkin, "Di Ershte Yidishe Shprakh-Konferents," *Di Naye Tsayt* (Vilna, 1908), pp. 86–87.
32. *Di Ershte Yidishe . . . ,* p. 110.

in general, deal only with matters strictly pertaining to language. Zhitlovsky (representing the Seymists) and Khazanovitsh went along with her on this minimalist type of organization, but when there was some talk of permitting the organization to establish schools and libraries she called the plan a "falsification" and resigned from the Conference.[33]

The functions of the new organization were carefully limited to preparations for the next conference, the publication of the minutes of the first Conference, the publication of Sholem Asch's translation of the Book of Ruth and Mieses's address, and the preparation of a program of activities for the organization to be discussed at the next conference.[34] None of these projects was ever carried out by the organization.

The actual achievements of the organization were limited to two items that appeared in Birnbaum's *Vokhnblat* a short time after the Conference. One was a proclamation inviting Jews of all classes and parties to participate. Institutions were asked to pay minimum dues so that they would be entitled to send delegates to the next conference, and it was suggested that local representatives be designated to help carry out the aims of the organization and supply it with information on local activities. The other item was a letter to the Central Committee of the Zionist Organization in Galicia protesting the negative attitude of its newspaper to the Yiddish-language movement.[35]

In 1928, on the occasion of the twentieth anniversary of the First Yiddish Language Conference, Zhitlovsky published an evaluation of it in which he wrote that it had indeed signified an ideological and moral victory for Yiddishism. However disparate the theoretical views of the delegates, they had all been suffused with the same basic mood of love for Yiddish and respect for its literature. They had shared a hatred for those

33. *Ibid.*, p. 120.
34. *Ibid.*
35. *Ibid.*, pp. 123f., 245f.

assimilationists and Hebraists who had the "despicable audacity to look derisively and with ridicule at the language of our great folk masses and of the awakened intellectual leaders of the folk." They had sorrowed over the disrespect and abuse heaped upon the Jewish people when its language was declared to be an "ugly jargon." The "spirit of Czernowitz" had worked as a disinfecting and purifying stream in the life of Jewry and had served to rid many intellectuals of their prejudice against Yiddish.

> And in everything that we have achieved during these twenty years in the construction of our modern secular culture, in all of our finest achievements in the fields of education, literature, press and theatre, the spirit of Czernowitz lives, acts, and gives strength to continued life and work.[36]

Zhitlovsky lamented the fact that the practical results of Czernowitz that were to have been carried out by the organization created by the Conference were nil. The Yiddishists had failed to organize themselves effectively the way the Zionists did after the First Zionist Congress in Basle in 1897. The Yiddishists had failed to foil the "reactionary" and "chauvinistic romanticism" of the Zionists. The "internal logical essence" of Zionism for Zhitlovsky was its striving for the politicoeconomic liberation of Jewry. But the spiritual liberation of Jewry was equally significant. Such a liberation, meaning both the legitimation of pluralism in Jewish life and the assertion of the unity of the Jewish people, could be effected only by a uniform national language. "National unity is sought and found in the uniform psychic threads with which a language ties the members of a people together into a uniform culture-producing organism." The "wonderful power" of a language consisted in its being able to free the individuals belonging to a people while simultaneously binding them together.

In order to free itself of the spiritual restrictions foisted upon it by religious and philosophical movements, a people had to

36. Chaim Zhitlovsky, "Tshernovits un der Yidishizm," *Yidishe Kultur* (May 1958), p. 14.

remove all barriers to freedom of expression and permit absolutely free cultural activity in the language spoken by its masses. The "national mission of Yiddishism" was to protect, develop, and strengthen Yiddish, and embrace with its psychic threads all elements of the Jewish people everywhere. "Yiddishism is therefore nothing but and nothing less than the striving for full and complete national unity and full and complete spiritual freedom and independence." The powerful and harmful elements of Zionism could be countered by an effective organization proclaiming "Yiddish—our national language, our only unity and freedom."[37]

The Yiddishists had failed to reckon with the healthy and progressive elements of Zionism, said Zhitlovsky. They had still been under the influence of utopian beliefs and thought that Yiddish culture could develop naturally without deep roots in a land of its own. That "cardinal error" could have been avoided, because Zionists and Territorialists had participated in the Czernowitz Conference. But the organization created by the Conference had been short-lived. The equivocation at the Conference concerning the status of Yiddish had robbed it of its ability to establish itself ideologically. Zhitlovsky felt that the adoption of the formulation "a" national language rather than "the" national language confused the organization from the very start and sentenced it to a rapid demise.

Nevertheless, the "spirit of Czernowitz" remained a potent force for creativity in the Yiddish cultural sphere. Had the time come for the establishment of a new Yiddishist organization that would strive for both spiritual liberation and national cultural uniformity in Jewish life? Zhitlovsky was not certain. There were still too many enemies ready to attack these principles. There were pious religionists, Hebraists, and assimilationists who prevented the realization of such ideas. But Zhitlovsky nevertheless remained confident of the ultimate triumph of his cause.[38]

37. *Ibid.*, p. 15.
38. *Ibid.*, p. 16.

In 1937, Zhitlovsky had occasion to reevaluate the achievements of the Conference once again. Its purpose, he said, had been two-fold: the formulation of the place of Yiddish in Jewish life and the creation of an international organization to help develop political and social conditions for the growth of Yiddish culture.

> With all its compromising, the Czernowitz language resolution signified first of all, the democratic elevation of the Jewish folk masses. The Jewish people came to be equated principally with the great Jewish folk masses whose language the resolution raised, if not to the status of the Jewish national language, at least to that of a national language, equal to Hebrew in national significance. That also signified the mightiest battle against assimilation.[39]

Zhitlovsky recalled that the entire duration of the Conference had been taken up with the question of the status of Yiddish and no time was left for cultural and organizational matters. Immediately following the Conference, the language controversy flared up again in the Hebrew and Yiddish press. One of the principal arguments the Hebraists used was the notion that not form, that is, language, but content is of primary significance. They accused the Czernowitz Conference of having put all its eggs in an empty basket, the Yiddish tongue.

Zhitlovsky pointed out that "content" and "form" could not be separated except in abstract thinking. Moreover, "content" and "form" were relative concepts. What was "form" in one context was "content" in another. There were times in the history of a people when it had to devote its energies to "form" in the political, economic, or social sphere.

> In the same way, among all peoples which live as minorities among others and which wish to maintain their national existence, public interest is concentrated on this very matter of national language-form. . . . Czernowitz demonstrated to the

39. Chaim Zhitlovsky, *Mayne Ani Mamins*, p. 397.

Jewish world that, for the Jewish minorities too, the time had
come to concentrate the interest of the Jewish public on
the question of which language-form was to be used for the
expression of the life and creativity of the Jewish cultural
sphere.[40]

Zhitlovsky also took pride in the fact that the Conference
had been imbued with a militant anti-assimilationist spirit.

The purpose of the Czernowitz Conference was the creation of
an international "spiritual-national home," in which all classes
and groups of the dispersed Jewish people could live; a spiritual-
national territory—"Yiddish-land" we call it today—whose
atmosphere consists of the fresh air of our folk language and
where with every breath and every word one helps maintain
the national existence of one's people.[41]

At the Conference, the strengths, weaknesses, and inner
conflicts of the emerging Yiddishist program were already
apparent in the differences between its leading architects and
spokesmen. The failure of the Conference to create an effective
organization was destined to reduce Yiddishism to the status of
an ideological trend rather than an activist movement. Nevertheless, the First Yiddish Language Conference may be credited
with putting Yiddishism on the map of Jewish history and
bringing it to the attention of world Jewry as both a serious
interpretation of modern Jewish life and a challenging alternative to other theories and programs.[42]

40. *Ibid.*, p. 402.
41. *Ibid.*, p. 403.
42. For an analysis of a negative Hebraist reaction to the Conference,
see G. Kresel, "Veidat Tshernovits Be-aspaklaryat (Zevi) Scharsfstein Hat-
sair," *Sefer Scharfstein*, ed. Z. Ravid (Tel Aviv, 1970). Recent Yiddishist
views are those of A. Zak, *Geven a Yidish Poyln* (Buenos Aires, 1968), pp.
210–16; H. S. Kazdan, "Tshernovits—Kholem un Vor," *Undzer Tsayt*
(New York, January 1969), pp. 17–21; J. Kisman in *Undzer Tsayt* (July-
August, 1958), pp. 8–13; Y. Mark in *Forverts* (New York, August 25, 1968);
M. Ravitch in *Tsum Yoyvl fun der Ershter Yidisher Shprakh Konferents*
(Montreal, 1958); E. Schulman in *Der Veker* (New York, September 1968);
M. Weichert in *Letste Nayes* (Tel Aviv, May 15, 1969); A. Glantz-Leyeles
in *Der Tog-Morgn Zhurnal* (New York, August 11, 1958).

Five Yiddish writers at the Czernowitz Conference (left to right: Abraham Reisen, Y. L. Peretz, Sholem Asch, Chaim Zhitlovsky, H. D. Nomberg).

9
AFTERMATH

AT THE TIME OF THE CZERNOWITZ CONFERENCE, NATHAN
Birnbaum settled in Czernowitz with the hope of shaping a
vibrant Jewish cultural life there. He felt that conditions in
Austria were ripe for the recognition of Yiddish as the basis and
recognizable sign of Jewish national autonomy.[1] He issued the
Yiddish journal *Dr. Birnbaum's Vokhnblat* and the German
publication *Das Volk*. He opened a Jewish bookstore and
founded a Yiddish theatrical union. He published theater
reviews and the plays *For the Sins of the Parents* and *I Am
Solomon*. The former was produced on the Yiddish stage in
1909 and the latter, in the author's own German translation, on
the German stage. Birnbaum also published many reviews of
Yiddish plays during this period.

In 1910, Birnbaum was active in the movement to have

1. Cf. S. Rozenhek, "Beyn Haketsavot," *Karmelit* nos. 6-7 (Haifa,
5720), p. 248 and S. Birnbaum, "Fun Mayn Foters Arkhiv," *Fun Noentn
Over* (Warsaw, April-June, 1938), pp. 157f.

Yiddish included in the Austrian census as one of the official languages of the Austrian empire. This was an important part of the struggle of Galician Jewry for national rights. Galician Bundists, Zionists, and Poaley Zionists cooperated in encouraging Jews to list Yiddish as their language of daily communication in the census, although the government regarded this as a criminal offense liable to punishment. In Czernowitz, Birnbaum led thousands of Jews in a march through the main streets of the city to the provincial government building, where a delegation of Bundists, Zionists, and Poaley Zionists presented a memorandum to the government on behalf of the entire Jewish population. However, the movement failed to convince the government that it should alter its policy. In Galicia, persons who registered Yiddish were added to those who listed Polish and, in Bukovina, to those who listed German as their tongue. In addition, they were fined or jailed. Although the entire movement miscarried and a serious blow was dealt to the struggle for Jewish national rights in Austria, this effort represented the first mass manifestation of Jewish national solidarity on behalf of Yiddish.[2]

In 1911 Birnbaum embarked on a lecture tour of the larger cities of Russia, Poland, and Lithuania, where he expounded his theories of *Golus* Nationalism, Yiddish, and Yiddish literature. All the while, as he later explained, his ideas were taking a new turn. He began to doubt his secular and materialistic world view and to appreciate the role of religion in human life. Following a lecture that he attended in St. Petersburg, he rose and in a passionate address gave voice to his newly acquired religious convictions. He moved his family to Berlin, which was rapidly becoming a meeting ground for Jewish intellectuals from Eastern and Western Europe, and began publishing articles on religious themes. His first address in Germany was a defense of the "Chosen People" doctrine of traditional Judaism, a theme to which he continually returned in his articles in the German

2. Cf. *Di Geshikhte fun Bund,* vol. 3 (New York, 1966), pp. 421–25 and O. Janowsky, *The Jews and Minority Rights* (New York, 1933), pp. 149–51.

monthly *Die Freistatt* and in his later publications in Yiddish and German. He also sought a synthesis between his former secular *Golus* Nationalism and his religious ideas.

In an article published in 1912, Birnbaum sought to defend Yiddish from the attacks of well-meaning, religious Jews who saw a conflict between the language and the "absolute idea" of Judaism. He felt that he was now qualified to do this because he was himself a "convinced believer." In the "absolute idea" of Judaism he also now perceived the source of the Jewish people's greatness.

Birnbaum developed the distinction he had made between "civilization" and "culture" in *Jewish Modernism* in 1897. "Culture," he now wrote, "is the unique process, the method of a people, by which it follows the path of general human civilization. There is no product of civilization which is unstamped by one or another culture, by the people which created it." Where the individual stamp was of little significance as in politics, economics, and science, one could speak of products of civilization. Where the individual stamp was of more significance, as in philosophy, art, and relgion, one referred to products of culture. On occasion a particular people chooses an aspect of civilization and so completely makes it its own and infuses it with its own individuality that it becomes identified with the people and in turn influences every aspect of its national life. It then becomes the essential content of the people's culture. Like the nineteenth-century Jewish philosopher of Galicia, Nahman Krochmal (1785–1840), Birnbaum believed that the Jewish people had made or was chosen to make the "absolute idea," rather than art or law, for example, its national cultural idea. The Jewish religion was the school that brought this idea to the people and thus taught it how to approach the absolute or God.

But the absolute idea of Judaism also possessed indirect means of influencing the Jewish people. It entered other aspects of the life of Jewry, its civilization and culture and even the "remotest corners" of its life.

It does not ask what forms these are and whence do they come. It does not declare : take this form and do not take that form. What is important to it is only to enter the forms which life —relative, provisional life—submits to it and breathe its soul into them.[3]

It was wrong to attack Yiddish from the standpoint of the "absolute idea" of Judaism, because the latter had no need of any particular language. What was necessary was only that the language the people used was its own or one that the absolute idea could transform into a language of the Jewish people. Foreign languages were unacceptable because they bound the people to foreign cultural forms and concepts.

Those who insisted on Hebrew rather than Yiddish, however, were not altogether wrong, said Birnbaum. In Hebrew the Jewish religion had organized and crystallized itself. Hebrew had "emerged from provisional life and entered eternal life." It had become a language that itself served the absolute Jewish idea in the synagogue and school. But Hebrew was not found everywhere in Jewish life. It was absent from the mouths of the people. Modern Hebrew literature was not associated with the absolute idea of Judaism. The spoken Hebrew of Palestine would only be another one of the spoken languages of Jewry. Modern Hebrew might eventually even become linguistically different from the Hebrew of the past.

Yiddish, Birnbaum insisted, had a unique function to perform on behalf of the absolute idea of Judaism as a living spoken language. The absolute idea of Judaism had certain tasks to fulfill in this language that were quite different from those it accomplished through Hebrew.

The Yiddish language plays a tremendous role in the working economy of the absolute Jewish idea. It has thus far had sufficient opportunities to prove how suited it is to this role. In Yiddish Jewish women for hundreds of years related their noblest and most beautiful feelings to God. In Yiddish they

3. N. Birnbaum, "Di Absolute Ideye fun Yidntum un di Yidishe Shprakh," *Di Yidishe Velt*, no. 1 (St. Petersburg, 1912), pp. 48–49.

hallowed Sabbaths and festivals. In a Yiddish translation God's Torah was transmitted from generation to generation. In Yiddish the rabbis preached and the Bar Mitzvah lads recited their discourses. In Yiddish were related all those tales and legends which are also associated with the service of the absolute Jewish idea. All of this can and will continue in Yiddish. But should our people merit that which so many Jews hope and wish for today—a new vibrant, creative religious epoch—then Yiddish will really be able to show forth its treasures and demonstrate the full range of religious emotion which it has gathered for hundreds of years. The absolute idea of Judaism will once again peacefully breathe its sanctity into the Yiddish language. And even Hebrew will not be angry but fulfill its eternal role as eternal witness to the eternity of our people.[4]

In 1914 Birnbaum could still write in *Die Freistatt* :

I have now cast off my former rationalism. But I should like to say that in these matters, too, all my expectations are pinned on the East European Jews and the living organism which they constitute, and that I have neither theoretically nor practically given up my aspirations regarding the national culture of East European Jewry, who in my view constitute the major and living exponent of the Jewish people. It is imperative that they should be preserved as a people. For although the Jewish people is a *God-ordained* people, it can never and must never be anything but a people.[5]

With the outbreak of the First World War, Birnbaum's three sons were drafted into the Austrian army. Two of them served on difficult battlefields and one lost a leg. These experiences seem to have intensified his religious convictions. He returned to Vienna with his wife and served as director of the newly established Jewish War Archives. He also published a pamphlet on behalf of Jewish cultural autonomy in Eastern Europe following the War (*Der Ostjuden ihr Recht!*, 1915).

Birnbaum now felt that Jewish religion and culture were

4. *Ibid.*, pp. 50–52.
5. Quoted in S. A. Birnbaum, "Nathan Birnbaum," *Men of the Spirit*, ed. L. Jung, p. 532.

both divine in origin and that one could not exist without the other.[6] He accepted the discipline of Jewish religious law in his personal life. His religious conversion now complete, he felt the need to rejuvenate Yiddish-speaking Jewry in the spirit of traditional Judaism. He spoke of a "spiritual ascent" spearheaded by a disciplined order of "Ascenders" or "guardians of the faith," which would constitute the spiritual authority of world Jewry. The "Ascenders" were to actively hasten the coming of the Messiah by establishing agricultural communities in which Jewish religion, language, and attire would be preserved and the threefold holiness of *Da'at* (understanding God in fervor and humility), *Rahamim* (performing deeds of mercy toward our fellowmen), and *Tiferet* (striving for beauty, purity and harmony) be attained. These ideas were set forth in *Divrey Ha-Olim,* which appeared in Hebrew and Yiddish editions (Vienna, 1917).

The following year, *Gottes Volk (God's People)*, which Birnbaum wrote in German, created a sensation. It was reprinted several times and a Yiddish edition appeared in 1921. In this work the full implications of Birnbaum's religious world view based on Jewish chosenness and Messianism are spelled out and he repudiates the "pagan-Jewish" elements, that is, the Jewish nationalists, with whom he had formerly been associated.

> What goes for the modern Jewish nationalists of Western Europe, also applies to their Eastern European fellows-in-arms. I must give [to] them even more credit than to the others. I respect the great Hebrew and Yiddish writers, who draw their power from the eternal fount of Jewish life, even though they do not share in its profound and fervent faith and great religious self-discipline. I also acknowledge that particularly the younger generation among them seeks the spiritual soul of the Jewish people; they have not fallen prey to the fallacy of those nationalists who are proud of the sacred Jewish past, but in effect, deny this past by excluding our spiritual traditions from their own picture of national life.

6. *Yubileum Bukh,* p. 16.

But, on the other hand, the nationalists of the Eastern European brand are even more dangerous than their more assimilated Western friends, because of the closer contact and greater influence upon the Yiddish-speaking religious masses. And I notice the same unhappy aberrations spreading among them which I spoke of before—all the more crudely and repulsively because their Eastern European devotees are quite new to them. I see them argue and debate in small and smaller parties and groups, all the more confused and narrow-minded the more radical and materialistic they are.

The traces of their pagan rebellion can be found not only in their manners but also in their goals and desires. Instead of penetrating to the core of the Jewish soul, they stick to petty and superficial features of it, and know nothing of the real holiness of Judaism. Their efforts for a national culture are based upon the time-bound ideas of our age, and not upon the eternal Jewish values. Their aspirations for national autonomy among the nations are governed by worldly desires, and in their struggle for the Yiddish language (however meritorious in itself) they do not consider this an expression of the spirit but a tool of the people, like any other language. Thus, I can only conclude that, no matter how successful they will be, they too are only pagan rebels in a Jewish garb.[7]

In 1919 the international organization of Orthodox Jews opposed to political Zionism (*Agudas Yisroel*), which had originally been formed in 1912, was reorganized. Birnbaum attended the founding conference of the organization in Zurich and became its first General Secretary. In 1920 and 1921 he traveled to Lithuania, England, and the United States on its behalf, warning Orthodox Jews of the perils of paganism and atheism and prodding them to become the leaders of Jewry. "Why have you let the reins out of your hands and given them to irresponsible people (*hefker-mentshn*)?" he asked. He warned them, however, against adopting the type of political activism favored by the Zionists and secularists. Such an approach, he felt, was inimical to the spirit of traditional Judaism.[8] Toward

7. N. Birnbaum, *Confession*, pp. 36, 37. See also A. Zeitlin, "Dr. Nathan Birnbaum un Zayn Veg fun Veltlekhkayt tsu Emune," *Der Tog* (New York, June 8, 1952).

8. *Yubileum Bukh*, p. 20.

the end of his life he advocated the vocational restratification of Jewry and the establishment of agricultural bases for the Jewish economy. He preached "religious territorialism" to his new Orthodox audiences, for whom he was the traditional penitent (baal-teshuvah).

Birnbaum's later writings include *Vom Freigeist zum Glaubigen* (1919), *Vor dem Wandersturm* (1920), *Um di Ewigkeit* (1920), *In Golus bay Yidn* (1920), *Im Dienste der Verheissung* (1927), *Rufe* (1936), and *Eys Lasoys* (1938). In 1911 he moved to The Hague-Scheveningen, where he published a journal, *Der Ruf* (1934-7).

In the course of a response to a request from the Yiddish Scientific Institute in Vienna to reevaluate the Czernowitz Conference on its twentieth anniversary, Birnbaum wrote the following:

> I am afraid that those workers set out on a false path. At the time of the conference I did not and could not see this. But today—because I have returned to the Jewish Torah and to those who do not abandon it—I see it and am worried. The radical parties have virtually monopolized the Yiddish language and in so doing have made it somewhat suspect among the masses of pious Jews, the first and true creators of Yiddish. They have also placed Yiddish in danger of losing its linguistic independence, its true Jewishness, its strong colors, and of becoming a gray shadow of itself, a kind of dry creation or just another European tongue.
>
> Would that this danger be overcome and Yiddish remain the Jewish treasure, for which purpose the calling of the Czernowitz conference was worthwhile.[9]

Two commemorative volumes, one in German and the other in Yiddish, were published in honor of Birnbaum's sixtieth birthday in 1925. While the first was limited to Orthodox contributors, the second contained contributions by representatives of all the factions in Jewish life with which Birnbaum had been associated during his long career.[10] He died on April 2, 1937.

9. *Di Ershte Yidishe Shprakh-Konferents* (Vilna, 1931), p. 11.
10. *Vom Sinn des Judentums,* ed. M. Landau and A. E. Kaplan, (Frank-

On October 2, 1908 the *Sotsyaldemokrat* of Cracow published Peretz's response to its request that he clarify his position on the Hebrew-Yiddish question.

Yiddish is not German. Jews do not know German and Germans do not know Yiddish. That Yiddish was once a form of German is of no account since it did not remain German. After the word "Taytsh" was changed to "Daytsh," the phrase "Vos Taytsh?" came to mean "How is it expressed more clearly?" or "What is its meaning?" and not "How is it said in German?" It became "Yiddish" because it is the vernacular of ninety per cent of the Jewish people. The people does not call it "Jargon."

But it is not a national language even today. A language is "national" if it is born and develops together with a people and possesses the treasury of its entire culture in all places and times. Abraham, Isaac, Jacob, the Prophets and the later classical writers did not know Yiddish. Our modern intellectuals have to use various national languages, our Yiddish intellectuals have to use Hebrew.

We actually conduct our life in three languages: the people —in Yiddish, the semi-assimilated intellectuals—in the languages of their countries, and the Jewish *intelligentsia* in the *former* national language of our past.

A nation must have a national language and it must be one, not two or three.

Which language should be our national language in the future? The languages of the various lands cannot become our national languages. For us they are anti-national. If we adopt the languages of the various lands, we sign our own horrible death sentence.

Shall our future language be Hebrew?

A language cannot be mechanically revived and I do not believe in dead languages for living peoples. One cannot go back to his cradle. What remains is Yiddish.

Without the language of the land we have little culture, without Hebrew the people has no past, without Yiddish we have no people. . . .

fort M., 1925) and *Yubileum Bukh* (Warsaw, 1925). See also S. A. Birnbaum, "Fun Mayn Foters Arkhiv," *Fun Noentn Over* (Warsaw, April-June 1938); S. Bickel, *Detaln un Sakhaklen* (New York, 1943), pp. 169–74; S. Gorelick, *Eseyen* (Los Angeles, 1947), pp. 265–72; J. Kisman, "Dr. Nathan Birnbaum—Zayne Gaystike Zukhenishn un Vandlungen," *Di Tsukunft* (New York, September, 1962), pp. 319–27; and N. Mayzel, *Noente un Eygene* (New York, 1957), pp. 53–62.

The folk language must therefore become a national language. As many cultural treasures must be created in it as are necessary to enable the cultured Jew to live his life in Yiddish. And as many cultural treasures of our past must be brought into it as are necessary to make it the language of the entire culture of the Jewish nation everywhere and at all times. The path to the free, unified, inter-territorial Jewish nation is from folk language to national language. We will consider all other living languages either friendly or alien. Hebrew will be our revered language of the past, our "sacred tongue." It is a long and difficult path but the only one possible.

Cracow, September 22.

Y. L. Peretz[11]

Peretz clarified his position even further in an article entitled "Hebrew and Yiddish," which he published in his own short-lived weekly, *Di Yidishe Vokhnshrift*, a few months later (January 28, 1909). He believed that as the language of the Bible, Hebrew was and would continue to remain sacred. Every Jew who was able to do so had the duty of acquainting himself with the Bible in its original tongue. Although a Yiddish translation would be closer to the original than translations into other languages, perfume could not be transferred from one container to another without damage. The spirit of a work of art was lost even in the best of translations. In addition, Hebrew seemed to have a magical effect on the Jewish spirit.

Its exalted, winged words; its pure metallic ring, its sculpture-like forms—all of this, illumined with the golden reflections of a proud past, is an eternal enchantment which is incomprehensible to those who have forgotten or never known the tongue of the Bible.

Nevertheless, to ask Jews to live their lives in the language of the Bible was like asking them to become color blind and tone deaf, to impoverish themselves and live on atavistic feelings alone. They would have to renounce seven hundred years of

11. *Di Ershte* . . . , pp. 133f.

Jewish culture and create what would be tantamount to a new "jargon" far removed from the Bible. In trying to modernize Hebrew, they would also become guilty of desecrating something truly sacred.

The contemporary cultural instrument of the Jewish people was that which it referred to as "Yiddish."

> The people could not call it anything else. It is their own language in which their entire life is lived. It is a language which they assimilated, altering form and structure, pouring into it their entire spirit, their sorrow and anger, their longing, hope and prayer.
>
> The people took a strange branch but implanted it within their own heart and watered it with blood. . . . And it sprouted and bloomed into—"Yiddish."

Yiddish was ugly only to those for whom Jewish life was ugly and a "jargon" only to those, estranged from their people, who could not speak it or write it. Where Hebrew bound Jews to the past, Yiddish united them in the present. Without Yiddish, there could be no Jewish life. With the disappearance of Yiddish the assimilationist dream would come true and only "Communities of the Mosaic Confession" survive. Once again Peretz addressed the intellectuals. If they wished to remain Jews and influence their people, they would have to address it in its own living language.[12]

The last public statements that Peretz made concerning the language question are part of an address that he delivered at a banquet in Vilna in 1912. When the leader of their movement was introduced in Hebrew by the toastmaster, the Yiddishist elements in the audience felt insulted. Peretz is reputed to have stated that

> Hebrew is ours. The soul of Yiddish is its Hebrew content. But I would not speak in Hebrew at a meeting where the majority will not understand me.[13]

12. *Ibid.*, pp. 286–88.
13. S. Niger, *Y. L. Peretz*, p. 398.

In the course of his address, Peretz compared Hebrew and Yiddish to two rivers flowing together. In spite of the turbulence at the point of commingling, they eventually flow together peacefully and are united as one.[14]

During the last several years before his death in 1915, Peretz was intensely involved in a variety of literary and general cultural projects. The upsurge of Polish anti-Semitism before the First World War also brought him into the political struggle for Jewish rights. In numerous articles he attacked both Polish anti-Semites and Jewish assimilationists. He helped organize assistance for Jewish refugees when the war broke out and established the first kindergarten for refugee children in Warsaw. From Yiddish writers he increasingly demanded a return to Jewish authenticity and Jewish tradition. Disillusioned by liberalism, democracy, and the general turn of events, Peretz urged a return to Jewish sources and the millennial aspirations of the Jewish people. The slogans of Czernowitz, he felt, had not been realized. Yiddish writers had not succeeded in bringing the great works of the Jewish tradition into Yiddish and were merely engaged in aping European models. They had failed to reflect the true spirit of the Jewish people throughout the world and down through the ages.

Peretz apparently arrived at a new stage in his developing conception of the role of Yiddish and Yiddish literature toward the end of his life. Although he began his career with a view of Yiddish as a means of spreading education and worldliness among Jews and gradually came to view Yiddish literature as an end in itself, he now saw the primary task of Yiddish as the preservation and development of the historic religio-ethical values of Judaism. Without succumbing to the dictates of Orthodoxy, it was necessary and possible, he believed, for Jewry to reassert its spiritual tradition. This was now to be the mission of the Yiddish writer.[15]

14. *Ibid.*, and S. Rozenhek, "Beyn Haketzavot," p. 250.
15. Cf. Z. Kalmanovitch, "Y. L. Peretz' Kuk af der Yidisher Literatur," *Di Goldene Keyt,* no. 2 (Tel Aviv, 1949), pp. 114–26.

Peretz's call to tradition was probably the result of his frustration with the Jewish situation in Russia and Poland shortly before his death. When all hope for Jewish autonomous existence in Eastern Europe on the basis of the Yiddish language foundered on the rocks of nationalism and anti-Semitism, Peretz called for a "return to the synagogue" as the only hope for Jewish survival in Eastern Europe.[16]

> I am talking to those who struggle to secure cultural rights, the right to create Jewish cultural values—it is not enough to talk Yiddish. You must have something to say!
>
> If you have nothing to say, you may talk Yiddish from the cradle to the grave, you may talk it everywhere, at home, in the street, in the synagogue during the Reading of the Law, in the Philharmonia, in the middle of a concert, in the theater, at the opera—what you say will not be Jewish, because it will not mean anything real, it will be an imitation, dead.
>
> We stand firm like a wall for Yiddish! We are ready to give our lives for Yiddish! Yet before our eyes the Jewish content, what is essentially Jewish disappears, the Jewish soul dies. We are flooded with plagiarisms, with substitutes, with spurious goals and false trademarks.
>
> And people are happy about it—they say it's European. Where is the original, the distinctively, genuinely Jewish? . . .
>
> Creation is the elevation of the soul. Only the Jewish soul can be the Jewish writer's *Shekinah,* his holy spirit, his one inspiration and creative force. It must be the eye in his head, with which he sees the world, its past, present and future. He must live and die for the Jewish soul, for the Jewish spirit.[17]

Whatever its source, however, Peretz's final message to Yiddish literature and to the Yiddishists had a profound effect. It added a new spiritual dimension to the Yiddish cultural movement and, because it was taken seriously by many writers, made Yiddish literature an even more significant aspect of Jewish culture generally.

16. Cf. M. Klaynman, *Demuyot Vekomot* (Paris, 1925), pp. 201–2.
17. Y. L. Pertez, "What Is Missing in Our Literature?" *The Way We Think,* ed. J Leftwich, 2:33, 35.

Matisyohu Mieses's polemic with Ahad Haam, "On the
Question of the Yiddish Language," published in *Heatid* in
1910, may be considered an important result of the Czernowitz
Conference. The proclamation of Yiddish as "a national language of the Jewish people" marked a new stage in the development of Ahad Haam's attitude toward the language. Although
he had no faith in the future of Yiddish, the philosopher of
cultural Zionism had been instrumental in the establishment of
the first Yiddish literary weekly, *Der Yid*, in 1898, and in the
appointment of Y. Ravnitsky, a distinguished scholar and author,
as its editor. Ahad Haam saw the Czernowitz Conference, which
he referred to mockingly as a "Purim-shpil," as an act of
betrayal against Hebrew. With the decline of religion, Hebrew
was one of the few remaining pillars of Jewish survival. He
declared open war against Yiddish after the Conference, utiliz-
ing every opportunity to show that it was no more than a
palliative and a temporary phenomenon.[18]

In 1910 Ahad Haam published an essay entitled "The
Language Controversy" in the Hebrew journal *Hashiloah*. In
this essay he defined the concept "national language" and maintained that Yiddish had no greater hold on the Jewish people
than any of the other Diaspora languages it had created during
the centuries of exile.[19]

> A national language does not mean the language spoken by the
> masses. . . . It is an essential requisite of a national language
> that it be not merely a "mother tongue," but the vehicle of
> the national self-expression in successive ages. . . . However
> unorthodox it may be, I feel bound to say frankly that for me
> Yiddish holds no terrors. By all means let good books be written
> in Yiddish for the better education of the masses. No national
> literature will be produced in Yiddish. Anything that may be
> worth preserving will be preserved in Hebrew translation, as
> has happened with Jewish literature written in Arabic and
> other languages; the rest will all disappear completely with

18. Cf. Z. Zilbercweig, *Ahad Haam un Zayn Batsiung Tsu Yidish* (Los
Angeles, 1956), p. 6.
19. Cf. L. Simon, *Ahad Haam:Asher Ginzberg, A Biography*, p. 238.

the disappearance of Yiddish itself. Can anybody doubt that Yiddish will be forgotten in two or three generations? Whether we like it or not, we cannot change the course of events. What language we speak is determined by the requirements of our daily life; and if conditions are such that we have to speak some other language, Yiddish is doomed, and no amount of propaganda will save it. And when it ceases to be a language of speech, it cannot survive for a moment as a literary vehicle, as Hebrew has survived these two thousand years. Not a single Jew will regard it as a national duty to learn Yiddish or to teach it to his children; whereas there always have been and always will be Jews who recognize this obligation to our real national language.[20]

Mieses opened his response to Aham Haam's essay with an attack against the latter's definition of the concept of a "national language."

Until now, we knew that every people strives to express its thoughts and feelings in its own mother-tongue. We considered this striving just and suited to the laws of cultural development. But a new doctrine has reached our ears. Ahad Haam proclaims it. A mother-tongue is not the national language of a people. We were all mistaken, decides Ahad Haam with absolute certainty. In order for its language to be exalted to the status of a national language, it is not enough for a people to have a mother-tongue. That tongue must also contain "the spiritual treasury of the nation for many generations."[21]

Mieses set out to prove that there were a number of mother tongues which, although not encompassing the literary treasures of their respective peoples, were nevertheless recognized as national languages. Among the examples he cited were the Norwegians, who created a national language out of their mother tongue despite the fact that their cultural heritage was in the Finnish language. The Lithuanians, too, viewed their Lithuanian mother tongue as their national language rather than Polish in which their leading authors wrote. The

20. Ahad Haam, *Essays, Letters, Memoirs* (London, 1946), pp. 228f.
21. M. Mieses, "Lishelat Halashon Hayehudit," *Heatid* (1910), p. 209.

Ruthenians, whose spiritual heritage was recorded in Russian, refused to acknowledge that their own mother tongue was a dialect and insisted on viewing it as their national language instead of Russian. After discussing several additional examples that supported his thesis, Mieses drew the conclusions that,

> What is decisive here is not what this language has garnered of a people's spirit in the past, but what it can garner in the present and the future. He who deals only with the past addresses himself to a museum of antiquities. The people which senses that its literary tongue has become estranged and too removed from the living language; which realizes that its literary tongue is incapable of fulfilling all of its spiritual needs naturally, is compelled to turn its back on this literary tongue and elevate its living spoken language with its beating pulse to the level of a new literary tongue. (p. 210)

Mieses used the Romance languages, Palestinian Aramaic, and some of the languages of India to illustrate the point that "every linguistic period begins primarily with a folk language abolishing a literary language and taking its place" (p. 210).

> The literary language must derive all its strength from the living language of the people. The entire people must feel that the literary language gives complete expression to the soul of the people. (p. 211)

Mieses offered a large number of illustrations from European linguistics to show that a point is reached in the history of language when the spoken language and the literary language part. The literary language then ceases to draw sustenance from the spoken language and becomes artificial. The spoken language then takes the place of the literary language even when the spoken language is no more than a dialect of the literary language, when etymologically and grammatically the two languages are very close. This is even more true in the case of Yiddish, which "a mighty philological abyss separates from the Hebrew language and whose relationship to our literary language cannot be compared to that of any dialect to its official language" (p. 211).

Mieses took Ahad Haam to task for suggesting that the relationship of Yiddish to Hebrew was that of a dialect to an independent language. Yiddish, he maintained, was never a dialect of Hebrew. Although it was once a German dialect (*Taytsh*), the Jewish people reworked it, digested it, and adjusted it to its own spirit. It brought its own folklore into it, and created a unique world of feelings and logical associations in it, so that the dialect became its own language and was given the new name "Yiddish."

> A language of this kind cannot be considered a "dialect" today. It has become an independent, autonomous tongue. The Yiddish language is our language, the language of our people. This is the first time since the people ceased speaking Hebrew that it proclaimed any language it accepted as "Jewish." Neither Aramaic, Alexandrian Greek, Ladino, or any other language accepted by the dispersed of our people was crowned with this honorable designation. (p. 212)

According to Mieses, Ahad Haam was wrong when he said that "even women and ignoramuses knew that this language was not the national language." Although Yiddish was not the sacred tongue for them, they nevertheless considered it their mother tongue, part and parcel of themselves. Jews of previous generations never scolded their children for speaking "Jewish" as they did when they found them speaking "Gentile." The average Jew was neither philosopher nor philologist, but he felt that the language he called "Yiddish" was his language and his treasure. He felt the need to preserve it from disappearing. Yiddish did not have to be "restored to its throne," as Ahad Haam would have had it, because, said Mieses, it achieved its own greatness by means of the labor of the generations contained within it. Attesting to this fact were Yiddish folk poetry, which could not be dismissed so lightly, original riddles, idioms, and Hebrew grammatical rules. (Here Mieses referred the reader to his previous article in *Haolam*.)

Mieses asked his readers to consider Yiddish a "small

sanctuary," which came into being under conditions unique in
the history of the Jewish Diaspora. The major part of Jewry
had lived in one country, where it pursued a segregated existence. Nothing of significance interfered with the internal evolution of Polish Jewry during that period. Out of the Jewish
refugees of various lands a new type emerged, marked more
strongly than the Jews of the East (Sephardim and Jews in
Arab lands) by profound Jewish national characteristics. Along
with the Polish Jew, his language had emerged. The destiny of
the language was linked to the destiny of the Polish-Jewish type.
"As the Jew gradually loses his national characteristics and
consciously or unconsciously assimilates, resembling the gentile
mentally and spiritually, his language retreats before the language of the gentile which replaces it" (p. 212).

Mieses agreed with Ahad Haam that Yiddish was destined
to be forgotten. Indeed, it was already being forgotten. But
along with it, said Mieses, all of Judaism was gradually being
forgotten! As Mieses saw it, the major question before Jewry
was: Given the secular life in which Jews now found themselves, what could preserve their national essence? Mieses dismissed religion as a potent factor against assimilation and pointed
to the Orthodox Jews of Frankfurt as evidence of the fact that
religion could not stem assimilationist trends. He described
Hebrew as being unable to descend from its throne to dwell in
the streets of the ghetto and strengthen the people's sense of its
identity. "Of such a possibility no one can dream." (The editor
of *Heatid* politely added a question-mark to this statement by
Mieses. He apparently felt that it had to be countered or denied
immediately (p. 213).)

Mieses feared the disappearance of Jewish national identity.

For the time being our eyes behold a magnificent sight in the
midst of the Jewish people: From Riga to Bucharest, from
Odessa to Pest and to Cracow they all speak one language. The
remnant of our nationhood has not ceased. Will what is left
of these communities be able to maintain their traditional
culture after Yiddish which unifies them is no more? (p. 213)

Mieses predicted that the ranks of the Hebraists who declared war on Yiddish would be diminished and pass away as Yiddish declined. Everywhere only those who knew Yiddish also knew Hebrew. In Germany, he pointed out, the demise of Yiddish brought with it the disappearance of Hebrew.

> Yiddish is the bridge which unites us with Hebrew. It is the dam and wall protecting Hebrew from the waves of assimilation. Yiddish does not fight against Hebrew. A notion as strange as that is the product of the imagination. There is no language controversy among us at all. The Yiddish language is fighting, wrestling, struggling—but only with the alien tongues, and to our sorrow the hands grow weak, the knees totter, courage flags. . . . The languages of the peoples in whose midst we dwell utter forth a shout of victory. The foundations of the Yiddish language shake, but—let those who curse Yiddish remember this!—when the foundations give way, the destructive winds will penetrate the sanctuaries of the Hebraists. It will not be long before even ruins cease to mark our nationalism which will have passed away. The sword which devours the life of the Yiddish language is not drawn against it alone. It hovers over all our national existence. Our entire national essence is in danger. (p. 213)

Mieses asked the Hebraists, whom he considered the leaders of the nation, to ponder the situation and reconsider their position vis-à-vis Yiddish. For their struggle against Yiddish, he felt, supplied those who sought the destruction of all that was Jewish with a sword with which to accomplish their aims.

Ahad Haam, said Mieses, responds to his own question, "What will become of us?" by positing the existence of a national will to live that would eventually discover an answer to the question. Mieses addressed himself to what he called Ahad Haam's metaphysics in the latter's famous phrase, "This is not the way!" He directed these words to the Hebraists who had taken a great responsibility upon themselves in their struggle with the "Jargonists" and who, he said, might be castigated by future generations for their impetuousness.

With Herzl's famous words, "If you will it, it is no dream,"

Mieses told his readers that, were its importance recognized, Yiddish might play a role not unlike that of Aramaic in the Hellenistic period. Yiddish had an important function to perform in the life of the people despite those who were unable to forget its date and place of origin. The Jewish people, he said, had the same right to speak a German-derived language that the Gauls and Franks had to speak a Latin-derived language. What was significant, he said once again, was the powerful individuality that left its mark upon the language. The spiritual configuration of Yiddish was a positive asset. Ahad Haam, he said, had compared Yiddish to the pauper who equaled the wealthy in what they lacked but not in what they possessed.

> But Yiddish has as much of a literature as do the Rumanians and Bulgarians and we have no less a national right to Yiddish than those peoples have to their languages. . . . In addition, we possess a past which we are not relinquishing. We cannot even imagine tearing the thread which ties us to the periods which precede Yiddish for Yiddish is dependent upon those earlier periods and it bears the spiritual stamp of Hebrew. (p. 214)

Yiddish and the Romance languages resembled each other not only for the negative reason of their derived status. The relationship between the Romance languages and Latin was similar to that between Yiddish and German in a positive sense. There were similar ties between the languages in terms of development, grammar, and phonetics. Some of these similarities were discussed by Mieses in detail.

Mieses also dealt with the contention that because of Yiddish the Jews were a laughingstock to their neighbors. Since the non-Jews recognized the corruption of their own language in Yiddish, ran the argument, they saw it as a sign of the degeneration and corruption of the Jews.

> To this we reply : We are not frightened by the arguments of the gentiles. Like them, we too have conferred of our spirit on the borrowed language and, like them, we have a national right to it. The spirit which we have conferred upon the Yiddish language is a real thing, a positive matter. (p. 215)

The non-Jews were not such purists as the detractors of Yiddish maintained. Mieses mentioned that plays by Asch and Jacob Gordin had been presented on the stages of Europe with success. No one took offense at the fact that they had originally been written in Yiddish. Mieses drew the conclusion that if the works of Yiddish literature were original and profound enough, the nations would be compelled to admit the national individuality of Jewry.

Ahad Haam had warned that because of Yiddish, the nations might deny the Jews their national rights. Was that any reason for Jews to surrender their language? asked Mieses. Should they forfeit Yiddish and stand unprotected before assimilation for a pottage of lentils and mere promises?

> To alter our language and dance to the tune called by the non-Jews while they toss us a few crumbs would be a national disgrace, a double servitude, a national decline unbefitting even for gypsies. . . . Ahad Haam would have us renounce our language so that we may be considered a nation and acquire national rights. If Yiddish disappears we will cease to be a nation and there will be no one to whom to give national rights. . . . We will constitute a Synagogue, a semi-religious community without color and an identifiable life, a disintegrating community or perhaps even less. (p. 216)

Mieses urged his readers to disregard anti-Semitic arguments. As he saw it, the attitude of the Hebraists to Yiddish was a result of the influence of anti-Semitism. German anti-Semites were opposed to Yiddish because of its Jewish elements. But surely there was no reason for Jews to disparage it.

> May a spark of pride be awakened in the heart of the eternal people! Let us not destroy the values of our people in order to afford pleasure to our neighbors. The eternal people whose essence is "absolute justice" must not forfeit its national possessions because of the unjust demands of others. (p. 216)

With his polemic against Ahad Haam, Mieses apparently ceased writing apologetics on behalf of Yiddish. He did not play any official role in the Yiddish cultural movement, although his achievements in the field of Yiddish linguistics are considerable. He did scientific work in Hebrew, German, Polish, and Yiddish, but he went almost completely unnoticed in the Yiddishist circles.

In 1915 Mieses published *Die Entstenhungsursache der Juedischen Dialekte (The Reason for the Development of the Jewish Dialects)*, in which he sought to account for the emergence of the Diaspora tongues. Mieses held that neither oppression, racial characteristics, nor economic conditions could account for the emergence of those tongues. The Diaspora tongues, he believed, had come into being because of the fact that the Jews possessed a religion of their own. The Jewish languages had developed because Jews had possessed a different faith from the peoples from whom they took the languages. Mieses also believed that those languages, and especially Yiddish, could emancipate themselves from their religious overseers. The work is important primarily because of the large amount of material that Mieses collected.[22]

Mieses developed these ideas further in *Die Gesetze der Schriftgeschichte (The Laws of the History of Script* [Vienna-Leipzig, 1919]). In this work he dealt with the relationship between religion and written language in general and with Yiddish script in particular.

Mieses's principal work in the field of Yiddish linguistics was *Die Jiddische Sprache,* a historical grammar of the Yiddish language (Berlin-Vienna, 1924). It is one of the most important studies of the Yiddish language, with material on phonetics, grammar, vocabulary, and borrowings from Yiddish in other languages. It also deals with the derivation and spread of the Yiddish language and its relationship to the various dialectical groups of German.[23]

Mieses's concern with religion, which suffused all of his

22. Cf. M. Weinreich, *Shtaplen: Fir Etyudn tsu der Yidisher Shprakh-Visnshaft un Literatur-Geshikhte* (Berlin, 1923), p. 10.
23. Cf. Z. Reisen, *Leksikon fun der Yidisher Literatur,* pp. 377–78.

work on the Yiddish language, eventually became his major interest. He was preparing an encyclopedic work on comparative religion, of which more than ten volumes were ready for publication at the time of his death, while enroute to Auschwitz in 1945.[24]

During the years immediately following the First Yiddish Language Conference and, for that matter, for the rest of his long life, Zhitlovsky labored assiduously on behalf of the prestige and development of Yiddish. His arguments on behalf of the language, however, became more and more dogmatic. He tended to consider Jews who knew no Yiddish as not belonging to his "Yiddishistic" nation.[25]

In the introduction to his work *Philosophy: What It Is and How It Developed* (New York, 1910), he expressed the hope "that this first philosophical work in Yiddish which is now being published will help create an intelligentsia that writes and thinks in Yiddish and which occupies itself seriously with philosophical problems."[26]

In 1911, Zhitlovsky published two essays in which he elaborated his Yiddishist theories. In "Yiddish and Hebrew," he wrote that if membership in the Jewish people was to be as "natural and voluntary" as that in any other nation, there had to be a common cultural atmosphere in which all kinds of thinking, both secular and religious, could be included. Such an atmosphere could be provided by a culture in a common language. "Language is that cohesive power which makes of an individual person a uniform organism and clearly delineates his independence and uniqueness for the surrounding world."[27] Any language could serve that purpose but only Hebrew, Yiddish, and Ladino could aid the Jewish people in its struggle for existence. Since the Hebraists had raised the cry "One people—

24. G. Kresel, *Leksikon Hasifrut Haivrit Badorot Haaharonim*, 2 : 344.
25. Cf. M. Epstein, *Profiles of Eleven*, p. 312.
26. *Zhitlovsky Zamlbukh*, p. 235.
27. C. Zhitlovsky, *Gezamlte Verk*, 4 : 128.

one language," Zhitlovsky felt it his duty to put forth the reasons why that language should be Yiddish.

All languages were originally "jargons," according to Zhit-lovsky, and if the term was meant to imply that Yiddish was a young language, there could be no objection to it. But what was permissible in linguistics could not be tolerated in the political arena. Yiddish could not be held responsible for the fact that other Germanic languages still existed and made it relatively easy to determine her origins. For political scientists and sociologists, languages were simply sums of words in which groups expressed themselves. If a group found its sum of words sufficient for that purpose, it automatically lifted its "jargon" to the status of a language.

> The future development of our Jewish people has become so closely intertwined with the development of our Yiddish language that if the Hebraists do not want to be left alone out in the open they will be compelled to turn to the people in its language, to propagandize their anti-Yiddishist thoughts in Yiddish. No matter how much poison there is in the content of their propaganda, the Yiddish form of their speech will make the Balaams bless where they would curse. With every new sum of Yiddish speech which they pour into the people's conscious-ness they will involuntarily enrich the aspiring stream of Yiddish.[28]

Yiddish was still in a developmental stage, as the large number of Yiddish dialects and the unsettled nature of its grammar demonstrated. But in spite of this it was unhampered in its ability to serve the people. The claim that Yiddish was ugly was due to subjective considerations and the idea that it was an impoverished language was not important because literature and life were constantly enriching it. To the argument that Yiddish was an alien tongue, Zhitlovsky responded that in the consciousness of the people Yiddish was unlike any other language ever spoken by Jews and was not regarded as alien. Although Yiddish was not spoken by all Jews, it was spoken by

28. *Ibid.*, p. 136.

the overwhelming majority and was therefore more suited to become the one language of Jewry than Hebrew. The claim that Yiddish was disappearing was absurd in the mouths of Hebraists, whose language had completely disappeared. Yiddish was struggling for survival where Hebrew was already dead. It was more feasible to heal a living language than play the part of God and revive a dead one.

> Yiddish is like a young forest growing on an oasis in the desert. Sandstorms cover parts of it and choke the young plants. Native and foreign Bedouins intentionally uproot whole sections. But the part of the forest that remains grows, spreads and strikes deep roots in the soil. Hebrew, however, is philologically a cemetery. Life may no longer be expected of it.

Since religion was no longer compulsory, the Jewish people would eventually have to stress the language factor the way other nations did. It would recognize in Yiddish "the cement which could unite its separate parts into a uniform organism." There was therefore every reason to expect that Yiddish would not disappear.[29]

Assimilationism had become a reactionary force in Jewish life, according to Zhitlovsky, and only Jewish nationalism was truly progressive. He now considered himself a Zionist but disapproved of Zionism's pinning all its hopes on revolutionary changes instead of dealing with evolutionary developments and the Jewish people's capacity for life. "The Yiddish language, Yiddish literature and the Yiddish spiritual atmosphere constitute an antibody which the folk organism is now emitting and developing on its own more and more in order to paralyze the poison of *Golus*."[30] Hebrew, like the Jewish religion, was hampered in its ability to serve as a survival factor in Jewish life because learning it required a prior belief or commitment. Yiddish, on the other hand, reached the masses unconsciously.

The Yiddish cultural world was achieving the self-conscious-

29. *Ibid.*, pp. 148–49
30. *Ibid.*, p. 154.

ness necessary to its furtherance and Zhitlovsky was confident of its future. He suggested that in Palestine Yiddish as well as Hebrew be permitted to flourish. There was no need for a war between the two languages, but if Hebrew sought to restrict Yiddish in any way, a war would inevitably result and in time of war, concluded Zhitlovsky, the rules of war are followed.

In "Yiddish Culture and the Yiddish Language," Zhitlovsky admitted that the theoretical bickering between Yiddishists and Hebraists was of little avail to either side. Practically speaking, however, the Yiddishists had every reason to be optimistic. They had the upper hand because even the Hebraists, if they desired to reach the masses, had to use Yiddish. Moreover, they were compelled to fight for Yiddish and treat it as the national language of Jewry whenever they fought for national rights for their people. The Yiddishists, on the other hand, were able to dispense with Hebrew and merely recognize its pedagogic, aesthetic, and philological value.

But new enemies of Yiddish had arisen in those Jews who championed Jewish cultural creativity in the languages of their respective countries. According to their view, language was only the means, and content the true end of the national culture of any people. Zhitlovsky pointed out, however, that as long as talented Jews continued to produce their works in non-Jewish languages, their works would be attributed to other peoples. The Jewish people would then continue to be considered impoverished by other nations no matter how many geniuses it produced. The struggle for the development of Yiddish was therefore "the struggle for a normal, free, comprehensive, rich and fertile culture of the Jewish people; the struggle for its life and development, for its respect and value."[31]

In 1912 the twenty-fifth anniversary of Zhitlovsky's literary activity was celebrated and a committee was formed to help publish his *Collected Works* in ten volumes (New York, 1912–1919). During this period he was active in a large number of American Jewish organizations of both a political and cultural

31. *Ibid.*, p. 183.

character, including the Socialist-Territorialist party, the Labor Zionist party, the Workmen's Circle, and the Jewish National Worker's Alliance (Farband).

Zhitlovsky also headed a group known as "Serp," which combined some of the ideas of the Bundists with those of the Territorialists. It sought Jewish cultural autonomy everywhere and political autonomy wherever Jews lived in compact masses. In 1908 and 1909 conferences were held to unite the Labor Zionists, the Territorialists, and the "Serpists" into one larger party. The merger took place in Chicago in September 1909. There were a number of heated arguments during these conferences between Zhitlovsky, the Yiddishist, and Nachman Syrkin, the Hebraist, who headed the Socialist-Territorialist movement. Zhitlovsky got the new party to engage in work in the Diaspora and to conduct its cultural activities in Yiddish and Hebrew. He prepared the way for the eventual establishment of the "national radical" supplementary schools for Jewish children in the United States sponsored by the Labor Zionist movement. When this idea finally took hold, it was duplicated by the Workmen's Circle and other organizations, and a secular Yiddishist school system developed in the United States and Canada.[32]

In 1914, Zhitlovsky visited Palestine but was forbidden by militant Hebraists to deliver his lectures in Yiddish. He became a regular contributor to the New York Yiddish Daily *Der Tog* in 1914 and played a significant role in the formation of the American Jewish Congress in 1915. He traveled to Western Europe on a lecture tour in 1913 and to Eastern Europe in 1924. In 1925, his sixtieth birthday was celebrated by his followers everywhere and a number of publications were issued in his honor.

In 1925 Zhitlovsky's colleagues, friends, and disciples issued a special volume on the occasion of his sixtieth birthday and in 1929 and 1930 he toured Poland, Lithuania, Latvia, and other

---

32. Cf. M. Brown, *Mit Yidishe Oygn,* pp. 253–55.

European countries. In an address devoted to the language question, delivered in Kovno on October 27, 1930, Zhitlovsky explained that his opinion on this question was based on his concept of progress, the striving for maximum happiness for the maximum number of people. That concept consisted of four basic principles: the principle of personal freedom and fulfillment, the principle of cultural enrichment, the principle of social justice or equality, and the principle of international brotherhood or equal rights for nations. It was the task of progressive parties of all nations to fight for these principles. The progressive parties of oppressed peoples had the additional obligation of fighting for the national freedom of their peoples.

It was the principle of cultural enrichment that was of greatest importance for the national question. Cultural creativity resulted from contacts between various cultures, and for that reason the idea of cosmopolitanism was false. A nation is a living organism, the purpose of which is the creation of culture. Progressive parties are responsible for seeing to it that such cultural creativity takes place by ensuring the security of their nations in their national homes. Such homes were either physical or, as in the case of the Jewish people, spiritual and portable.

In the past, the spiritual home of the Jewish people was its religion, and for that reason language was considered of no importance. But since the basis of Jewish life had become secularized, language had become most significant. Without it, Jewish cultural creativity, contact with other cultures, and progress were unattainable.

The former Hebrew-Yiddish bilingualism of Jewish culture was precluded by the secularization of Jewish life and modern conditions. The Jewish people had to choose between Hebrew and Yiddish. In the past, Hebrew had been the language of the Jew's written culture and Yiddish of his oral culture. The essence of the relationship between the two languages was expressed in the proverb "He who knows no Hebrew is an ignoramus, he who knows no Yiddish is a gentile."

Since Hebrew had been the language of the intellectuals and

Yiddish that of the masses, a gulf had existed between the two groups that was no longer feasible. The Hebraists and Yiddishist camps each had its own answer as to how to overcome it. Both Hebraism and Yiddishism were revolutionary and sought to eradicate bilingualism from Jewish culture. Like all revolutionary movements, both required sacrifices. Both had to struggle against assimilation. Moreover, only one million of the sixteen million Jews in the world spoke Hebrew and the majority of Jews had a psychological stumbling block with regard to Yiddish. The Jewish middle classes were psychologically opposed to Yiddish. Among all nations, the middle classes always followed the educated class and the aristocracy.

The Hebraists claimed that Hebrew would enhance Jewish life culturally and aesthetically because of its rich literary treasures. But was that any reason to require that all Jews speak Hebrew? Jews were well acquainted with Hebrew literature in the past although they did not speak the language. Zhitlovsky discredited the Hebraists' counterclaims that Yiddish was only a "jargon," that it was culturally impoverished, and that it was an alien tongue. A language became a people's own when that people loved it and invested it with their spirit. The Yiddish revolution would be much more easily accomplished than the Hebrew because ten million Jews spoke it; others spoke Germanic languages and would be able to learn Yiddish without too much effort. The Hebraist contention that not all Jews spoke Yiddish therefore carried no weight.

The Hebrew poet Bialik, who also wrote poetry in Yiddish, had predicted the demise of Yiddish on the basis of his reading of Jewish history. All the languages other than Hebrew that Jews had spoken eventually disappeared from Jewish life. No lessons could be drawn from the past, argued Zhitlovsky, because conditions had become so radically altered. Language had been a relatively insignificant factor in Jewish life in the past due to the pervasiveness of religion. But secularization had changed that. In addition, no other languages had been given the name "Jewish," a name conferred upon Yiddish by the people themselves and not by the Yiddishists as their Hebraist opponents sometimes contended.

Zhitlovsky reminded Bialik that in the past the masses had usually played an insignificant cultural role. Yiddish culture, however, was the product of the cultural awakening of the Jewish masses and of the principles of democracy and progress. Hebraism would lead to the adoption of the languages of their countries by all those Jews who did not go to Palestine. Hebrew might serve as a counterweight to assimilation but only Yiddish could be an antitoxin. It was only with Yiddish that the Jewish people could fight for minority rights and thus contribute to human progress. Hebraism was a block to the achievement of those rights.

The Zionist spokesman, Yitzhak Gruenbaum, had argued that Jews were mystically bound to Hebrew. That was no reason for beginning to speak it now, countered Zhitlovsky. Gruenbaum foresaw a victory for Hebrew because the Jewish middle class favored it over Yiddish and the Jewish proletariat was declining in numbers. Zhitlovsky retorted that since the middle class followed the lead of the intellectuals they might be persuaded to favor Yiddish. There were already some pro-Yiddish intellectuals and some members of the Jewish bourgeoisie had already become Yiddishists.

Before our eyes, simultaneously battling both Hebraism and assimilation, a wonderful culture has sprouted in the Yiddish language, works of which are already included in the spiritual wealth of all mankind. One hundred and fifty daily newspapers in Yiddish, theatres in every Jewish settlement, art-theatres around the world which the English press writes about and points to as an example. In every Jewish community islands of Yiddish culture have emerged as links which join Jewish life and the Jewish people of Buenos Aires, New York, Paris, Warsaw, Kovno, and of every community where life pulsates and where the song of the Yiddish word is heard. . . . And we already have the pinnacles of our culture—the Yiddish Scientific Institute which studies the history of our people in Yiddish. And minds such as Einstein and Sigmund Freud are honorary curators of Yivo. Did the Yiddishists accomplish this themselves?

The Hebraists helped because when they wished to approach the people they did so in its own language—Yiddish. So they wrote and spoke in Yiddish. . . . The growth of our culture in Yiddish is proceeding with such zest that perhaps in a generation or two we will be able to match the most cultured of peoples because of the achievements of our culture and the recognition it has already won from other peoples. Modern Yiddish secular culture is already a colossal oak tree deserving of equal rights with other cultures; it is our national home which binds the entire people together, the intellectuals with the masses in one international unity. And as our ability to withstand assimilation grows, we gather strength with which to fight for the principles of progress, for personal freedom and fulfillment, for cultural enrichment, for social justice and equality, for international brotherhood, equal rights for all nations.[33]

In an article written in 1931, "Should We Build Our Culture Here in English?" Zhitlovsky argued that a dispersed people required the voluntary spiritual unity provided by a common culture. American Jewry, he felt, should strive to become the avant-garde of world Jewry. It would also be able to increase its own chances for national survival if it drew closer to other Jewish communities.

If American Jewry was to create an all-embracing, highly developed, and creative culture, it would have to do so in Yiddish. Jewish culture in English was, of necessity, one-sided. The works of Morris Raphael Cohen and Horace Kallen were attributed to American culture. The one-sidedness of a Jewish culture in English, a culture devoted exclusively to Jewish themes, precluded the attainment of excellence because it could hardly expect to attract Jews of genius. Nor could such a culture be fertile. It would fail to attract the masses, which were always more concerned with universal human matters than with specific

33. C. Zhitlovsky, *Undzer Shprahkn-Frage*, ed. Z. B. Mink (Kovno, 1930), pp. 29–31. On Bialik's attitude to Yiddish, see J. Glatstein, *Homeward Bound* (New York, 1969). pp. 111–14; Y. H. Biletsky, *H. N. Bialik ve-Yidish* (Tel Aviv, 1970); A. Zeitlin's introduction to his Hebrew translation of Bialik's Yiddish poems. *H. N. Bialik: Shirav Ha-idiyim* (Tel Aviv, (1956); F. Schulman, "Bialik's Yiddish Poetry," *Yiddish: A Quarterly Journal Devoted to Yiddish and Yiddish Literature* 1, no. 2 (Fall 1973): 66–74.

national ones. An Anglo-Jewish culture in America would lead to "Judaistic assimilation," whereas one in Yiddish would lead to the development of a comprehensive, rich, and fertile cultural life.[34]

In 1931 and 1932, Zhitlovsky participated in the establishment of the influential Jewish Cultural Society (*Yidishe Kultur Gezelshaft*) and its monthly journal, *Yidish*, to which he contributed. He published several important series of articles on social and philosophical themes in the New York daily *Der Tog* and the monthly *Tsukunft*. He also continued to lecture extensively throughout the United States and Canada.

On the occasion of his widely celebrated seventieth birthday, in 1935, the first volume of Zhitlovsky's memoirs was published (two additional volumes appeared in 1940). In an essay surveying his career of half a century, he summarized what had been accomplished in the Yiddish cultural field during those years.

> The right of the Jewish people to a national life of its own in many countries of residence was recognized officially by the Versailles peace treaty. The same national right to self-government is being realized by the Jewish population of the Soviet Union to a degree which evokes our deepest respect. . . . All of these cultural and autonomous activities have made of the Yiddish language and the works written in it, the "national spiritual home" which ties the overwhelming majority of the Jewish people throughout the world together in one unique cultural sphere. It is increasingly becoming a protective wall surrounding Jewish national existence and free development; a secular, national protective force which can in this capacity compete with the ancient Jewish religion.[35]

In 1937, Zhitlovsky also participated in the establishment of the politically leftist Yidisher Kultur Farband (YKUF) and its journal, *Yidishe Kultur,* which began to appear in New York the following year. Although opposed to Bolshevism, he was heartened by the prospects of a Jewish agricultural territory in

34. *Yid un Velt,* pp. 153–59.
35. *Ibid.,* pp. 172f.

Birobidjan and by Stalin's determination to create a multi-national country, which seemed to augur well for Jewish culture in the Soviet Union. He also saw in Russia a potential ally of the Jewish people against Hitler. Although Zhitlovsky left YKUF during the period of the Nazi-Soviet pact (1939–1941), he returned to it after Hitler attacked Russia, and remained associated with it for the rest of his life. A pro-YKUF address, "Religion, Culture, Language," delivered in several American cities, was Zhitlovsky's most extreme formulation of his Yiddishist and secularist doctrines.

> A Jew who lives in the language sphere of Yiddish can be a Jew by religion, a Christian by religion, of no religion or even against religion. He still remains a Jew and all cultural works by Jews in the Yiddish language will belong to the Jewish people, will be part of the Jewish spiritual national home now being created in Yiddish. . . .[36]
> The creation of a new progressive, secular culture sphere in Yiddish which will unite the folk masses with the creative spirits of our people is a tremendous revolution in our life. Nothing like it ever occurred in the cultural history of our people. The development of this new cultural sphere depends upon the historical destiny of our people and the historical destiny of our people depends to a large extent upon the revolution in our cultural life, on the new cultural sphere in Yiddish.[37]

For Zhitlovsky the essence of secularism was the idea that religion is a private matter. Church and state had to be kept separate. Since the Yiddish language was the Jewish people's substitute for a state, it too had to be kept free of religion. "No religious faith must make the pretense of representing official Judaism which every Jew must accept in order to be considered a Jew."[38] All religious and anti-religious faiths and ways of life were to have equal rights in the spiritual-national home of the Jewish people, which was the Yiddish language.

From 1941 on, Zhitlovsky served as chairman of the pro-

36. *Ibid.*, p. 191.
37. *Ibid.*, p. 193.
38. *Ibid.*, p. 197.

Soviet "Committee of Jewish Writers and Artists." In an article published in the Yiddish communist daily, *Morgn Frayhayt,* on August 1, 1941, he again disavowed Communism but called upon his fellow American Jews to support the Soviet Union in its war against Hitler.[39] Unfortunately, Zhitlovsky's blind faith that the Soviet Union was solving the problem of its Jewish population in accordance with his own theories also blinded him to even the grossest miscariages of justice in the U.S.S.R. and turned him into a pro-Soviet propagandist.

Zhitlovsky died on May 6, 1943, abandoned by many of his former disciples, who now considered him a traitor to his former principles and to the Jewish people. Following his death and for several years thereafter, hundreds of articles and several books appeared evaluating his contributions to Jewish life from various points of view.[40]

39. *Leksikon fun der Nayer Yidisher Literatur,* 3 : 704.
40. Cf. the highly critical *Yidn un Yidishkayt in di Shriftn fun Dr. C. Zhitlovsky* by Chaim Lieberman (New York, 1944) with the articles in *Yidishe Kultur,* May 1953 and December 1965. See also N. Summer, *Mentsh un Vort* (New York, 1950).

אידיש

אַ מתנה מיין ליבן און איידעלן
פריינט און קאָלעגע, דיכסער און
ליבהאַבער פון אידיש — אהרן
קאָרלין.

אידיש, שפּראַך און לשון מיין,
וואונדער פון מיין בלייבן זיין ;
צווישן פרעמדע דאָ און דאָרט —
ביזט מיין היים אין יעדן אָרט...

וואו איך קום, אָפּט מאַט און מיד,
קלינגט מיר אויף דיין היימיש ליד ;
דורך מיין פענסטער, וואו ס'זאָל זיין —
דרינגט דיין ליד אַרום, אַריין...

און ניט ליד אַליין — דיין וואָרט,
מיר דערנעענט וויַיטסטן אָרט ;
איז מיר ליב וואוהין איך קום,
ברידער רינגלען מיך אַרום...

ווערט ניט נאָר וואָרט — דיין בוך אַליין
אידיש בוך, ווי ליב און שיין !
פּרץ, מענדעלע — נאָכאַנאַנד —
ווערט מיין היים שוין, אידיש-לאַנד :

ניין, קיין פרעמדער ערגיץ ניט,
מיט מיין אידיש ווערט און ליד ;
מיט מיין צייטונג-בלאַט און בוך
פאָר איך אַלע לענדער דורך !...

"Yiddish," a popular poem by Abraham Reisen.

10

THE GROWTH
OF YIDDISHISM

THE EMERGENCE OF YIDDISH AS A MAJOR FACTOR IN JEWISH LIFE
at the beginning of the twentieth century actually resulted from
the confluence of five major forces:

(1) the growing awareness that the tongue of the East
European Jewish masses had developed from a vernacular
dialect and corrupt "jargon" to a language of national significance and literary status;

(2) the large measure of success that the *Haskalah,* or Jewish
Enlightenment movement, had achieved in secularizing and
modernizing Jewish life in the nineteenth century;

(3) the spirit of modern nationalism that was gradually
pervading all Jewish parties and movements;

(4) the growing Jewish working class and the development
of the Jewish socialist and revolutionary movements; and

(5) the flowering of modern Yiddish culture (press, theater,
literature, and education).

The arguments that the devotees of Yiddish set forth as the basis for its official recognition by the Jewish people at the beginning of the twentieth century were not unlike those which had been used by the champions of the various Western European vernaculars in the Middle Ages. In 1550, for example, Joachim Du Bellay, in his *La Deffence et illustration de la langue francoyse,* urged the recognition of French and expressed the hope that it might one day equal Greek and Latin. According to Du Bellay, French did not deserve to be called a "barbarian" tongue. While explaining why French was not so rich as the Classical tongues, he also tried to prove that it was not so impoverished as some thought.[1] The philosopher Johann Gottfried Von Herder (1744–1803), associated with the German romantic movement, believed that language was the essential attribute of each *Volk,* the fundamental expression of the national soul. He considered it "the organ of social activity and cooperation . . . the bond of social classes and a means for their integration."[2] Similar arguments were used by the leading Yiddishists, but what was a gradual evolutionary process lasting several centuries for the languages of Europe was a radical revolutionary development over a few short decades for Yiddish.

In their attempts to modernize East European Jewry, the Russian and Galician *maskilim* had discovered that the linguistic program of their predecessors in Germany was ineffective, simplistic, and self-defeating. That program consisted primarily of getting the Jews to adopt the national languages of their respective countries as their own vernaculars. Gradually, the East European *maskilim* came to an awareness of the fact that only through the medium of the despised "Jargon" could their message reach the masses. Thus, along with Hebrew, Yiddish became a vehicle of Europeanization and secularization among the Jews of Eastern Europe. In turn, it gradually grew in stature and significance among the intellectuals as well as the

    1. See H. Kohn, *The Idea of Nationalism* (New York, 1944), p.131 and Y. Elzet, "Undzer Folks-Oytser," *Yidish Amerike,* ed. N. Steinberg (New York, 1929), pp. 244–45.
    2. Cf. K. R. Minogue, *Nationalism* (New York, 1967), pp. 57–62.

masses. The success of the *Haskalah* contributed immeasurably to the emergence of Yiddish as an important cultural factor.

The awareness of the significance of national languages is essentially a product of the growth of modern nationalism. Before the age of nationalism, people were scarcely conscious of the fact that the same language was spoken in a particular territory. Language was rarely stressed as a significant factor in the life of a society.[3] The attitude of the revolutionary government in France immediately following the Revolution adumbrates the emergence of national languages in many countries. At first it translated official decrees into the minority languages of France and the use of those languages was encouraged. Later, however, the policy was reversed, with the justification that French would become the official language, since it was the language of liberty. "Meanwhile," said the revolutionaries, "let French become the language of all Frenchmen."[4]

In modern times, imperialistic nations sought to use national and uniform languages to consolidate their empires while oppressed minorities often linked their struggles for self-determination and sovereignty to their own tongues. At the beginning of the twentieth century, many minorities, including those of the Russian and Austrian empires, were asserting themselves and stressing the values of their own national languages and cultures. Yiddish is not unique in this respect. Its achievements are similar to those of Finnish, Estonian, Latvian, Lithuanian, Ukranian, Flemish, Icelandic, and Scottish-Gaelic.[5] A number of little-known, or dormant, languages developed vigorous and diversified poetry and prose in the nineteenth and twentieth centuries, largely as a result of modern nationalism.

Since Jews are linked by many ties, the most important of which is an indigenous religion, language was never a factor

3. H. Kohn, pp. 6, 7.
4. M. Pei, *The Story of Language*, Mentor Book (New York, 1949), p. 219.
5. A. Rannit, "Speaking of Finnish, Estonian, Latvian, Lithuanian . . . ," *The New York Times Book Review*, November 16, 1969, p. 2.

of major significance in Jewish life. The modern Jewish political movements began to assert the importance of language on the model of other modern nations. In addition, with the diminishing importance of religion, other factors unifying Jewry had to be emphasized. Hebrew and Yiddish both became factors in the growth of Jewish nationalism which, in turn, increased the significance attached to them.

The growth of the Jewish working class and its gradual modernization made the tongue of the masses the inevitable tool of Jewish socialist and revolutionary movements. As the workers and socialists gradually absorbed the nationalistic mood of the times, and as they met with the opposition to Jewish individuality of their European counterparts, Yiddish became more and more important. For many Jewish workers, Yiddish became the major if not the only distinguishing characteristic of Jewish nationality.

The phenomenal rise of Yiddish literature and the growth of the Yiddish press, theater, and educational trends increased the significance of the language in the twentieth century. Yiddish literature attracted many of the leading literary talents of the Hebrew and Russian press. The works of Mendele, Sholom Aleichem, Peretz, Asch, Pinski, Reisen, Leivick, and other writers became classics of the Jewish heritage, which made the language in which they were written more significant than ever. Yiddish became a valuable expression of Jewish identity for a significant segment of East European Jewry, and one of the most powerful forces linking it to the Jewish people and its historic destiny. Yiddish literature mirrored the diversity and variety of Jewish life and the international character of the Jewish people. By and large, Yiddish literature managed to avoid the pessimism, nihilism, and brutality of much of modern Western literature. It faithfully reflected the traditional values and ethical emphases of Jewish civilization. It strengthened the Jewish will to live and the Jew's commitment to a better future for his people and for mankind as a whole.

The bitter controversy between Yiddishists and Hebraists,

despite some of its narrower manifestations, was a sign of the vitality of the Jewish people as it entered the world of the twentieth century. The struggle, symbolizing as it did conflicting interpretations of Jewish history and destiny, unlocked many powers that had been dormant in Jewry for centuries. The major Hebrew and Yiddish writers were bilingual. Their work in one language deepened and enriched their work in the other. Such conflicts have proved to be fruitful many times in history. We may recall that Dante wrote his defense of Italian, *De Vulgari Eloquentia,* in Latin, and that while he composed "The Divine Comedy" in Italian, he wrote his reflections on politics in the classical tongue.

In the struggle for supremacy between Hebrew and Yiddish, partisans of Hebrew failed to realize that no tongue is "pure," as no nation or race is "pure," with the possible exception of minor primitive tribes and their languages.[6] The pleas for special recognition of their favored tongues by Hebraists and Yiddishists frequently sounded like the prayer of the eighteenth-century Russian poet-physicist Michael Lomonosov.

> Lord of many languages, the Russian tongue is far superior to all those of Europe, not only by the extent of the countries where it is dominant, but also by its own comprehensiveness and richness. Charles the Fifth, Emperor of the Holy Roman Empire, said that one ought to speak Spanish to the Deity, French to one's friends, German to one's enemies, and Italian to the fair sex. But had he been acquainted with Russian, he would assuredly have added that one could speak it with each and all; he would have discovered in it the majesty of Spanish, the vivacity of French, the strength of German, the sweetness of Italian, and, in addition, energetic conciseness in its imagery, together with the richness of Greek and Latin.[7]

Yiddishism scored its greatest triumphs and became a leading force in Jewish life during the first several decades of the twentieth century. It drew its basic strength from the fact that,

6. M. Pei, p. 136.
7. *Ibid.*, p. 159.

at the turn of the century, Yiddish was spoken by three out of every four Jews in the world.[8] The Yiddish press was the chief medium of enlightenment and entertainment for millions of Jews, their primary source of information and interpretation of Jewish and general life. Yiddish theater and literature were unrivaled as the basic cultural fare of the vast majority of Jews. Yiddish was the language of instruction in the overwhelming majority of tradition-oriented Jewish schools and in the newly emerging Jewish secularist school systems that resulted from the alliance of Yiddishism and the various Jewish political parties. Yiddish culture was also winning the recognition of West European Jews and even of non-Jews who appreciated its authenticity and artistic excellence.

Yiddishism was essentially an ideological movement with a mystique, theory, and program of its own. The ideology of Yiddishism fired the Jewish people's imagination with a new interpretation of Jewish history and destiny. It stimulated the Jew's will to live and his determination to survive as a Jew. It aroused creative potentialities and artistic impulses within Jewry, engendering a cultural renaissance of magnitude and significance. Yiddishism, together with its counterpart, Hebraism, spelled the cultural rebirth of the Jewish people in modern times.

The mystique of Yiddishism derived not only from the unprecedented flowering of Yiddish language and culture. It stemmed principally from the fact that Yiddishism represented the serious attempt of a major portion of Jewry to confront itself, as well as the world of the twentieth century, as a modern, "normal" nation. In this respect, Yiddishism was the product of forces similar to those which gave rise to the Zionist movement in Western Europe. It set out to relieve the unbearable psychological pressure and tension that the Jew experienced as he emerged from a segregated world of outcasts into the spiritual and mental climate of twentieth-century Europe. It was no accident that the four architects of Yiddishism whose contributions we have surveyed were all modern intellectuals who had undergone the processes of secularization and sociocultural

8. A. Tartakover, *Hahevrah Hayehudit* (Tel Aviv, 5717), pp. 210f.

assimilation. Nor was it accidental that the field commanders of the Yiddishist campaigns were largely university students who had suffered humiliation, degradation, and ostracism in the course of their attempts to obtain European education.

The mystique of Yiddishism also drew inspiration from the attitudes of the major groupings within Jewry to the Yiddish language.[9] The religious traditionalists, who constituted the largest portion of the Jewish population of Eastern Europe, viewed Yiddish as an indispensable aspect of the Jewish way of life. They pointed to the fact that Yiddish had been the language of religious study for countless generations, that it had been employed by the great European rabbis and sanctified by the Hassidic leaders. Conservatism and fear of the secularizing influences of European culture motivated traditionalist opposition to the use of European languages by Jews. The traditionalists were convinced that the abandonment of Yiddish would invariably lead to the abandonment of the religious regimen and ultimately to apostasy. The fact that the Haskalah movement had bitterly opposed Yiddish was enough to raise its esteem in their eyes.

The rising Jewish middle class in Eastern Europe actually looked somewhat favorably upon the development of the Yiddish language and culture. It sought to combine a respectful attitude to both Hebrew and Yiddish with knowledge of the national languages of Europe, which had become indispensable to participation and advancement in general society. The Jewish middle class feared the success of assimilation in destroying the ties of the younger generation with the Jewish community. Secular education had created a generation gap between parents and children and seriously threatened the stability of the Jewish home. The middle-class Jewish family was heartened at the sight of young Jews defending the dignity and rights of Yiddish and taking an interest in the works of the Yiddish writers and dramatists.

The conferment of status upon Yiddish was viewed by the

9. Cf. Zvi Woislawski, ""Esrim Shanah Le-Tshernovits," *Hatekufah* 25 (1928): 613–20.

Jewish proletariat as symbolic of its own emergence as an important sector of the Jewish community. Jewish workers saw Yiddish as an integral part of their socialist faith and defended its honor as they did their own. The Yiddish language was the principal sign of their Jewishness and the tie that bound them to world Jewry.

The Zionist movement, like the Jewish socialist parties, made Yiddish the chief instrument of its propaganda throughout the world. Zionist opinion at the beginning of the century was veering away from "the negation of the Diaspora" toward the furtherance of Jewish political and cultural objectives wherever Jews lived. The affirmation of the Diaspora of necessity included a significant role for Yiddish. Despite the language controversy within the Zionist camp itself, it was Zionism which, in fact, did most to advance the status and further the development of Yiddish.

Yiddishist theory was intent upon demonstrating that the Yiddish language was a language like all others, deserving of respect and recognition by the people who used it. It also set out to demonstrate the "normalcy" of Jewry and the inevitability of a future for it on the model of the modern nations of Europe. The two most difficult problems that confronted the Yiddishists and with which they were unable to deal objectively without weakening the basic foundations of Yiddishism, were the phenomenon of Hebrew and the landlessness of the Jewish people.

Yiddishism attempted to solve the problem posed by the Hebrew language by drawing an analogy between Hebrew and Yiddish, on the one hand, and Latin and the modern European languages, on the other.[10] Just as Latin had been gradually replaced by the national languages of Europe, so Yiddish was destined to replace Hebrew as the dominant national language

10. See L. Lehrer, *Yidishkayt un Andere Problemen* (New York, 1940), pp. 74f.; R. Mahler, "Yidish Ve-Ivrit Leor Hametsiut shel Yameynu," *Klal Yisrael*, ed. B. Dinur, A. Tartakover, Y. Lestchinsky (Jerusalem, 1954), pp. 374–76; A. Tartakover, p. 221.

of Jewry. Moreover, just as the victory of the national vernaculars over Latin had signaled the emancipation of the European nations from medievalism, autocracy, and clericalism, so too would the victory of Yiddish signify the emancipation of the Jewish people in Eastern Europe from bondage to otherworldly superstitions, a medieval communal structure, and a leadership unable to cope with the problems of modern, secular civilization. The victory of Yiddish would spell the victory of Jewish modernism and this-worldliness over antiquarianism and provincialism. It would mean the emancipation of Jewry from the bondage of its own past without the surrendering of its integrity and identity to the nations of Europe.

The landlessness of the Jewish people in Eastern Europe was a much more difficult problem. It emerged as the crucial socio-political problem of Jewish life in modern times and began to be resolved only with the establishment of the State of Israel in 1948. Yiddishists were unable to suggest any original solutions to this problem or even to unite among themselves on one of the several solutions suggested by other Jewish groups. In the main, they were divided among themselves on this issue and exhibited the full range of ideological approaches to it that were found in Jewish life as a whole.

The program of Yiddishism involved agitation for the acknowledgment by Jews of Yiddish as the national living language of Jewry and the central factor of Jewish life, and its legal recognition by the international community as the official language of the Jewish people. During the period under discussion, Yiddish became an official language of such significant Jewish international welfare agencies as ORT, OZE, HIAS, the Zionist and Jewish Socialist movements, and all Jewish political parties in Eastern Europe. The distinguished Yiddish poet Abraham Walt Lyessin referred to Hebrew as the national language of Jewry, and Yiddish as its international language.[11] Yiddishists not only involved themselves in the

11. Quoted by R. Mahler, p. 375. Lyessin penned the most celebrated poem about the Yiddish language. See his *Lider un Poemen* (New York,

political struggles for the recognition of Yiddish; they also fought for Jewish national rights and, in the Soviet Union, for Jewish national autonomy.

The Yiddishist program also involved the promotion of cultural institutions such as schools, libraries, literary societies, cooperative publishing houses, theaters, drama clubs, folklore circles, and glee clubs. Yiddishism stimulated the attempts of Jewish writers and artists to raise Yiddish literature and theater to the level of the European nations. It encouraged Yiddish scholars in their attempts to purify and refine Yiddish and develop an academic literature in the language.

The mystique of Yiddishism suffered severe setbacks and began to disintegrate as conditions in Eastern Europe once again demonstrated the anomalous position of Jewry. "Normalcy" might be achieved in the distant future in Palestine, or some other national territory. But, in the meantime, anti-Semitism and social, economic, and political discrimination continued to underscore that Jews were indeed different. As the urge to be like others became more and more impractical and therefore diffuse, and as the essential otherness of the Jewish situation became ever more salient, Yiddishism lost its appeal. Zionism and the increasing growth of Jewish national aspirations and romantic sentiments inevitably turned the eyes of Jewry toward Palestine and Hebrew, and away from the ever-disillusioning *Golus* and Yiddish.

The mystique of Yiddishism also withered as the various sectors of Jewry that had been staunch supporters of Yiddish turned their backs on the language. The overwhelming majority of traditionalists in lands of immigration who made contact with West European Orthodoxy were impressed with the fact that uncompromising religious observance could be maintained by Jews who spoke European languages and were integrated into Western culture. The realities of linguistic assimilation compelled

1938) 1:13–18. Cf. also the anthology of poems about Yiddish edited by S. Rozhanski, *Yidish in Lid* (Buenos Aires, 1967).

them to adopt the concept of a Western-style, linguistically assimilated orthodoxy as the one hope of holding on to the younger generation. Only traditionalist fringe groups that remained oblivious to the modern development of Yiddish and to the achievements of modern Yiddish culture remained loyal to the language. The traditionalists feared the materialism, secularism, and atheism of avowed leaders of Yiddishism such as Zhitlovsky and their influence on traditionalist youth.

The fascination of middle-class Jewish youth for Yiddish proved evanescent as more and more of them became integrated into the culture of their lands. They became more proficient in the various national languages of Europe and became imbued with the cultural traditions of the countries in which they lived. The Jewish national sentiments of the bourgeoisie found their basic outlet in Zionist work and *aliyah* to Palestine.

Even the various socialist groups eventually loosened their ties to Yiddish. Their collaboration with socialist groups of other nationalities in the improvement of economic and political conditions for workers, and in the struggle for socialism, necessitated their adoption of the various national languages. As the Jewish worker sought to advance himself professionally, he found it imperative to learn other languages. In America and other lands, Jewish laborers gradually abandoned the labor movement as they became members of the middle class. This often entailed the abandonment of the proletarian culture with which they associated Yiddish.

The successful Hebraization of Palestine ensured the victory of Hebrew over Yiddish in the Zionist movement and increased Zionism's theoretical loyalty to Hebrew in the Diaspora as well. In actuality, the Zionist apparatus adapted itself to linguistic assimilation in the various Jewish settlements outside of Palestine. As Zionists militantly fostered Hebraic education, they knowingly diminished the chances of Yiddish for survival. Unfortunately, it was the various national languages of Europe and America that reaped the major harvest from Zionism's attempt to replace Yiddish with Hebrew.[12] The prediction of the Yiddishists in this regard was fully validated.

Yiddishist theory failed to come to grips with the complex nature of the relationship of Jewry to Hebrew, which only superficially resembled that of the European nations to Latin. Unlike Latin, which was the sacred language of Christendom but completely divorced from the national aspirations of the peoples of Europe, Hebrew was the historic national language of Jewry. The national awakening of the European peoples was generally associated with the development of their national tongues. The latter were viewed as symbols of national liberation and freedom from foreign domination. For Jewry, however, the hope of national liberation was expressed in the sacred Hebrew texts, and the national revival of the Jewish people had always been associated with the revival of that language. Moreover, unlike Latin, Hebrew was never reserved exclusively for sacred purposes. It served as a major means of communication between Jews of various lands and was even used as the medium of business transactions among Jews. While knowledge of Latin was restricted to the Catholic hierarchy and clergy, every Jew had some knowledge of Hebrew, both because of the frequency of Hebrew words in Yiddish and because traditional Jewish education and culture were based exclusively on Hebrew and Aramaic texts and their translation into Yiddish. Whereas Catholic laymen were forbidden to study the Bible in any language in the thirteenth century, Jews traditionally spent their leisure hours in societies organized for the study of various parts of the Bible or Talmud.

The inability to unite on any program that would lead toward an ultimate solution of the Jewish territorial question was probably the major factor in the decline of Yiddishism after the First World War. The almost unqualified support that Yiddishists throughout the world gave to Soviet attempts to establish an autonomous Yiddish-speaking region in Birobidjan

12. Cf. H. Leivick, "The Individual Jew," trans. E. S. Goldsmith, *Reconstructionist*, 23, no. 17 (December 27, 1957), p. 10.

in the 1920s, even though it entailed the complete submission of Yiddish culture to communist dogma, was the closest that Yiddishists ever came to taking a united stand on the territorial issue. Many Yiddishists were deluded into believing that the temporary blossoming of Yiddish culture in the Soviet Union in the twenties augured the salvation of Yiddish culture. The disillusionment of the thirties proved to be another severe blow for Yiddishism. The espousal of Yiddishist radicalism by communists tended to discredit even the positive values of Yiddishism and Yiddish culture.

Despite its successes in the linguistic and cultural fields, Yiddishism was never able to compete with other modern Jewish ideologies because it failed to deal with the full range of issues in Jewish life.[13] Its concentration on language as the *sine qua non* of modern Jewish existence, which was essentially the application of an alien norm to Jewish life, blinded Yiddishism to the totality of Jewish civilization and the complexity of Jewish problems. Its association with secularism divorced it from the deepest sources and strivings of Jewry and made it suspect among the many Jews who continued to harbor positive sentiments toward the Jewish religion. Birnbaum, Peretz, and Mieses sensed this, while Zhitlovsky, the principal exponent of Yiddishism, became its worst enemy and helped undercut the relevance of Yiddish culture to Jews and Judaism. It was not until the 1940s and 50s that Yiddishist writers and thinkers such as Leybush Lehrer, Samuel Niger, Solomon Simon, Yisroel Efroykin, Abraham Menes, Yudel Mark, and Abraham Golomb stressed the need for a tradition-oriented, nondogmatic Yiddishism. Unlike Hebraism, which always regarded itself as but one aspect of the total Zionist approach to the Jewish question, and which fostered an attachment to Jewish religious values and *sancta,* Yiddishism painted itself into a linguistic corner and assumed that the solution of the language problem would automatically solve all of the other ills of Jewish life.

13. Cf. L. Lehrer, pp. 63, 82, and "Yidish un Yidishizm" in L. Lehrer, *In Gayst fun Traditsye* (Tel Aviv, 1966), pp. 341–49.

The world of Yiddish culture provided a satisfying form of Jewish association and involvement for millions of Jews during the first half of the twentieth century. Only the ever-accelerating pace of linguistic assimilation and the European holocaust were able to radically diminish its power and influence. The integration of Jewry into the body politic of other nations spelled the end of the process of Jewish language creativity that began in antiquity. The new world in which Jewry found itself after the First World War made the maintenance of cultural differentiation in lands of immigration more and more difficult. The German war against the Jewish people resulted in the destruction of the heartland of Ashkenazic Jewry and of the Jewish communities in which Yiddish language and culture had reached their apogee. The holocaust brought an end to that sector of the Jewish world, without which Yiddish remained bereft of the principal source of its vitality and influence. In the Soviet Union, what Hitler failed to accomplish was achieved by Stalin and his henchmen, who viewed Yiddish and Yiddish culture as embodiments of Jewish separatism and internationalism.[14]

The Yiddishists hit upon several significant truths which, as we have seen, they reiterated continually. However, they did not sufficiently examine them or adjust them to the historic realities and contemporary complexities of the Jewish condition. The

14. On the liquidation of Yiddish culture in the Soviet Union, see the following: S. W. Baron, *The Russian Jew Under Tsars and Soviets* (New York, 1964); Y. Gilboa, *Al Horvot Hatarbut Hayehudit Bivrit Hamoatsot* (Tel Aviv, 1959); Y. Gilboa, *The Black Years of Soviet Jewry, 1939–1953* (Boston, 1971); B. Z. Goldberg, *The Jewish Problem in the Soviet Union* (New York, 1961); N. Mayzel, *Dos Yidishe Shafn un der Yidisher Shrayber in Sovetnfarband* (New York, 1959); A. Pomerantz, *Di Sovetishe Harugey-Malkhes* (Buenos Aires, 1962); N. Rozntal, *Yidish Lebn in Ratnfarband* (Tel Aviv, 1971); Ch. Shmeruk. Introduction to *A Shpigl oyf a Shteyn*, ed. B. Hrushovski, Ch. Shmeruk, A. Sutskever (Tel Aviv, 1964); S. Schwarz, *Di Yidn in Sovetn-Farband* (New York, 1967); Y. Yanasovitsh, *Mit Yidishe Shrayber in Rusland* (Buenos Aires, 1959); S. Niger, *Yidishe Shrayber* in *Sovet-Rusland* (New York, 1958); L. Kochan, ed., *The Jews in Soviet Russia Since 1917* (London, 1970); G. Aronson, J. Frumkin, A. Goldenweiser. J. Lewitan, eds. *Russian Jewry, 1917–1967* (New York, 1969); A. Tartakover, *Shivtey Yisrael*, vol. 2 (Tel Aviv, 1966); E. Schulman, *Di Sovetish-Yidishe Literatur* (New York, 1971), and *A History of Jewish Education in the Soviet Union* (New York, 1971). See also J. Rothenberg. *The Jewish Religion in the Soviet Union* (New York, 1971).

Yiddish language, they stated, had emerged from the ghetto and become one of the great pillars of Jewish life, a major factor in the modernization of Jewry and a prominent bulwark against the disintegration and erosion of Jewish loyalty and identity. The recognition and development of Yiddish would ensure the survival and growth of Jewry. The flowering of Yiddish culture would spell both a Jewish renaissance and the victory of Jewish self-respect over self-abasement. It would proclaim the entry of the Jewish people into the world of the twentieth century as a nation like all others, with a significant culture of its own that could make a contribution to mankind.

The Yiddishists simply did not realize that, however significant an attribute a habitually spoken language or "mother tongue" may be to an ethnic group, nationality, or nation, it is neither indispensable nor all-sufficient. Moreover, the notion that a language expresses a national or folk soul is essentially mystical and incapable of rational demonstration.[15] The Yiddishists were guilty of what may be termed "obsessional thinking," but theirs was a magnificent obsession—one that brought new dignity, vitality, and beauty to the life of Jewry in our time.[16]

15. Cf. B. Akzin, *States and Nations,* Anchor Book ed. (New York, 1966), pp. 141, 143, and Minogue, p. 124.
16. See K. Mannheim, *Diagnosis of our Time* (London, 1943), pp. 89f. Contemporary Yiddishist and neo-Yiddishist writings exhibit a wide diversity of viewpoints. See for example: E. Auerbach, *Getrakht mit Ivri-Taytsh* (New York, 1955), pp. 100–108; H. Bass, *Shrayber un Verk* (Tel Aviv, 1971), pp. 91–104, 548–59; S. Birnbaum, "Judaism and Yiddish," *The Way We Think,* ed. J. Leftwich (New York, 1969) 2:513–18; M. Boreisho, *Eseyen* (Buenos Aires, 1956); J. Botoshansky, *Mame Yidish* (Buenos Aires, 1949); L. S. Dawidowicz, "Yiddish: Past, Present and Perfect," *Commentary,* May 1962, pp. 375–85; L. Domankevitsh, *Verter un Vertn* (Tel Aviv, 1965), pp. 11–26; Y. Entin, *Yidishe Dertsiung* (New York, 1960); L. Finkelstein, *Loshn Yidish un Yidisher Kiyum* (Mexico, 1954); J. Glatstein, *In der Velt mit Yidish* (New York, 1972); *Oyf Greyte Temes* (Tel Aviv, 1967); A. Golomb, *Tsu di Heykhn fun Yidishn Gayst* (Paris, 1971); *Tsvishn Tkufes* (Tel Aviv, 1968); *Eybike Vegn fun Eybikn Folk* (Mexico, 1964); *Undzer Gang Tsvishn Felker* (Buenos Aires, 1961); *Oyf di Vegn fun Kiyum* (Buenos Aires, 1959); E. S. Goldsmith, "Yiddish in Modern Judaism," *Reconstructionist,* June 2, 1961; S. Goodman, *Traditsye un Banayung* (New York, 1967); M. Gross-Zimerman, *Intimer Videranand* (Tel Aviv, 1964), pp. 310–20; Y. Hofer, *Mit Yenem un mit Zikh* (Tel Aviv, 1964), pp. 11–95; A. Koralnik, "Without Mazl," *Voices from the Yiddish,* ed. I. Howe and E. Greenberg (Ann Arbor, Mich., 1972), pp. 326–28; L.

Kenig, *Folk un Literatur* (London, 1947); *Dos Bukh fun Lesterungen* (London, 1948); J. C. Landis, "Who Needs Yiddish?" *Judaism* (Fall 1964); "The Relevance of Yiddish," *Jewish Heritage* (Fall 1969); L. Lehrer, *In Gayst fun Traditsye* (Tel Aviv, 1966); *Azoy Zenen Yidn* (New York, 1959); *Fun Dor tsu Dor* (New York, 1959); *Mentsh un Ideye* (New York, 1960); *Yidishkayt un Andere Problemen* (New York, 1940); *Di Moderne Yidishe Shul* (New York, 1927); H. Leivick, *Eseyen un Redes* (New York, 1963); A. Lis, *In Zkhus fun Vort* (Tel Aviv, 1969), pp. 315–31; S. Margoshes, *In Gang fun Doyres* (Tel Aviv, 1970); Y. Mark, "Veltlekhe Yidishkayt," *Forverts*, May 21, 1972; "The Yiddish Language: Its Cultural Impact," *American Jewish Historical Quarterly* (December 1969); *"Trakhtenishn Vegn Kiyum Ha-ume,"* Di Tsukunft (May-June, 1973); N. Mayzel, *Tsurikblikn un Perspektivn* (Tel Aviv, 1962); W. Nathanson, *Tsu der Revizye fun Natsyonal-Radikaln Gedank* (Chicago, 1935); S. Niger, *Fun Mayn Togbukh* (New York, 1973); J. Opatoshu. *Yidn un Yidishkayt* (Rio de Janeiro, 1952); J. Pat, *Shmuesn mit Yidishe Shrayber* (New York, 1954); *Shmuesn mit Shrayber in Yisroel* (New York, 1860); Y. Rapoport, Zoymen in Vint (Buenos Aires, 1961), pp. 251-310; M. Ravitch, *Eynems Yidishe Makhshoves in Tsvantsikstn Yorhundert* (Buenos Aires, 1949); A. A. Roback, *Di Imperye Yidish* (Mexico, 1958); *Di Folksgayst in der Yidisher Shprakh* (Paris, 1964); M. Samuel, *The Professor and the Fossil* (New York, 1956), pp. 40–45; *In Praise of Yiddish* (New York, 1971); E. Schulman, *Sugyot Betoldot Sifrut Yidish* (Tel Aviv, 1969); *Yisroel Tsinberg: Zayn Lebn un Shafn* (Paris, 1971); M. Shtrigler, *Shmuesn mit der Tsayt* (Buenos Aires, 1961) 2:7–76; Y. Shpigl, *Geshtaltn un Profiln* (Tel Aviv, 1971), pp. 254–9; H. Steinhart, *In Kamf far Yidish* (New York, 1954); D. Sadan, *Heymishe Ksovim*, vol. 2 (Tel Aviv, 1972); S. Simon, *Tokh Yidishkayt* (Buenos Aires, 1954); *Emune fun a Dor* (New York, 1970); *Yidn Tsvishn Felker* (New York,, 1949); H. Sloves, *In un Arum* (New York 1970), pp. 230–96; "Yidish un Moderne Yidishkayt," *Yidishe Kultur*, January 1971; J. S. Taubes, *Yidish—Nisht Hebreyish* (New York, 1952); J. I. Trunk,, *Kvaln un Beymer* (New York, 1958), pp. 407–53; M. Tsanin, *Oyf di Vegn fun Yidishn Goyrl* (Tel Aviv, 1966); M. Weinreich, "Yidishkayt and Yiddish," *Mordecai M. Kaplan Jubilee Volume* (English Section) (New York, 1953); A. Zeitlin, "Yidish un Yidishkayt," *Der Tog-Morgn Zhurnal*, February 11, 1959; "Yisroels Manger Prayz far Shafung oyf Yidish," *Der Tog-Morgn Zhurnal*, April 18, 1969; Y. Efroykin, *A Kheshbn Hanefesh* (Paris, 1948); *Oyfkum un Umkum fun Yidishe Golus Shprakhn un Dialektn* (Paris, 1951); Y. Goldkorn, "Yidish farn Vendpunkt," *Di Tsukunft* (May–June 1974); W. Glicksman, "Yidish Loshn, Der Driter Khurbn un Klal Yisroel," *Di Tsukunft*, March 1964; M. Zeldner, "Yiddish—A Living Language," *Jewish Frontier*, April 1974; A. Menes, *Der Yidisher Gedank in der Nayer Tsayt* (New York, 1957); *Shabes un Yontev* (Tel Aviv, 1973); H. Lieberman, *In Kamf far Yidisher Dertsiung* (New York, 1941); *Bikher un Shrayber* (New York, 1933); A. Zak, *Geven a Yidish Poyln* (Buenos Aires, 1968); *In Opshayn fun Doyres* (Buenos Aires, 1973); Y. Horn, *Arum Yidisher Literatur un Yidishe Shrayber* (Buenos Aires, 1973); P. Rubin, *"The Vitality of Yiddish,"* Congress Weekly, March 4, 1957; J. L. Teller, "Secular Hebrew and Esoteric Yiddish," *Commentary*, June 1956; A. Glantz-Leyeles, "Der Koyekh fun Yidish," *Der Tog-Morgn Zhurnal*, Dec. 7, 1957; "Mizrekh un Mayrev," *Der Tog-Morgn Zhurnal*, Dec. 14, 1957; L. Rosten, *The Joys of Yiddish* (New York, 1968); L. M. Feinsilver, *The Taste of Yiddish* (New York, 1970); Y. Yanasovitsh, *On Oysruf-Tseykhns* (Tel Aviv, 1975), pp. 153–59.

What is the legacy of Yiddishism to the Jewish people and to mankind? It is, on the one hand, the awareness of the inestimable value of the Yiddish language and culture as bearers of the millennial religio-cultural and humanistic values of the Jewish tradition for all Jews—American and Israeli, Western and Oriental, Ashkenazi and Sephardi, Orthodox and liberal. Those values include the religious quest and Messianic vision of the Jewish people, its Sabbaths and festivals, its heritage of history, learning, and lore, and its attachment to the land of Israel as the ancestral and reclaimed homeland of Jewry. Yiddish language and literature are keys to the understanding of the East European Jewish experience, the Hassidic and Mussar movements, the rise of Jewish socialism, Zionism and Labor Zionism, the Jewish immigrant experience in the United States, Canada, South America, South Africa, Israel, and other lands, the heroism and martyrdom of Jewry during the Holocaust, and the resettlement and readjustment of the surviving remnant.[17]

On the other hand, Yiddishism points to a future for all mankind in which ethnic, cultural, or religious differentiation will be viewed as a blessing instead of a curse, when man's gregarious and creative instincts will lead to harmony and mutuality, respect and brotherhood. It may be that ethnic groupings and religious or cultural ideologies recognizing the unity of mankind will one day be called upon to extricate us from the drab uniformity imposed by totalitarian regimes or the conformist tendencies of democratic states. Yiddishism, as an enduring expression of Judaism, portends a time when the earth will be filled with a knowledge of the preciousness of all that fosters and enhances man's humanity, enabling him to transcend himself and bring the world closer to the vision of the prophets and the rabbis.[18]

17. On Mussar see L. Eckman, *The History of the Musar Movement, 1840–1945* (New York, 1975); L. Ginzberg, *Students, Scholars and Saints* (Philadelphia, 1928), pp. 145–94; M. G. Glenn, *Israel Salanter, Religous-Ethical Thinker* (New York , 1953); C. Grade, *Musarnikes* (Vilna, 1939), *The Seven Little Lanes* (New York, 1972), *Tsemakh Atlas (Di Yeshive),* 2 vols. (New York, 1967–68); D. Katz, *Tenuat Hamusar,* 5 vols. (Tel Aviv, 1952–63); J. Mark, *Gedoylim fun Undzer Tsayt* (New York, 1927); Z. F. Ury, *The Musar Movement* (New York, 1970); J. J. Weinberg, "Lithuanian Mussar" in *Men of the Spirit,* ed. L. Jung (New York, 1964), pp. 213–83.
18. Cf. K. E. Boulding, *The Meaning of the Twentieth Century* (New York, 1964), pp. 19–20, and M. M. Kaplan, *The Religion of Ethical Nationhood: Judaism's Contribution to World Peace* (New York, 1970).

טראָגט זיך איצט ווידער, פֿון האָרץ ווי פֿון סידור,

די תפילה די שטילע, איינציק און ריין:

ה׳ עוז לעמו יתן!

גאָט זאָל ישראל איצט שטאַרקייט פֿאַרשאַפֿן,

שטאַרקייט אין ווילן און שטאַרקייט אין וואַפֿן,

און שטאַרקייט אין איינהייט, סיי אַלט און סיי ניי,

סיי פֿרומע סיי פֿרייע — אַלע געטריי.

און ליבע זאָל פֿלייצן פֿון האָרץ ווי אַ שטראָם,

פֿון יעטוועדן ייִדן באַשר הוא שם.

ה׳ יברך את עמו בשלום!

1955.XI.20

A Yiddish prayer for Israel by Zalman Shazar, third President
of Israel.

11

YIDDISHISM
AND JUDAISM

EVER SINCE THE EMANCIPATION AND THE ENLIGHTENMENT, THERE SEEMS
to have been no end to the making of definitions of Judaism.*
Although Aristotle spoke of a definition as "a sentence signifying
what a thing is," Samuel Butler was probably more to the point
when he described a definition as " 'the enclosing of a wilderness
of ideas within a world of words.' "[1] Nevertheless, definitions are
useful.

Judaism has been defined by Mordecai M. Kaplan as "the ongoing life of a people intent upon keeping alive for the highest conceivable purpose, despite changes in the general climate of opinion."[2]

---

*An earlier version of this chapter was published in *Judaism: A Quarterly
Journal*, 38, No. 4 (Fall 1989), 527–536.
   1. Quoted in Michael McKenna, *The Stein and Day Dictionary of Definitive
Quotations* (New York, 1983), p. 50.
   2. Mordecai M. Kaplan, *The Purpose and Meaning of Jewish Existence* (Philadelphia, 1964), p. 40.

This definition takes into account both the existential dimension (the ongoing life of a people) and the essential dimension (the highest conceivable purpose) of the Jewish phenomenon. It takes into account both peoplehood, or nationalism, and civilization, or culture. Religion is subsumed under the rubric "highest conceivable purpose," since religion is that aspect of human culture or civilization which consciously seeks cognizance of, and contact with, the transcendent or highest aspects of human experience. In Judaism, the latter are conceived of as Divinity, Deity, or God. Finally, the words "intent upon keeping alive" remind us that whatever other objectives it may assume, the survival of the Jewish people (*kiyem ha-ume*) remains a *sine qua non* of Judaism.

Yiddishism, which has alternatively been called the Yiddish language movement, the Yiddish culture movement, or the Yiddish language and culture movement, is a modern expression of Judaism which came into being at the end of the nineteenth and the beginning of the twentieth centuries as a result of the revolutionary upheavals in the life of the Jewish people and the consequent redefinitions of its selfhood which had begun in the middle of the eighteenth century with the emergence of Hasidism or Jewish pietism, on the one hand, and Haskalah, or Jewish enlightenment, on the other. Hasidism, without intending to, unleashed both a populism, or awareness of the folk aspects of the Jewish religion, and a questioning of the halakhic or legalistic emphases of traditional Judaism that would emerge only a century later.

Even more than Hasidism, the Haskalah (a word which, translated literally, means "rationalism") called into question the exclusive hegemony of Torah or traditional religious culture as the overriding preoccupation of the Jewish mind. It also caused a rift in the symbiosis of peoplehood and religion that had been the hallmark of Jewish civilization for millennia. Now that Torah was no longer the be-all and end-all of Jewish intellectual concern and romantic idealization, new forms of Jewish existence and interpretations of Jewish religion and culture evolved. The officially monolithic structure of Judaism was shattered forever, and numerous Judaisms competed for the allegiance and support of the modernized Jew. The picture was further complicated by the fact that this modern Jew now no longer belonged exclusively to the Jewish community, but was on the way to becoming (or already was) a citizen of the country in which he lived and a participant in its culture which, ironically, when it was not overtly hostile, still harbored resentments against him and his Judaism.

In Western Europe, where Jewish communities were small and widely scattered, the road to emancipation, enfranchisement, and the integration of the Jew into the general body politic resulted in a general sloughing off of the folk and national aspects of Judaism and in attempts at creating new forms of Jewish identity based upon diverse interpretations of the religious heritage. The growth of Reform, Orthodoxy, and the Historical School of Judaism went hand in hand with cultural assimilation, including linguistic self-denial. It was sustained by the rise of the Science of Judaism, or modern Jewish historical and literary scholarship, which set out to prove to Jew and non-Jew alike that only the Jewish religious heritage separated them. Judaism, once freed of its nationalist entanglements, was, in fact, more like Christianity than different from it. Discrimination and persecution of the Jew was unenlightened and intellectually abhorrent.

In Eastern Europe, where Jews lived in compact, mass settlements usually removed from the general population, and where chances of integration and citizenship were, therefore, virtually non-existent, it was precisely the populist and peoplehood aspects of Judaism that came to be emphasized once Hasidism and Haskalah had taught their lessons to the small numbers of Jewish merchants, professionals, and disenchanted yeshivah students who were willing to read forbidden literature, buck the generally insecure Jewish communities, and proclaim themselves *maskilim*, or, later, socialist or Zionist revolutionaries. With the growth of modern nationalism throughout Europe and, especially, in the Czarist and Austro-Hungarian empires, the Eastern European Jewish intellectuals drew support for their growing awareness of Jews as a modern nation from the various exponents of modern European nationalism. Two elements of that nationalism were of particular significance to those Eastern European Jewish intellectuals who fathered Yiddishism: (1) language as the essence of national identity, and (2) anti-clericalism or secularism.

In Biblical Hebrew, the term "tongue" or "language" is a synonym for "nation."[3] In the Book of Psalms, the liberation of Israel from Egyptian slavery is described as its escape from a people of "strange speech."[4] In the *Dictionary of the History of Ideas*, we read that

> it is surely no mere accident that *nation* and *language community* tend on the whole to become coextensive terms. A common language and a common literary heritage have at all times been among the most powerful factors for creating a feeling for national unity.[5]

Language, writes Mordecai M. Kaplan,

> brings into play the remembrace of past heroes and events of history, the customs to which every member of the people is expected to conform, laws which regulate conflicts of interests and help maintain the peace, and folkways which include characteristic forms of esthetic self-expression.[6]

However mystical the concept, something of a nation's soul is always revealed in its language. Although national consciousness usually arises with concern for language, the relationship between language and nation is more than merely formal. "The difference between one language and another is not only a phonetic difference," writes Aryeh Tartakover, "it is also a difference of internal structure."[7]

This emphasis on the centrality of language in Jewish identity

3. See Solomon Mandelkern, *Kondordantsya Latanakh* (Tel Aviv, 1971), p. 651.

4. Psalm 114:1.

5. Philip P. Wiener, *Dictionary of the History of Ideas* (New York, 1973), vol 3, p. 660B.

6. Mordecai M. Kaplan, *The Future of the American Jew* (New York, 1948), p. 85.

7. Aryeh Tartakover, *"Hurban Hasafah Utehiyat Hasafah," Binetivey Hagut Vetarbut*, ed. Y. Shapiro (Tel Aviv, 1970), pp. 230–231.

first came into prominence at the First Yiddish Language Conference in Czernowitz, Bukovina, in 1908, where it was eloquently expressed by Matisyohu Mieses:

> Affording Yiddish the right to develop is a sacred national cause and a contribution to the progress of humanity. . . . Yiddish is our language with a distinct stamp of our spirit. . . .

The linguistic principle of modern nationalism, which became one of the primary bases of Yiddishism, inbued the creators and devotees of Yiddish literature, press, and theater with a sense of the significance of their work and a love for, as well as a dedication to, the Jewish people that extended far beyond the borders of the Yiddish-speaking world and benefited Jewish life everywhere. But, whereas the fruits that emerged from the implementation of this principle were warmly accepted, the principle itself was overwhelmingly rejected. While the primacy of language became the foundation of modern nationalism for many peoples, it could never serve as such for the Jewish people.

Jewish group consciousness had emerged millennia before modern nationalism enphasized either territoriality or linguistic uniformity as prerequisites of nationhood. Jewish group consciousness and loyalty were traditionally functions of the religious Torah culture and its halakhic regimen. Scripture and liturgy continuously reinforced the idea that all Jews were heirs of the Patriarchs and that they were all brothers responsible for one another. The laws and ideas of Judaism, rather than land or language, were considered primary in the scale of Jewish values and central to daily existence. This was also the major reason, until the holocaust, for some Jewish opposition to Zionism.

Having survived the disappearance of Hebrew and Aramaic as vernacular languages, Jews, in their hierarchy of values, could never accord centrality to any of their Diaspora tongues, however attached they may have become to them. In addition, unlike other oppressed peoples for whom national languages were emblems of liberation and self-assertion, Jewish national aspirations could never be divorced from the languages of the Bible and the Talmud. If land and language were central to the awakening peoples of Europe during the "springtime of nations," for most Jews religion superseded both territoriality and tongue as primary.[8]

Secularism, or anti-clericalism, was, similarly, a foreign norm and an alien ideal that Yiddishism sought to graft onto Judaism. According to Chaim Zhitlovsky,

> just as Jewish religion is absolutely independent of any national existence, so Jewish national existence is absolutely independent of any religious faith. . . . We Jews are a secular nation—for which religion is a personal matter as it is for every other people— struggling for its existence and for its free progressive development as do all other progressive peoples.[9]

For most European peoples, however, self-definition and independence were linked to liberation from the medieval church, which was usually seen as cosmopolitan and anti-national. In Eastern Europe, where Yiddishism took shape, the most powerful churches— Russian Orthodox and Polish Catholic—were linked to oppressive, reactionary regimes that had to be fought in the struggle for national identity and liberation. For Jews, on the other hand, religion was an indigenous phenomenon guarding the hope of national liberation and freedom from the yoke of foreign oppressors. While rabbis and scholars might sometimes be accused of insensitivity to the sufferings of the common people, they could not be considered inimical to Jewish national hopes and feelings. In the main, they themselves came from the lower classes and suffered, along with their people, the indignities of oppression and impoverishment.

The secularism of the Yiddishists was, for the most part, a dogmatic illusion which detached them from the deepest emotions of Jewry and robbed them of the sustaining power of the religious regimen and religious symbolism. They remained aloof from the mod-

8. Cf. Leybush Lehrer, *Yidishkeyt un andere Problemen* (New York, 1940), pp. 51–96.
9. Chaim Zhitlovsky, *Mayne Ani Mamins* (New York, 1953), pp. 270–271.

ern synagogue and from the various attempts of Jewry to adjust Jewish religion to the conditions of the twentieth century. All of this might have been defensible had the Yiddishists developed institutions to sustain their version of Judaism and to perpetuate it in the Diaspora, but the truth of the matter is that Yiddishism was, for many, merely a stepping stone to assimilation. Abraham Cahan, editor of the *Jewish Daily Forward* in New York, was, for many years, vigorously opposed to the establishment of Yiddish secular schools.[10] Americanization was his sole goal for his immigrant readers. The urge to assimilate was not limited, of course, to the Yiddishists. Zionism, Hebraism, and the modern Jewish religious movements could be similarly accused, to some extent, of harboring hidden assimilationist desires. But, to perpetuate their forms of Judaism, these other movements created institutional organs in which their theories could be constantly questioned and revised, while Yiddishism remained largely theoretical and lacking in institutions. The theory of Yiddishism failed to inspire the kind of devotion from its followers that would lead to deliberate planning for the future. The negative attitude to the synagogue prevented the establishment of Yiddishist synagogues that might have incorporated Yiddish culture in the worship and education of a modern house of assembly.[11] Yiddishists spent much of their energy in justly attacking the destructive attitude to Yiddish on the part of militant Hebraism in Palestine, or in blindly applauding the few crumbs thrown to Yiddish in the Soviet Union. But, when Hebrew culture was mercilessly silenced in the Soviet Union, the Yiddishists, with a few notable exceptions, failed to raise their voices adequately in protest.

With the decline of the *shtetl* and the destruction of Eastern European Jewry, the heartland of Yiddish culture in which Jewish secularism had emerged vanished forever, and both the Yiddishist and Hebraist versions of Jewish secularism were dealt severe blows. Despite its successes in Israel, Hebraist secularism has never suc-

10. Cf. David Shub, *Fun di Amolike Yorn* (New York, 1970), vol. 2, pp. 772–776.
11. Cf. Solomon Simon, *Emune fun a Dor* (New York, 1970), pp. 112–132.

ceeded in taking root in the Diaspora, while Yiddish secularism, on the other hand, has had to pay the price for what Abraham Golomb has called "an organic internal defect." Yiddishism, he writes,

> had no self-awareness, did not plumb its own depths. We were socialists with Yiddish, anarchists with Yiddish, Zionists with Yiddish. Yiddish was something extra, not an end in itself. We were Yiddishists only to the extent that [and for as long as] Jews spoke Yiddish.

Yiddishism failed to see itself as a movement of, by, and for the Jewish people. It denied its "folkist" or national character even to itself.

> Even in the one practical area—in our school system—we did not want to recognize Yiddishism as the ideal of a universal people with a language and culture of its own and its own fully organized peoplehood.[12]

This lack of a unifying principle may explain why Yiddishism allowed itself to become encumbered with anti-religionism.

Jewish secularism, in both its Hebraist and Yiddishist versions, has been in conflict with itself for many years. It denied the significance of traditional Jewish religious practices and symbols. Hebraists negated everything that smacked of exile (*shelilat ha-golah*) and attempted to create a new Biblical people, while Yiddishists avoided everything that smacked of religion. The result is that the Jewish people, both in Israel and in the Diaspora, is paying a heavy price for the failure of the secularists to articulate acceptable versions of secular Judaism for those Jews who become estranged from organized Jewish religious life.

Having exposed the theoretical inadequacies of Yiddishism or Yiddish secularism, we must not be oblivious to its achievements. The traditional Jewish concept that "practice, not theory, is what really counts" manifestly applies here. Yiddishism was, in no small measure, responsible for the Jewish survival of large numbers of

12. Abraham Golomb, *Tsu di Heykhn fun Yidishn Gayst* (Paris, 1971), p. 188.

Eastern European Jews, both in their native lands and in lands of immigration. Those who had abandoned what had become for them a rigid fundamentalist and intolerant way of life were, in very many cases, kept from abandoning Judaism and the Jewish people by the alternative offered to them by Yiddishism. Yiddish language and culture were barriers to disaffection and defection. In its still, small voice Yiddishism proclaimed: "*Ad kan!* this far you may go but no further!" The hidden agenda of the Czernowitz conference and of all subsequent Yiddish conclaves was *kiyem ha-ume*—the survival of the Jewish people and the maintenance and furtherance of Jewish distinctiveness and identity.[13]

The Yiddishists have remained the only organized Jewish trend to acknowledge publicly the incontestable value of the Yiddish language and literature as depositories and wellsprings of Jewish peoplehood and Jewish values in modern times. With all our respect for Hebrew and its ability to link us with ancient glories and with all our admiration for the miracle of the revival of spoken Hebrew, we must assert again and again that the creativity of the Jewish people did not cease in the Biblical or Rabbinic periods. We must also remember that the attempt to revive Hebrew included more than a dose of self-deprecation and the desire to sever ties with what were considered to be the despicable Jews of the *galut* and their culture. Yiddish, on the other hand, is, indeed, what Hyman Bass called

> the fullest, most complete and most faithful path to our people because it represents the most complete development of the creative forces in Jewish life; because it brings us the sincere love of Jewish generations that yearned and struggled; because Yiddish connects us with Jews of other communities; because Yiddish is the vehicle of the historical experience of a thousand years of Jewish life.[14]

Today, more than ever, Judaism needs Yiddishism. Now, more than ever, the survival of the Jewish people requires openness and

13. Cf. Yudel Mark, "Trakhtenishn vegn Kiyem Ha-Ume," *Tsuskunft* (May–June 1973).
14. Hyman Bass, *Shrayber un Verk* (Tel Aviv, 1971), pp. 558–559.

responsiveness to all Jewish generations and to the totality of our heritage. Once again the stone that the builders rejected must become the chief cornerstone. As Yehoshua Rapoport reminds us,

> the life that took place in the Yiddish language has in large measure disappeared. But that life survives in the language itself. That is why Yiddish must now be cherished and protected even more than when it was alive. Yiddish must be preserved so that the cultural treasure which it possesses in the liveliest and most contemporaneous format does not disappear.[15]

Even the secularism or anti-clericalism of Yiddishism, despite its misreading of Jewish history, has a role to play in the present. For modern Jews who tend to see authentic Eastern European Jewry in one-dimensional religious terms, it can serve as a reminder of the complexity of Eastern European Jewish society. Jewish pluralism was already in the making in Eastern Europe in the nineteenth century when new forms of Judaism were aborning. *Teshuvah* or return to Judaism can legitimately take many forms.

Ever since the Emancipation and the Enlightenment, Yiddish language and literature helped sustain Jewish identity and helped bring new life and new hope to our people. Now Yiddish and Yiddish literature must call upon all organs of Judaism and the Jewish people to rally to *their* aid and help sustain the culture that gave life to generations of the dry bones of our people the world over. As Leyzer Domankevitsh has argued, when Judaism needed Yiddish, Yiddish was there. Now, when Yiddish needs Jewry and Judaism, they must be there for it.[16] The task of Yiddishism today must be to get all sections and branches of our people to help support and sustain Yiddish language and culture. Yiddish linguistic and cultural content must become part of the educational programs of all Jewish schools, organizations, and social agencies. Yiddishism must no longer content itself with being a trend. It must become part of the Jewish consciousness of every Jew.

15. Yehoshua Rapoport, *Zoymen in Vint* (Buenos Aires, 1961), p. 272.
16. Cf. Leyzer Domankevitsh, *Verter un Vertn* (Tel Aviv, 1965), p. 20.

The luminous significance of Yiddish in the heritage of generations still summons us today:

> I come to you, my child, from the silent exile,
> From crowded, sealed-off ghettos.
> I possess only the beauty of pious prayers,
> I have naught but the loveliness of martyrdom.
> And if I have no lightning flashes that blind one
> Or flaming sun-like words that perform miracles,
> I do have the sparkle of starry legends,
> The precious moonlight of the spirit.
> From Worms, from Mainz, from Speyer,
> From Prague and Lublin to Odessa,
> One fire continued to burn,
> One miracle continued to glow.
> Wherever mortal enemies lay waiting
> And death was ready nearby—
> There, alone and in sorrow,
> I accompanied your parents.
> For hundreds of years together
> We faced every danger.
> I absorbed all the anger
> And I took in all the pain.
> I forged through the generations
> The wonder of will power and woe:
> To live for sacred teachings
> And die for them with strength.
> If pure holiness
> Be reflected in suffering,
> Then, my child, I am yours,
> I am your most sacred one.

(Abraham Lyessin)

The goal of a revitalized Yiddishism can be nothing less than the fulfillment of the prophet's words: "Your sons shall build once more the ancient ruins, and old foundations you shall raise again. You shall be called the repairer of ruins, the restorer of wrecked homes."[17]

17. Isaiah 58:12 (Moffatt translation).

BIBLIOGRAPHY

Abramovits, Z. "Tenuat Poaley Zion Be-Rusya." In *Katsir, Kovets Lekorot Hatenuah Hatsiyonit Be-Rusya.* Tel Aviv: Masada, 1964.

Ahad Haam. *Essays, Letters, Memoirs.* Edited by L. Simon. London : East and West Library, 1946.

————. *Selected Essays.* Translated by L. Simon. Philadelphia : Jewish Publication Society, 1912.

Akzin, Benjamin. *States and Nations.* Anchor Books. New York : Doubleday, 1966.

Algemeyne Entsiklopedye, Yidn. Vols. A, B, G, D, E. Paris and New York : Dubnov-Fond and Central Yiddish Culture Organization, 1950–1957.

Aronson, G., et al., eds. *Di Geshikhte fun Bund.* 3 vols. New York : Farlag Undzer Tsayt, 1960–1966.

Aronson, Gregor. "Ideological Trends Among Russian Jews." In *Russian Jewry: 1860–1917,* edited by J. Frumkin et al. New York : Thomas Yoseloff, 1966.

Asch, Sholem. "My First Meeting with Peretz." In Y. L. Peretz,

In This World and the Next, translated and edited by M. Spiegel. New York : Thomas Yoseloff, 1958.

Baal Makhshoves. *Geklibene Shriftn.* 2 vols. Vilna : Shloyme Shreberk, 1910.

————. *Geklibene Verk.* New York : CYCO Bicher Farlag, 1953.

Baron, Joseph L., ed. *A Treasury of Jewish Quotations.* New York : Crown Publishers, 1956.

Baron, Salo W. *A Social and Religious History of the Jews.* 3 vols. New York : Columbia University Press, 1937.

————. *A Social and Religious History of the Jews.* 2d ed., vols. 1–14. Philadelphia : The Jewish Publication Society of America, 1952–1969.

Bass, Hyman B. "Di Tshernovitser Konferents vi a Kultur Ideye." In *Undzer Dor Muz Antsheydn.* Tel Aviv : Farlag Y. L. Peretz, 1963.

Bein, Alex. "The Origin of the Term and Concept 'Zionism'." *Herzl Year Book,* vol. 2. New York: Herzl Press, 1959.

————. *Theodore Herzl.* Philadelphia : Jewish Publication Society, 1941.

Berdichevsky, Mikha Yosef. *Kol Kitvey M. Y. Berdichevsky.* 2 vols. Tel Aviv : Dvir, 1960.

Berkovits, Y. D., ed. *Dos Sholom Aleichem Bukh.* New York : Farlag YKUF, 1958.

Bernfeld, Simon. "Dos Folk un di Inteligents." *Der Yid* (Cracow 1900).

Bickel, Shlomo. *Detaln un Sakhaklen.* New York : Farlag Matones, 1943.

————. *Shrayber fun Mayn Dor.* New York : Farlag Matones, 1958.

Birnbaum, Nathan. "Di Absolute Ideye fun Yidntum un di Yidishe Shprakh." *Di Yidishe Velt,* no. 1 (St. Petersburg, 1912).

————. *Ausgewahlte Shriften zur Judischen Frage.* 2 vols. Czernowitz, 1910.

————. *Confession.* New York : Jewish Pocket Books, 1947

――――. "Derekh-Erets far dem Golus-Yid!" *Di Yidishe Velt* (Vilna, October 1914).

――――. *Eys Lasoys: Geklibene Ksovim.* Lodz : Beys Yankev, 5698.

――――. "Iberblik iber Mayn Lebn." *Yubileum-Bukh* (Warsaw, 1925).

――――. *Festschrift der Kadimah.* Vienna, 1933.

――――. *Der Yikhus fun Yidish.* Berlin, 1913.

――――. *Vom Sinn des Judentums.* Edited by M. Landau and A. E. Kaplan. Frankfort M., 1925.

Birnbaum, Solomon A. "Fun Mayn Foters Arkhiv." *Fun Noentn Over* (Warsaw, April–June 1938).

――――. "Nathan Birnbaum." *Men of the Spirit.* Edited by L. Jung. New York : Kymson Publishing Co., 1964.

Bokher, Elye (Elijah Levita). *Poetishe Shafungen in Yidish.* vol. 1. Edited by J. A. Joffe. New York, 1949.

Borochov, (Dov) Ber. *Nationalism and the Class Struggle.* New York : Young Poale Zion Alliance of America, 1937.

――――. *Poaley Zion Shriftn.* New York : Poaley Zion Farlag, vol. 1, 1920, vol. 2, 1948.

――――. *Shprakh-Forshung un Literatur Geshikhte.* Tel Aviv : Farlag Y. L. Peretz, 1966.

Brown, Meyer. *Mit Yidishe Oygn.* New York, 1958.

Bukhbinder, N. *Di Geshikhte fun der Yidisher Arbeter Bavegung in Rusland.* Vilna, 1930.

Burgin, H. *Di Geshikhte fun der Yidisher Arbeter Bavegung.* New York, 1915.

Chernov, Victor. *Yidishe Tuer in der Partey Sotsyalistn-Revolutsyonern.* New York, 1948.

Cohen, Israel. *Jewish Life in Modern Times.* New York : Dodd, Mead and Co., 1914.

――――. *Theodor Herzl: Founder of Political Zionism.* New York : Thomas Yoseloff, 1959.

Dawidowicz, Lucy S. *The Golden Tradition: Jewish Life and Thought in Eastern Europe.* New York : Holt, Rinehart and Winston, 1967.

Dik, Isaac Meyer. *Di Eydele Rakhe.* Vilna : Haahim Vehaalmanah Rom, 1875.

Doroshkin, Milton. *Yiddish in America: Social and Cultural Foundations.* Rutherford, N. J. : Fairleigh Dickinson University Press, 1969.

Dubnow, Simon. *Briv Vegn Altn un Nayem Yidntum.* Mexico : Shlomo Mendelssohn Fund, 1959.

————. *Fun Zhargon tsu Yidish.* Vilna : B. Kletskin, 1929.

————. *Nationalism and History.* Edited by K. S. Pinson. Philadelphia : Jewish Publication Society of America, 1958.

Duker, Abraham G. "Introduction" to Ber Borochov, *Nationalism and the Class Struggle.* New York : Young Poale Zion Alliance of America, 1937.

Efroykin, Yisroel. *Oyfkum un Umkum Fun Yidishe Golus-Shprakhn un Dialektn.* Paris : Farlag Kiyum, 1951.

Eisenstadt, Shmuel. "Di Tshernovitser Yidishe Shprakh-Konferents." *Yidishe Kultur.* (December 1968).

————. *Pyonerishe Geshtaltn.* Tel Aviv : Farlag Oyfkum, 1970.

————. "Tshernovitser Yidisher Shprakh Konferents." *Letste Nayes* (Tel Aviv, September 1968).

————. "Tsum Yoyvl fun der Tshernovitser Shprakh Konferents." *Yidishe Kultur* (June–July 1958).

Elbogen, Ismar. *A Century of Jewish Life.* Philadelphia : Jewish Publication Society, 1944.

Elzet, Yehuda. "Undzer Folks-Oytser." *Yidish-Amerike.* Edited by N. Steinberg. New York, 1929.

Epstein, Melech. *Profiles of Eleven.* Detroit, Mich. : Wayne State University Press, 1965.

Epstein, Zalman, "Hasakana Hazhargonit Umahuta." *Hash:loah* 6 (1910).

Erik, Max. *Di Geshikhte fun der Yidisher Literatur.* Warsaw : Farlag Kultur-Lige, 1928.

Di Ershte Yidishe Shprakh-Konferents: Barikhtn, Dokumenten un Ophandlungen fun der Tshernovitser Konferents, 1908. Vilna : Yiddish Scientific Institute, Philological Section, 1931.

Falkovitsh, E. "Esther: Der Lebnsveg fun der Groyser Revolutsyonern." *Folks-Shtime* (Warsaw, May 1965).

Federbush, Simon. *Halashon Haivrit Beyisrael Uvaamim.* Jerusalem: Mosad Harav Kuk, 1967.

Fraenkel, J. "Halifat Hamikhtavim Beyn Nathan Birnbaum Leveyn Siegmund Werner," *Shivat Tsiyon* 2–3 (Jerusalem, 1953).

Freundlich, Charles. *Peretz Smolenskin: His Life and Thought.* New York: Bloch Publishing Co., 1965.

Frumkin, Esther. "'Di Ershte Yidishe Shprakh-Konferents." *Di Naye Tsayt* (Vilna, 1908).

Gamzu, Yehuda Leyb. "Teshuva Kahalakha." *Hamelitz,* no. 119 (St. Petersburg, 1889).

Gelber, N. M. *Toldot Hatenuah Hatsiyonit Be-Galitsya.* 2 vols. Jerusalem: Reuven Mass, 1958.

Glantz-Leyeles, Aaron. "Fuftsik Yor Nokh der Tshernovitser Konferents." Jewish Labor Bund Broadcast, 1958 (Yivo Archives).

———. "Vos Vegn Morgn?" *Der Tog-Morgn Zhurnal* (August 11, 1958).

Glatstein, Jacob. "Peretzes Yerushe." *In Tokh Genumen.* New York: Farlag Matones, 1947.

Glazman, S. "Der Opklang fun der Tshernovitser Konferents in der Prese fun der Tsayt." *Yidishe Kultur* (December 1968).

Glenn, Menahem. "Ivrit, Aramit Veidit." *Ahisefer.* Edited by S. Niger and M. Ribalow. New York: Louis Lamed Foundation for the Advancement of Hebrew and Yiddish Literature, 1949.

Goldberg, Itshe. "Nokh Zekhtsik Yor." *Yidishe Kultur* (December 1968).

Goldsmith, Emanuel S. *Masters of Yiddish Literature.* Waltham, Mass.: Brandeis University National Women's Committee, 1972.

———. "Judaism, Israel and Diaspora Zionism." *Jewish Frontier* (December 1975).

———. "Matisyohu Mieses: Defender of Yiddish." *Jewish Frontier* (March 1976).

——. "Reassessing Yiddishism." *Jewish Frontier* (February 1975).

——. "The Spiritual Odyssey of Nathan Birnbaum." *Conservative Judaism* (Spring 1975).

——. "Yitzkhok Leybush Peretz: On His Sixtieth *Yortsayt.*" *Jewish Frontier* (June 1975).

——. "Zhitlovsky and American Jewry." *Jewish Frontier* (November 1975).

——. "The Polarity of Mendele's Art." *Conservative Judaism* (Summer 1968).

——. "Morris Rosenfeld, 1862–1962." *Reconstructionist* (June 15, 1962).

——. "Yiddish in Modern Judaism." *Reconstructionist* (June 2, 1961).

Golomb, A. "Der Yidishizm afn Sheydveg." *Geklibene Shriftn.* vol. 4. Mexico, 1947.

——. "Di Oyfgabn fun Yidishizm (Tsvantsik Yor Nokh Tshernovits)." *Literarishe Bleter,* no. 35 (Warsaw, 1928).

Goodman, Saul. "Chaim Zhitlovsky—His Contemporary Relevance." *Reconstructionist* (June 25, 1965).

——. *Traditsye un Banayung.* New York: Farlag Matones, 1967.

Gore, Norman C. *Tzeenah-U-Reenah: A Jewish Commentary on the Book of Exodus.* New York: Vantage Press, 1965.

Gorelick, Shmaryohu. *Eseyen.* Los Angeles, Calif., 1947.

Greenberg, Louis. *The Jews in Russia.* 2 vols. New Haven, Conn.: Yale University Press, 1944.

Hakohen, Mordecai ben-Hillel. "Sefat Hagalut." *Luah Ahiasaf* (5663 [1903]).

Heller, Joseph. *The Zionist Idea.* New York: Schocken Books, 1949.

Hertz, J. S. "The Bund's Nationality Program and Its Critics in the Russian, Polish and Austrian Socialist Movements. *Yivo Annual of Jewish Social Science* 14 (1969).

Herzl, Theodor. *The Complete Diaries of Theodor Herzl.* Edited by R. Patai. Translated by H. Zohn. New York : Herzl Press, 1960.

Hofer, Yekhiel. *Mit Yenem un mit Zikh: Literarishe Eseyen,* vol. 1. Tel Aviv : Farlag Y. L. Peretz, 1964.

Janowsky, Oscar. *The Jews and Minority Rights.* New York : Macmillan, 1933.

Kahn, Lazar. "Af der Tshernovitser Konferents." *Literarishe Bleter,* nos. 35, 39 (Warsaw, 1928).

―――. "Di Tshernovitser Konferents : August 1908" (manuscript). Yivo Archives, New York, 1908.

Kalmanovitch, Zelig. "Y. L. Peretzes Kuk af der Yidisher Literatur." *Di Goldene Keyt,* no. 2 (Tel Aviv, 1949).

Kann, Robert A. *The Hapsburg Empire.* New York: Praeger, 1957.

―――. *The Multinational Empire.* 2 vols. New York : Columbia University Press, 1950.

Kazdan, H. S. *Fun Kheyder un "Shkoles" biz Tsisho.* Mexico : Shlomo Mendelson Fond, 1956.

―――. "Tshernovits―Kholem un Vor." *Undzer Tsayt.* (January 1969).

Kisman, Joseph. "Di Tshernovitser Yidishe Shprakh-Konferents : Bamerkungen fun a Bateyliktn." *Undzer Tsayt* (July–August, 1958).

―――. "Dr. Nathan Birnbaum―Zayne Gaystike Zukhenishn un Vandlungen," *Di Tsukunft* (September 1962).

Klausner, Joseph. *Historyah shel Hasifrut Haivrit Hahadasha.* 6 vols. Jerusalem : Ahiasaf, 1960–1963.

Klausner, Yisrael. *Behitorer Am.* Jerusalem : Hasifriya Hatsiyonit, 1962.

―――. "Halutsey Hadibur Haivri Beartsot Hagolah." *Leshoneynu Laam* 15, nos. 1–2 (Jerusalem, 5724).

―――. *Opozitsya Le-Herzl.* Jerusalem, 5720.

Klaynman, Moshe. *Demuyot Vekomot.* Paris, 1925.

Kling, Simcha. *Joseph Klausner.* New York : Thomas Yoseloff, 1970.

————. *Nahum Sokolow: Servant of His People.* New York: Herzl Press, 1960.

Knox, Israel. "Zhitlovsky's Philosophy of Jewish Life." *Contemporary Jewish Record* (April 1945).

Kohn, Hans. *The Idea of Nationalism.* New York: Macmillan, 1944.

————. *The Mind of Modern Russia.* New Brunswick, N. J.: Rutgers University Press, 1955.

Kresel, G. "A Historisher Polemik Vegn der Yidisher Literatur." *Di Goldene Keyt,* no. 20 (Tel Aviv, 1954).

————. *Leksikon Hasifrut Haivrit Badorot Haaharonim.* 2 vols. Merhaviah: Sifriat Poalim, 1967.

————. "A. S. Lieberman in Likht fun Zayne Briv." *Di Goldene Keyt,* no. 13 (Tel Aviv, 1952).

————. "Matisyohu Mieses un di Polemik Vegn Yidish." *Di Goldene Keyt,* no. 28 (Tel Aviv, 1957).

————. "Zelbstemantsipatsion." *Shivat Tsiyon* 4 (Jerusalem, 1956).

Kursky, Franz. *Gezamlte Shriftn.* New York: Farlag Der Veker, 1952.

Landis, Joseph C. "Who Needs Yiddish?" *Judaism* 13, no. 4 (New York, 1964).

Leftwich, Joseph. *The Golden Peacock: A Worldwide Anthology of Yiddish Poetry.* New York: Thomas Yoseloff, 1961.

————. "Introduction" to Y. L. Peretz *The Book of Fire.* Translated and edited by J. Leftwich. New York: Thomas Yoseloff, 1960.

————. *Israel Zangwill.* New York: Thomas Yoseloff, 1957.

Lehrer, Leybush. *In Gayst fun Traditsye.* Tel Aviv: Farlag Y. L. Peretz, 1966.

————. *Yidishkayt un Andere Problemen.* New York: Farlag Matones, 1940.

Leivick, H. "The Individual Jew." Translated by E. S. Goldsmith. *Reconstructionist* 23, no. 17 (December 27, 1957).

Leksikon fun der Nayer Yidisher Literatur. 7 vols. New York: Congress for Jewish Culture, 1956–1968.

Lerner, Herbert J. "The Tshernovits Language Conference : A Milestone in Jewish Nationalist Thought." Master's thesis, Columbia University (n.d.). Copy of MS in Yivo Archives.

Levinsky, Elhanan Leyb. "Hayey Olam Vehayey Shaa." *Hamelitz,* nos. 104–6 (St. Petersburg, 1889).

———. "Sefat Ever Usefat Yehudit Hameduberet." *Hamelitz,* nos. 58, 59 (St. Petersburg, 1889).

———. "Yohanan Hasandlar Lefanim Veata." *Hamelitz,* no. 113 (St. Petersburg, 1889).

Levinson, Avraham. *Hatenuah Haivrit Bagolah.* Warsaw : Executive of the Brith Ivrith Olamith, London, 1935.

———. *Leom Banekhar.* Tel Aviv : Yavneh, n.d.

Levinsohn, Yitzkhok Ber. *Teudah Beyisrael.* Vilna, 1828.

Lew, Simkha. *Prokim Yidishe Geshikhte.* New York : Shulsinger Brothers, 1941.

Lewinsky, Yom-Tov. *Entsiklopedya shel Havay Umasoret Bayahadut.* 2 vols. Tel Aviv : Dvir, 1970.

Lewisohn, Ludwig, ed. *Theodor Herzl: A Portrait for This Age.* New York : World Publishing Co., 1955.

Lichtheim, R. *Toldot Hatsiyonut Be-Germanya.* Jerusalem, 1951.

Liptzin, Sol. *The Flowering of Yiddish Literature.* New York : Thomas Yoseloff, 1963.

———. *The Maturing of Yiddish Literature.* New York : Jonathan David, 1970.

———. *Peretz.* New York : Yivo Institute for Jewish Research, 1947. .

Litvak, A. *Vos Geven.* Vilna, 1925.

———. "Di Zhargonishe Komitetn." *Royter Pinkes* (Warsaw, 1929).

Lubetsky, Yitzkhok. "Vegn a Muzeum." *Di Velt* (Vienna, 1900).

Luria, Yitshak. "Yidish un Zayn Natsyonaler Batayt." *Fraynd* (St. Petersburg, 1906).

Ma'aseh Book. 2 vols. Edited by M. Gaster. Philadelphia : Jewish Publication Society of America, 1934.

Macartney, Carlile Aylmer. *National States and National Minorities*. London : Oxford University Press, 1934.

Madison, Charles. *Yiddish Literature: Its Scope and Major Writers*. New York : Andre Ungar, 1968.

Mahler, Raphael. *Hahasidut Vehahaskalah*. Merhaviah : Sifriat Poalim, 1961.

————. *Historiker un Vegvayzer*. Tel Aviv : Yisroel Bukh, 1967.

————. "Yidish Ve-Ivrit Leor Hametsiut shel Yameynu." In *Klal Yisrael*, edited by B. Dinur, A. Tartakover, Y. Lestchinsky. Jerusalem : Mosad Bialik, 1954.

Malachi, A. R. "Der Kol Mevaser un Zayn Redaktor." In *Pinkes far der Forshung fun der Yidisher Literatur un Prese*, edited by S. Bickel. New York : Congress for Jewish Culture, 1965.

————. "Nahum Sokolow un di Yidishe Shprakh." *YKUF Almanakh*. New York: Farlag YKUF, 1961.

Mannheim, Karl. *Diagnosis of Our Time*. London : Kegan Paul, Trench, Trubner and Co., Ltd., 1943.

Maor, Yitzhak. *Sheelat Hayehudim Batenuah Haliberalit Vehamahaphanit Berusya*. Jerusalem : Mosad Bialik, 5724.

Mark, Yudel. "Introduction" to Chaim Zhitlovsky, *Geklibene Verk*. New York : Cyco Bikher-Farlag, 1945.

————. "The Yiddish Language : Its Cultural Impact." *American Jewish Historical Society Quarterly* 59, no. 2 (December 1969).

————. "Zekhtsik Yor Nokh der Shprakh-Konferents in Tshernovits." *Forverts* (August 25, 1968).

Marmor, Kalmen, ed. *Arn Liebermans Briv*. New York : Yivo Institute for Jewish Research, 1951.

————. *Der Onhoyb fun der Yidisher Litratur in Amerike*. New York : Farlag YKUF, 1944.

————. *Yankev Gordin*. New York : Farlag YKUF, 1963.

Mayzel, Nakhmen. *Briv un Redes fun Y. L. Peretz*. New York : Farlag YKUF, 1944.

————. *Dr. Chaim Zhitlovsky: Tsu Zayn Hundertstn Geboyrnyor*. New York : Farlag YKUF, 1965.

————. "Di Ershte Mobilizatsye." *Literarishe Bleter,* no. 35 (Warsaw, 1928).

————. *Noente un Eygene.* New York : Farlag YKUF, 1957.

————. *Tsum Hundertstn Geboyrnyor fun Shimen Dubnov.* New York : Farlag YKUF, 1961.

————. *Tsurikblikn un Perspektivn.* Tel Aviv : Farlag Y. L. Peretz, 1962.

————. *Yitzkhok Leybush Peretz un Zayn Dor Shrayber.* New York : Farleg YKUF, 1951.

————. *Y. L. Peretz: Zayn Lebn un Shafn.* New York : Farlag YKUF, 1945.

Medem, Vladimir. *Vladimir Medem: Tsum Tsvantsikstn Yortsayt.* New York : American Representation of the General Jewish Workers' Union of Poland, 1943.

Mendele Mokher Seforim. "Shtrikhn tsu Mayn Biografye." *Ale Verk,* vol. 19. Warsaw : Farlag Mendele, 1928.

Mendelsohnn, Eric. *Class Struggle in the Pale.* Cambridge : Cambridge University Press, 1970.

Mendelssohn, Moses. *Mendelssohns Schriften,* vol. 5. Leipzig, 1844.

Menes, Abraham, ed. *Der Yidisher Gedank in der Nayer Tsayt.* New York : Congress of Jewish Culture, 1957.

————. "Di Groyse Tsayt." *Arkady Zamlbukh.* New York : Farlag Undzer Tsayt, 1942.

Meyer, Michael A. *The Origins of the Modern Jew.* Detroit : Wayne State University Press, 1967.

Mieses, Matisyohu. "Bizehut Hasafah Hayehudit." *Haolam,* nos. 22–23 (Cologne, 1907).

————. "Lishelat Halashon Hayehudit." *Heatid* (1910).

Minkov, Nokhem Borekh. "Peretz in Amerike." *Literarishe Vegn.* Mexico : Farlag Tsvi Kesel, 1955.

————. *Pyonern fun Yidisher Poezye in Amerike.* 3 vols. New York, 1956.

————. *Zeks Yidishe Kritiker.* Buenos Aires : Farlag Yidbukh, 1954.

Minogue, K. R. *Nationalism*. New York : Basic Books, 1967.

Mlotek, Joseph. "Di Tshernovitser Konferents un di Yidishe Prese." *Forverts* (September 1, 1968).

Niger, S. *Bleter Geshikhte fun der Yidisher Literature*. New York : Congress for Jewish Culture, 1959.

———. "Dr. Nathan Birnbaum." *Di Yidishe Velt* 1, no. 2 (Vilna, 1914).

———. *In Kamf far a Nayer Dertsiung*. New York : Arbeter- Ring Bildungs-Komitet, 1940.

———. *Dertseylers un Romanistn*. New York : CYCO Bicher-Farlag, 1946.

———. *Di Tsveyshprakhikayt Fun Undzer Literatur*. Detroit : Louis Lamed Foundation for the Advancement of Hebrew and Yiddish Literature, 1941.

———. *Y. L. Peretz*. Buenos Aires : Argentiner Opteyl fun Alveltlekhn Yidishn Kultur Kongres, 1952.

Novershtern, Avraham. "Sholom Aleichem un Zayn Shtelung tsu der Shprakhn-Frage." *Di Goldene Keyt,* no. 74 (Tel Aviv, 1971).

Paner, Yitzkhok. "Amol iz Geven." *Letste Nayes* (Tel Aviv, December 6, 1953).

Passow, Isidore David. "The First Yiddish Language Conference." In *Gratz College Anniversary Volume,* edited by I. D. Passow and S. T. Lachs. Philadelphia : Gratz College, 1971.

Patkin, R. *The Origins of the Russian-Jewish Labour Movement*. Melbourne, 1947.

Pei, Mario. *The Story of Language*. Mentor Books, New York : New American Library, 1949.

Peretz, Yitzkhok Leybush. *Briv un Redes*. Edited by N. Mayzel. Vilna : Farlag fun B. Kletskin, 1929.

———. "What Is Missing in Our Literature?" In *The Way We Think,* edited by J. Leftwich, vol. 2. New York : Thomas Yoseloff, 1969.

Pinsker, Leon. *Auto-Emancipation*. Translated by C. S. Blondheim. New York, 1948.

Pinski, David. "Dray Yor mit Y. L. Peretz." *Di Goldene Keyt,* no. 10 (Tel Aviv, 1951).

―――. *Oysgeklibene Shriftn.* Buenos Aires : Literatur Gezelshaft Baym Yivo in Argentina, 1969.

Pinson, Koppel S. "Arkady Kremer, Vladimir Medem, and the Ideology of the Jewish 'Bund'." *Jewish Social Studies* 7 (1945).

Pyekazh, Mendl. "Vegn Yidishizm in Sof Zibetsntn Yorhundert un der Ershter Helft Akhtsntn Yorhundert." *Di Goldene Keyt,* no. 49 (1964).

Raisin, Jacob. *The Haskalah Movement in Russia.* Philadelphia : Jewish Publication Society, 1913.

Raisin, Max. *Recent History of the Jews in Both Hemispheres.* (Vol. 6 of H. Graetz, *Popular History of the Jews.*) New York : Jordan Publishing Co., 1918.

Rannit, Aleksis. "Speaking of Finnish, Estonian, Latvian, Lithunian. . . ." *New York Times Book Review,* November 16, 1969, p. 2.

Raphaeli, A. "Veidot Artsiyot shel Tsiyoney Rusya." *Katzir, Kovets Lekorot Hatenuah Hatsiyonit Be-Rusya.* Tel Aviv : Masada, 1964.

Ravitch, Melekh. "In Yoyvl-yor fun der Ershter Yidisher Shprakh-Konferents." *Tsum Yoyvl fun der Ershter Yidisher Shprakh-Konferents.* Montreal : Montrealer Komitet fun Yivo, 1958.

Ravnitsky, Yehoshua Hona. "Hayesh Tsorekh Basifrut Hazhargonit?" *Hamelitz,* nos. 96–98 (St. Petersburg, 1889).

―――. "Hebreyish un Yidish (Zhargon)." *Hoyzfraynd* (St. Petersburg, 1896).

―――. "Od Bizehut Sifrut Haam." *Hamelitz,* nos. 130–31 (St. Petersburg, 1889).

Reisen, Abraham. "Mit Finf un Tsvantsik Yor Tsurik." *Forverts* (August 26, 1933).

―――. "Nathan Birnbaum." *Forverts* (May 5, 1937).

Reisen, Zalmen. *Leksikon fun der Yidisher Literatur.* 4 vols. Vilna, 1926–1929.

―――. *Yidishe Literatur un Yidishe Shprakh.* Edited by S.

Rozhanski. Buenos Aires : Literatur Gezelshaft Baym Yivo in Argentina, 1965.

Roback, A. A. *The Story of Yiddish Literature.* New York : Yiddish Scientific Institute, American Branch, 1940.

Rozenhek, S. "Beyn Haketsavot." *Karmelit,* nos. 6–7 (Haifa, 1960).

————. "Hebreyish-Yidish." *Di Goldene Keyt,* no. 66 (Tel Aviv, 1969).

Rozenhek, Yehoshua. "Di Ershte Yidishe Shprakh-Konferents." *Folks-Shtime* (Warsaw, 1958).

Sadan, Dov. *Heymishe Ksovim.* 2 vols. Tel Aviv : Farlag Hamenorah, 1972.

Samuel, Maurice. *The Professor and the Fossil.* New York : Alfred A. Knopf, 1956.

————. *In Praise of Yiddish.* New York : Cowles Book Company, Inc., 1971.

Schulman, Elias. *Di Geshikhte fun der Yidisher Literatur in Amerike.* New York : Farlag YKUF, 1943.

————. *Sugyot Betoldot Sifrut Yidish.* Tel Aviv, 1969.

————. "Zekhtsik Yor Nokh der Tshernovitser Konferents—un vos Vayter?" *Der Veker* (September 1968).

Schweid, Mark. *Dos Lebn fun Y. L. Peretz.* New York : Farlag Peretz, 1955.

Shaanan, Avraham. *Hasifrut Haivrit Hahadasha Lizrameha.* 4 vols. Tel Aviv : Masada, 1962–1967.

Shatzky, Jacob. *Di Geshikhte fun Yidn in Varshe.* 3 vols. New York : Yivo Institute for Jewish Research, 1947–1953.

————. "Der Umbakanter Peretz." *Di Tsukunft* (July 1945).

Shohet, Azriel. *Im Hilufey Tekufot: Reshit Hahaskalah Beyahadut Germanya.* Jerusalem : Mosad Bialik, 1960.

Sholom Aleichem. "Lisheelat Hasafah." *Hamelitz,* no. 80 (St. Petersburg, 1889).

————. *Shomers Mishpet.* Berdichev, 1888.

Shomer-Batshelis, Rose. *Undzer Foter Shomer.* New York : Farlag YKUF, 1950.

Shtif, Nokhem. *Yidn un Yidish.* Warsaw, 1920.

Shub, David. *Fun di Amolike Yorn,* 2 vols. New York : CYCO Bicher-Farlag, 1970.

Shtrigler, Mordecai. "Tragedyes un Zkhusim fun der Yidisher Literatur." *Shmuesn mit der Tsayt,* vol. 2. Buenos Aires : Kiyum Farlag, 1961.

Simon, Leon. *Ahad Haam: Asher Ginzberg, A Biography.* Philadelphia : Jewish Publication Society, 1960.

Simon, Leon and Joseph Heller. *Ahad Haam: Haish, Poalo Vetorato.* Jerusalem : Magnes Press, 1955.

Skomorovsky, Shlomo. "Eeneh Af Ani Helki." *Hameltiz,* no. 133 (St. Petersburg, 1889).

Slipoy, Mordecai. *Haoleh Hagadol: Dr. Natan Birnbaum, Hayav Ufoalo.* Jerusalem : Hotsaat Peninim, 5723.

Slouschz, Nahum. *The Renascence of Hebrew Literature.* Philadelphia : Jewish Publication Society, 1909.

Sokolow, Nahum. "Peretz." In *The Way We Think.* vol. 2. Translated by J. Leftwich. New York : Thomas Yoseloff, 1969.

———. *Perzenlekhkaytn un Folk.* Jerusalem : Hasifriya Hatsiyonit, 1966.

Soltes, M. *The Yiddish Press: An Americanizing Agency.* Philadelphia : Jewish Publication Society, 1925.

Spiegel, Shalom. *Hebrew Reborn.* Philadelphia : Jewish Publication Society, 1930.

Syrkin, Nachman. "Der Zhargon." *Der Yid,* nos. 37–40 (Cracow, 1900).

Tartakover, Aryeh. *Hahevrah Hayehudit.* Tel Aviv: Masada, 5717.

———. *Toldot Tenuat Haovdim Hayehudit.* vol. 1 Warsaw, 1929.

Tsum Tsvantsikstn Yortog Fun der Tshernovitser Konferents. Vilna : Vilner Yidishe Bildungs Komitet, 1928.

Turkov-Grudberg, Yitzkhok. *Y. L. Peretz: Der Veker.* Tel Aviv : Farlag Y. L. Peretz, 1965.

Walter, Hermann. *Moses Mendelssohn: Critic and Philosopher.* New York : Bloch Publishing Co., 1930.

Waxman, Meyer. *A History of Jewish Literature.* 5 vols. New York: Thomas Yoseloff, 1960.

Weichert, Michael. "Nokh Vegn der Tshernovitser Shprakh Konferents." *Letste Nayes* (Tel Aviv, May 15, 1969).

Wiener, Leo. *The History of Yiddish Literature in the Nineteenth Century.* New York: Charles Scribner's Sons, 1899.

Weinreich, Max. *Di Geshikhte fun der Yidisher Shprakh.* 4 vols. New York: Yivo Institute for Jewish Research, 1973.

―――. *Oysgeklibene Shriftn.* Edited by S. Rozhanski. Buenos Aires: Literatur Gezelshaft Baym Yivo, 1974.

―――. "Prehistory and Early History of Yiddish." *The Field of Yiddish.* vol 1. Edited by U. Weinreich. New York: Linguistic Circle of New York, 1954.

―――. *Shtaplen: Fir Etyuden tsu der Yidisher Shprakh-Visnshaft un Literatur-Geshikhte.* Berlin, 1923.

―――. "Yidishkayt and Yiddish." In *Mordecai M. Kaplan Jubilee Volume* (English Section). New York: Jewish Theological Seminary of America, 1953.

Weiss (Slonim), S. "Oys di Tsaytn fun der Tshernovitser Konferents." *Fun Noentn Over* 1 (Warsaw, 1937).

Wohlgelernter, Maurice. *Israel Zangwill: A Study.* New York: Columbia University Press, 1964.

Woislawski, Zvi. "Esrim Shanah Le-Tshernovits." *Hatekufah* 24 (1928): 613–20.

Zak, Abraham. *Geven a Yidish Poyln.* Buenos Aires, 1968.

Zangwill, Israel. *The Voice of Jerusalem.* New York: Macmillan, 1921.

Zhitlovsky, Chaim. *Di Filozofye.* 2 vols. New York: Maisel & Co., 1910.

―――. *Gezamlte Shriftn.* 7 vols. New York: Dr. Zhitlovsky Farlag-Gezelshaft, 1912–1917.

―――. *Mayne Ani Mamins.* New York: Farlag YKUF, 1953.

―――. "Tshernovits un der Yidishizm." *Yidishe Kultur* (May 1958).

————. *Undzer Shprakhn-Frage.* Edited by Z. B. Mink. Kovno, 1903.

————. *Yid un Velt.* New York : Farlag YKUF, 1945.

————. *Yitzkhok Leybush Peretz.* New York: Farlag YKUF, 1951.

————. *Zikhroynes fun Mayn Lebn.* 3 vols. New York : Dr. Zhitlovsky Farlag-Komitet, 1935–1940.

Zhitlovsky Zamlbukh, Warsaw : Farlag Bzhoza, 1929.

Zilbercweig, Zalmen. *Ahad Haam un Zayn Batsiung tsu Yidish.* Los Angeles, 1956.

Zilberfarb, Moyshe. *Gezamlte Shriftn.* Paris, 1935.

Zinberg, Israel. *Di Bli-Tkufe fun der Haskole* (Vol. 11 of *Di Geshikhte fun Literatur bay Yidn*). Waltham, Mass. : Brandeis University, 1966.

————. *Di Geshikhte fun der Literatur bay Yidn.* 10 vols. Buenos Aires : Alveltlekher Yidisher Kultur-Kongress, 1964–1970.

————. "Der Kamf far Yidish in der Yidisher Literatur." *Filologishe Shriftn.* vol. 2. Vilna : Yidisher Visenshaftlikher Institut-Yivo, 1928.

————. *Kultur Historishe Shtudyes.* New York : Farlag Moyshe Shmuel Shklarski, 1949.

INDEX